FELIXSTOWE
THROUGH TIME

Michael Rouse

AMBERLEY PUBLISHING

Acknowledgements

The 2012 photographs were taken on two visits to Felixstowe. The first was from Tuesday 5 June until Thursday 7 June when I stayed at the Waverley, so thanks to the Manager and staff there. The second was on Wednesday 25 July during a really hot spell. My daughter Cassie and her friend Mollie accompanied me on that second trip and were kind enough to co-operate in many photographs in return for rides on the Waltzer at Mannings, rolling around in a large floating plastic sphere, food and a Peter's ice cream.

I would like to thank Corinne Cappell, Seafront Gardens Project Manager, Suffolk District Council for showing me all the exciting proposals for restoring the seafront gardens and promising me a hot day and crowds of people. She delivered the latter and I'm sure she will deliver some wonderful gardens. Thanks also to Caroline Barrett, the Clerk to the Council for helping me with queries, TIC staff and all those I pester with questions.

The photograph of the Beach Station was taken by Douglas Thompson. Copyright passed to Paul Bolger, but even with the help of Robert Humm & Co., who distributed the photograph, I have been unable to contact him.

For historical research I referred to *Coastal Resorts of East Anglia*, which I wrote for Terence Dalton in 1982. Photographs 53, 91 and 95 were taken by me while working on that book. I also collected some *Ward Lock Guides* and *Town Guides*, for 1936, 1947,1950, 1965, 1974 and 1980.

I consulted Robert Malster's *Felixstowe, A Pictorial History* (Phillimore, 1992); *Felixstowe at Leisure* (1996), by Phil Hadwen, John Smith, Ray Twidale, Peter White and Neil Wylie; and *Felixstowe – Then and Now* (2010), by Mike Durrant, along with various websites.

Many thanks as usual to Sarah Parker, Rosie Rogers and all at Amberley.

To those with the vision who created the resort of Felixstowe and to those with the vision to protect its heritage and ensure its future.

First published 2012

Amberley Publishing
The Hill, Stroud
Gloucestershire, GL5 4EP

www.amberley-books.com

ISBN 978 1 4456 1086 3

British Library Cataloguing in Publication Data.
A catalogue record for this book is available from the British Library.

Typeset in 9.5pt on 12pt Celeste.
Typesetting by Amberley Publishing.
Printed in the UK.

Introduction

In 1844 William White's *Directory* reported 'Felixstow (sic) is a delightfully situated village and bathing place on the sea coast... its parish has 552 souls, and about 1170 acres of land, forming a narrow tract, terminating in bold cliffs on the sea shore...' William White mentions that C. Meadows of Ipswich and other speculators had built houses and cottages to let to visitors, and J. C. Cobbold, who occupied a local mansion, had built a hotel there in 1839. At this time this stretch of coast must have been remarkable for the sheer number of Martello towers strung along it, as a reminder that in the event of a French invasion, or any other European country, Felixstowe was in the front line.

C. S. Ward for his *Thorough Guide* in the 1880s is hardly optimistic: 'This place consists of a row of shops, &c., facing the beach and some good villas, the Bath Hotel, and the Church on the cliff, and that is about all. It is bright enough on a bright summer's day, and as the spot chosen for the Suffolk Convalescent Home may be assumed to be healthy, but the marshes on two sides of the town suggest ague in winter. The bathing and sands are excellent, and the cliff of Red Crag ending in Felixstowe Point, with villas and trees above, is picturesque... Those who have heard of Felixstowe Pier will be surprised not to see one. The structure so named is at the mouth of the Orwell, opposite Harwich...'

The visit of the Empress of Germany, her children and servants in 1891 greatly boosted the town's fortunes and West Carnie in his book *In Quaint East Anglia* (1898) described the resort as 'fashionable'. 'It is not at all like any other watering place,' he wrote, '...the houses all suggest prosperous residential owners rather than the usual seaside landlady, and I fancy the ordinary lodgings must be at a premium in Felixstowe during the summer months... the houses are scattered about here, there and everywhere, over a huge area. The consequence is that there are three stations for a town of barely three thousand inhabitants.'

It was in Edwardian times though that Felixstowe really burst into life as a fashionable seaside resort with a pier and some magnificent hotels.

Talk of Felixstowe today and many will think of the vast and hugely successful container port and the streams of lorries to and fro along the busy A14. The rise of the port has been contrasted to the fortunes of the seaside resort. Some very attractive buildings like the Herman de Stern Convalescent Home and the Cavendish Hotel have been lost, and the part of Undercliff West Road near where the Suffolk Convalescent Home stood has a mid-1960s redevelopment that defines the architecture of that time. The 1986 leisure centre close to the pier, with its vast roof and dark brick, has the appearance of a building that could be anywhere in the town and does nothing to complement the seaside resort. But there are so many good buildings full of Victorian and Edwardian character in the town that there is still hope.

Plans are well advanced to restore the Cliff Gardens and the owner of the pier has ambitious plans for a new entertainment centre, which hopefully may extend to the former boating lake area. The resort needs a major investment like this, also to encourage others and bring more visitors to the town.

Currently around £10 million is being spent on coastal defences from the war memorial to Cobbold's Point, to give protection to some 1,500 homes. Volker Stevin and Mott McDonald are putting eighteen rock groynes in place and creating a rock revetment and walkway around Cobbold's Point to Jacob's Ladder, which they claim will give protection for fifty years. The beach has also been recharged between the Spa Gardens and Cobbold's Point with imported sand and shingle.

This book concentrates on Felixstowe as a seaside resort and with substantial investment it can have a bright future. Where once it was said that the easiest way to get to Felixstowe was to be born there, now it has the A14 and the road infrastructure that it didn't have in the early days and accessibility is very important to attracting visitors.

The Spa Pavilion, though, faces an uncertain future as a result of the Suffolk Coastal Council withdrawing funding. There is not enough local support and without a popular summer season programme, perhaps like Cromer's Seaside Special and a strong holiday trade, the future looks bleak for the building as it is:

Felixstowe was created by men of business vision and enterprise like Colonel Tomline, John Cobbold and Douglas Tollemache and the architect T. W. Cotman as a seaside resort, which is the town's heritage and will be the town's future. After all what is the point of being given at least another fifty years' lease of life, if it is not to be enjoyed? As the 1936 town guide says: 'Whatever one spends on a Felixstowe holiday is an investment in a sound concern; the yield of health value is higher than any other investment can offer in these days'.

Just after the last war the 1947 guide said: 'Many things have altered, and more will alter no doubt as time goes on, but one thing which has not changed is the situation of Felixstowe, perched on its cliff and overlooking the broad sweep of its beautiful Bay, with the Spa gardens and their riot of colour and flowers reaching down to the edge of the sea.'

There are future generations yet to discover 'the Sunspot of the East Coast'. So respect the past, enjoy the present and plan for the future.

Michael Rouse
Ely, July 2012

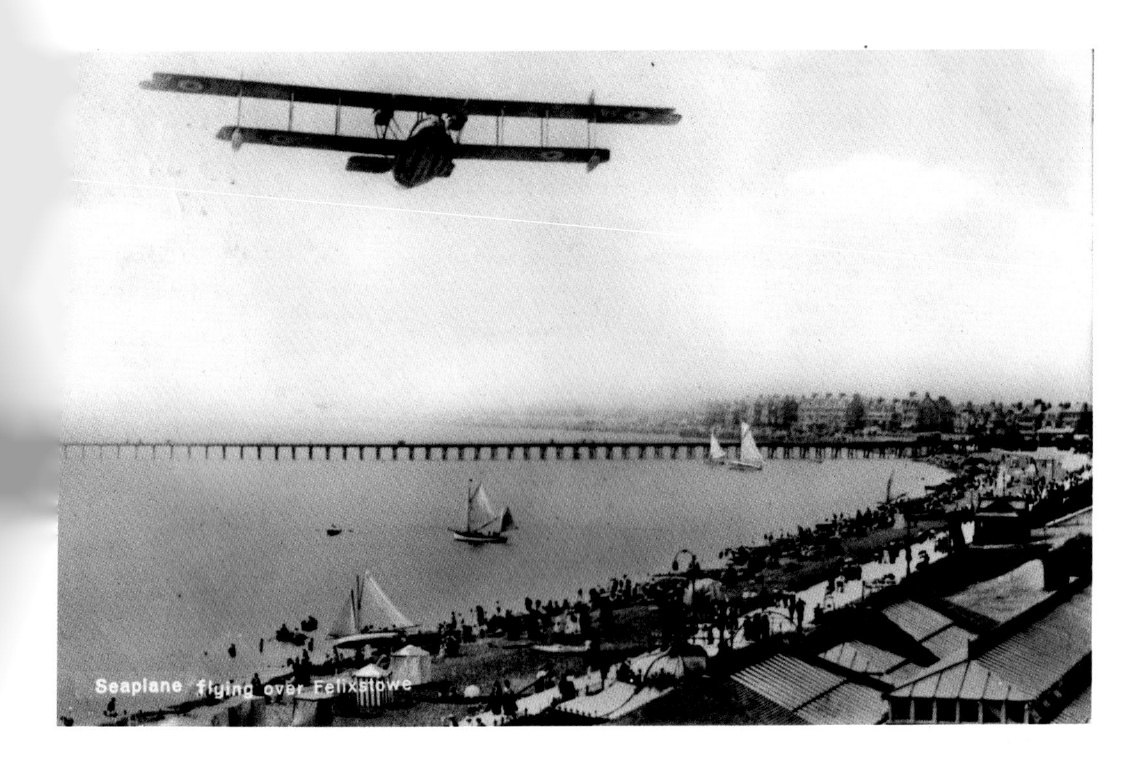

Seaplane Flying over Felixstowe *c.* 1927
The Waverley Hotel has allocated me the perfect room on a top floor corner. From the small balcony I can see up and down Wolsey Gardens and beyond the pier round the curve of the bay to the giraffe like cranes at the container port. I won't see the seaplanes that once flew from the air station between Landguard Fort and the dock, but, of course, I can see the sea stretching to the horizon and the cruise liners and container ships sliding by. I am at the seaside and I love it.

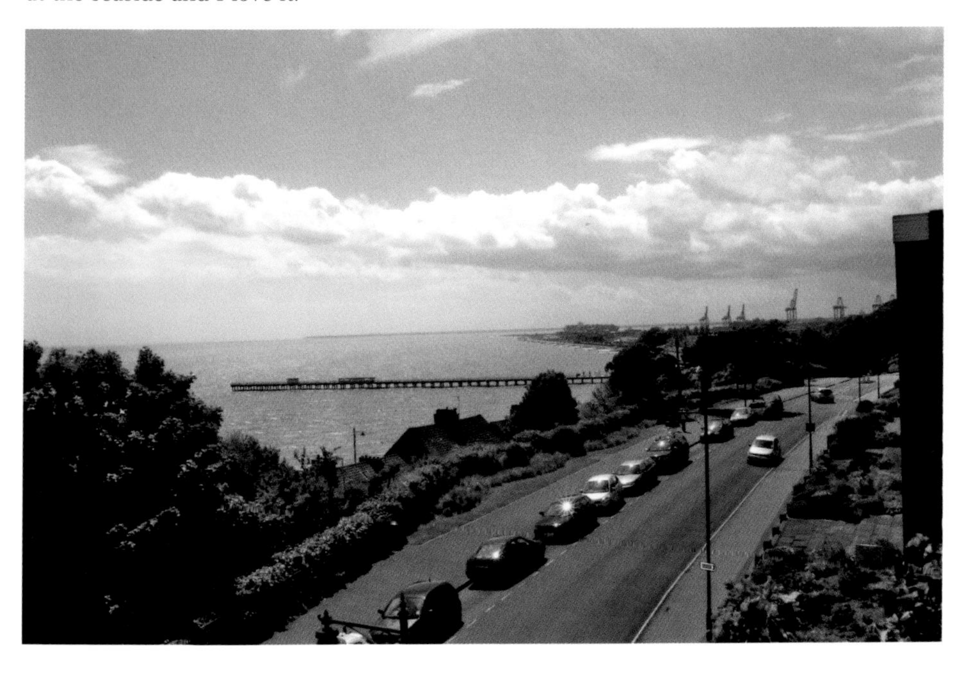

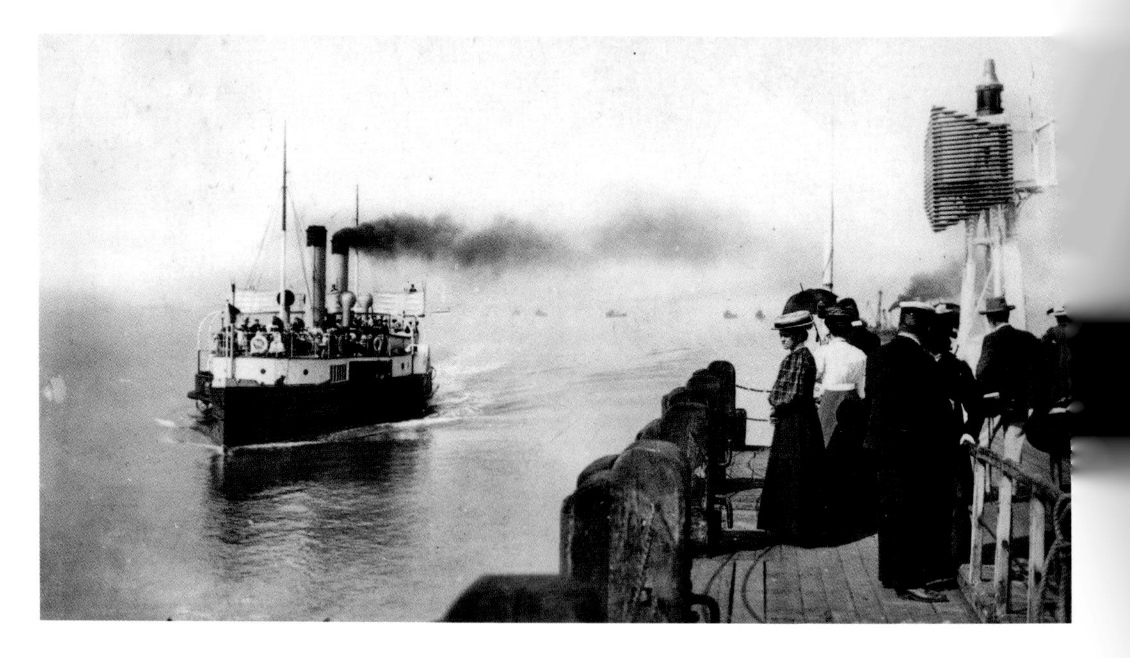

Felixstowe Old Pier *c.* **1910**

When in the 1870s Colonel George Tomline began to develop the new port of Felixstowe to rival Harwich, he planned a new rail link from Ipswich and a pier for the steamers to land. 'This is where we landed' is written on the front and the message sent to Chatham in Kent reads: 'Fancy Alf is going to take me to Brussels tomorrow Saturday night and returning Tuesday night...have lots to tell you am having a lovely time...' The successor to the Halfpenny Ferry to Harwich still operates with the ferry landing on the shore.

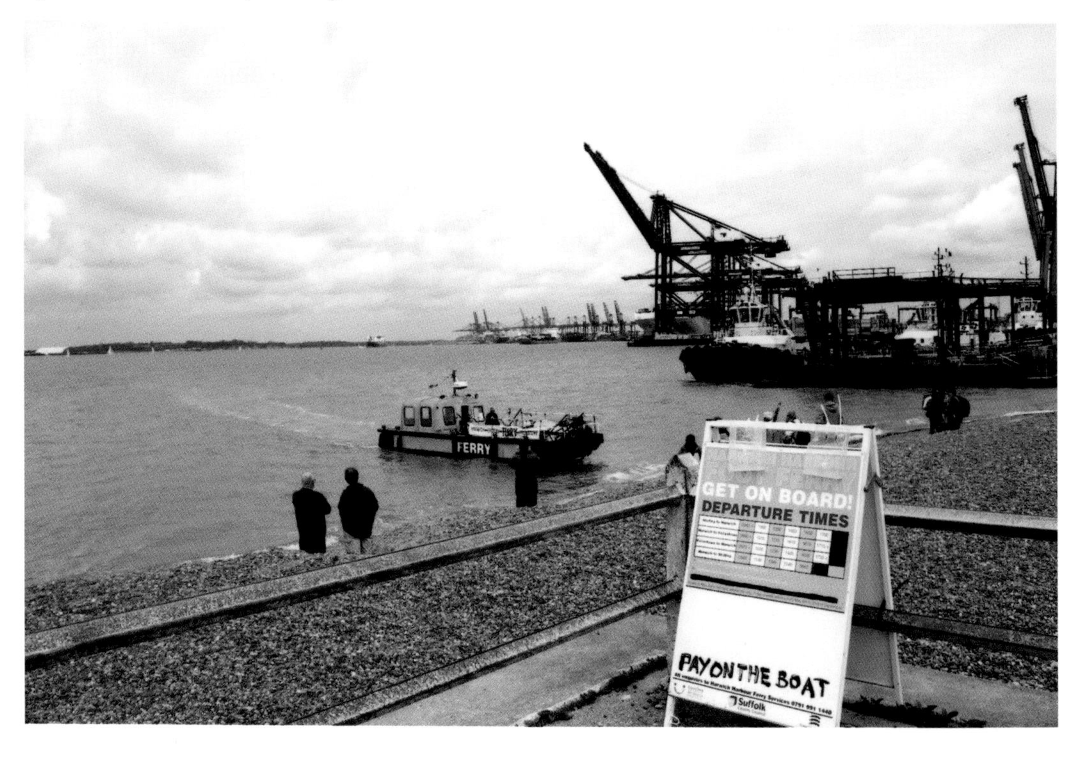

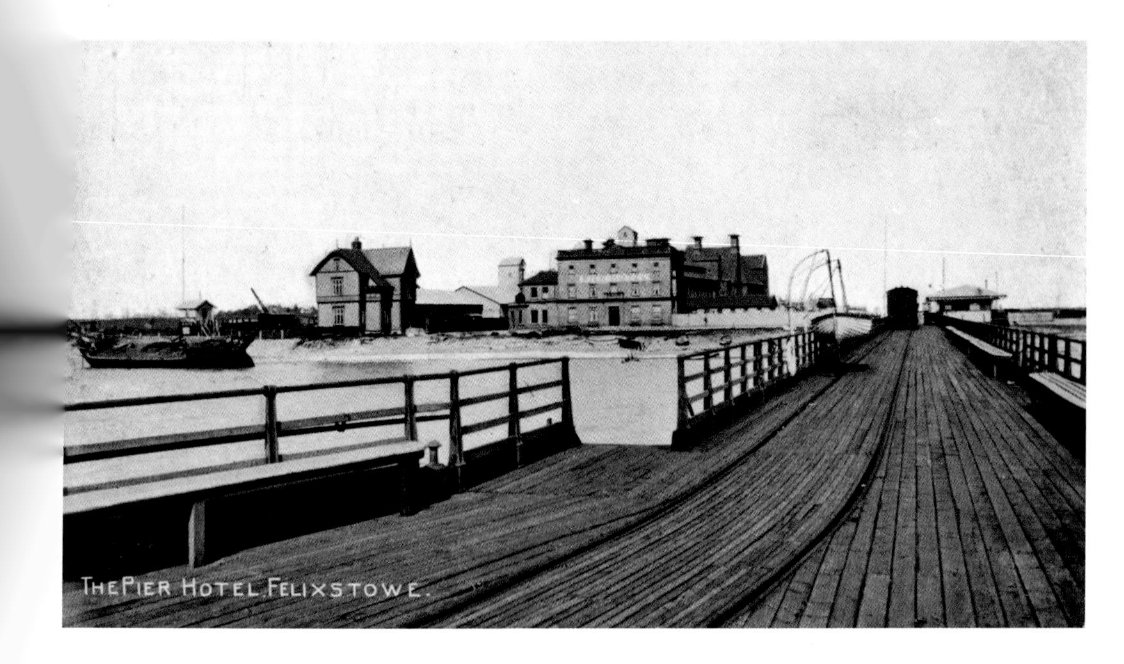

The Pier Hotel *c.* **1905**
The Felixstowe Railway and Pier Company took the railway line along the pier. Work began on the dock in 1881 and it was opened in 1884. The Pier Hotel, opened in 1877, was part of Tomline's ambitious plans for his new town. The hotel was primarily for passengers using the steamers that he hoped would operate to northern Germany. During the First World War the hotel served as a hospital and during Second World War it was the Headquarters for HMS *Beehive*, a Royal Naval Base for Motor Torpedo Boats, Motor Gun Boats and Motor Launches.

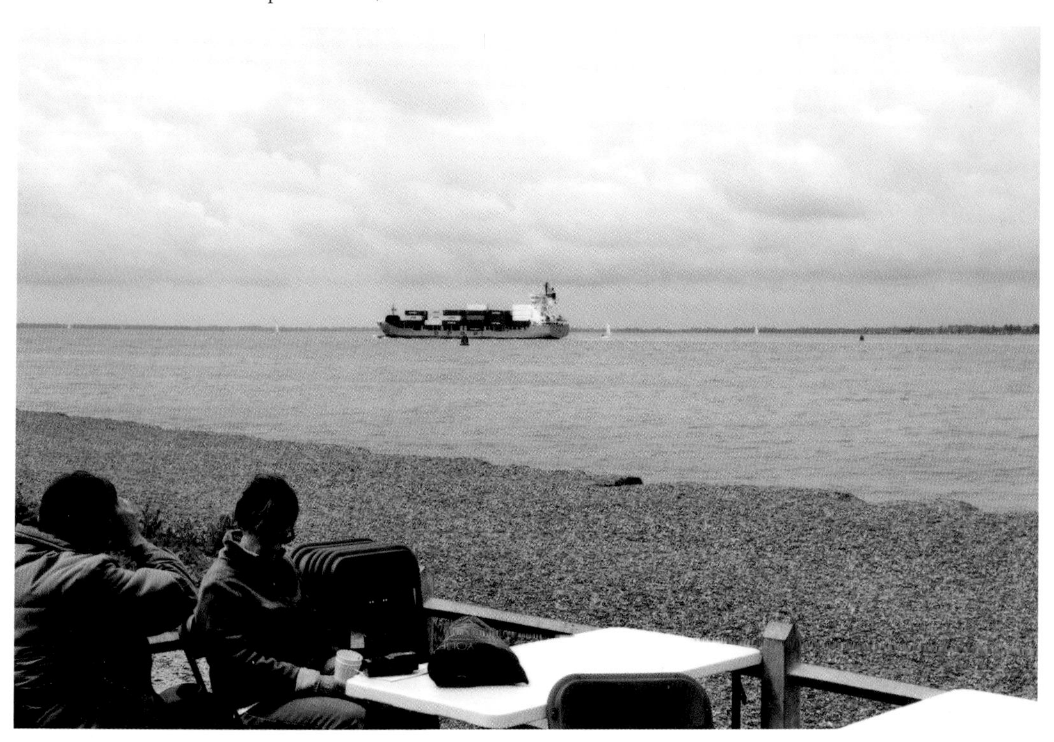

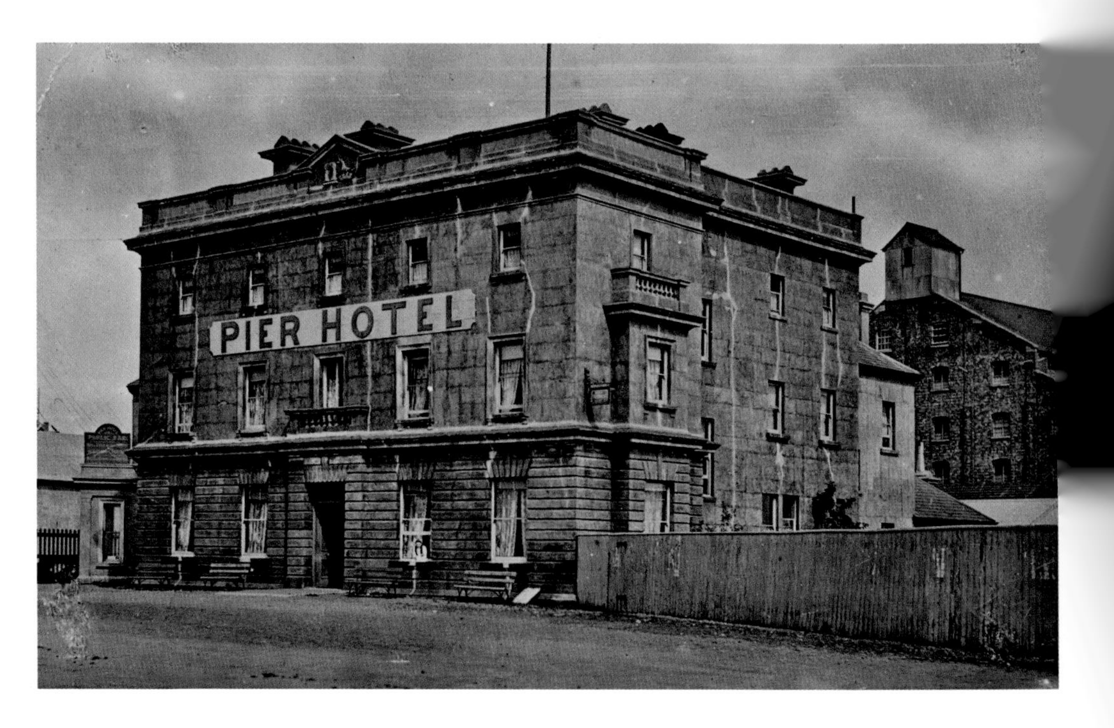

The Pier Hotel, Felixstowe
Known in later years as the Little Ships Hotel, it was swallowed up in the development of the port of Felixstowe, eventually closing in 1990 and lost in a fire soon after. Those who go to Landguard Point today to visit the historic fort, the nearby Museum, to see the activity of the container ships coming in and out of the busy port and the cruise ships, or to watch the sailing boats or catch the ferry, can still enjoy some traditional English refreshment.

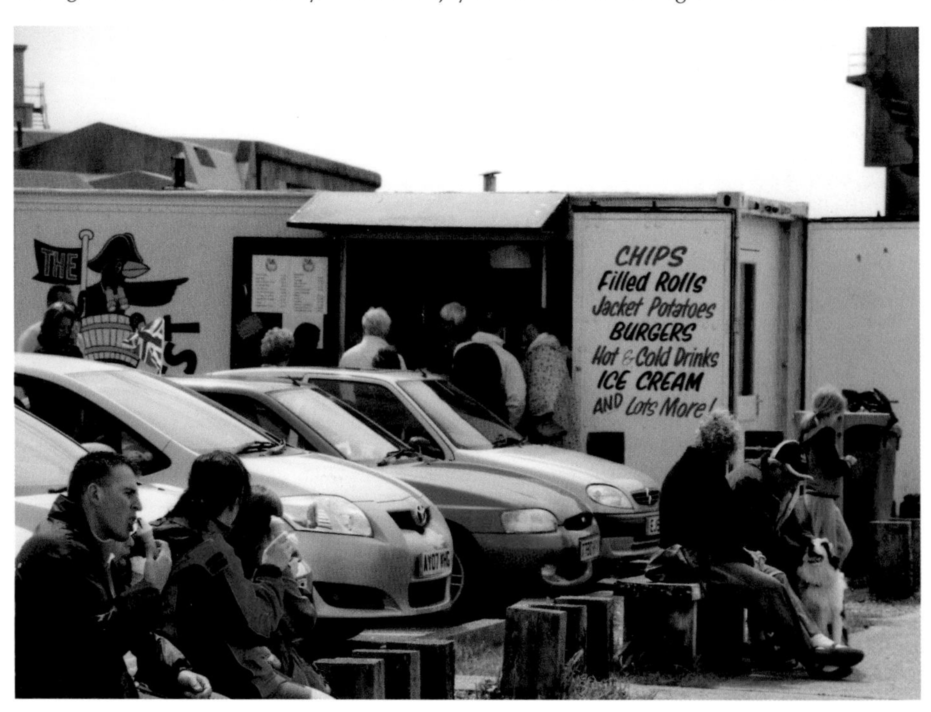

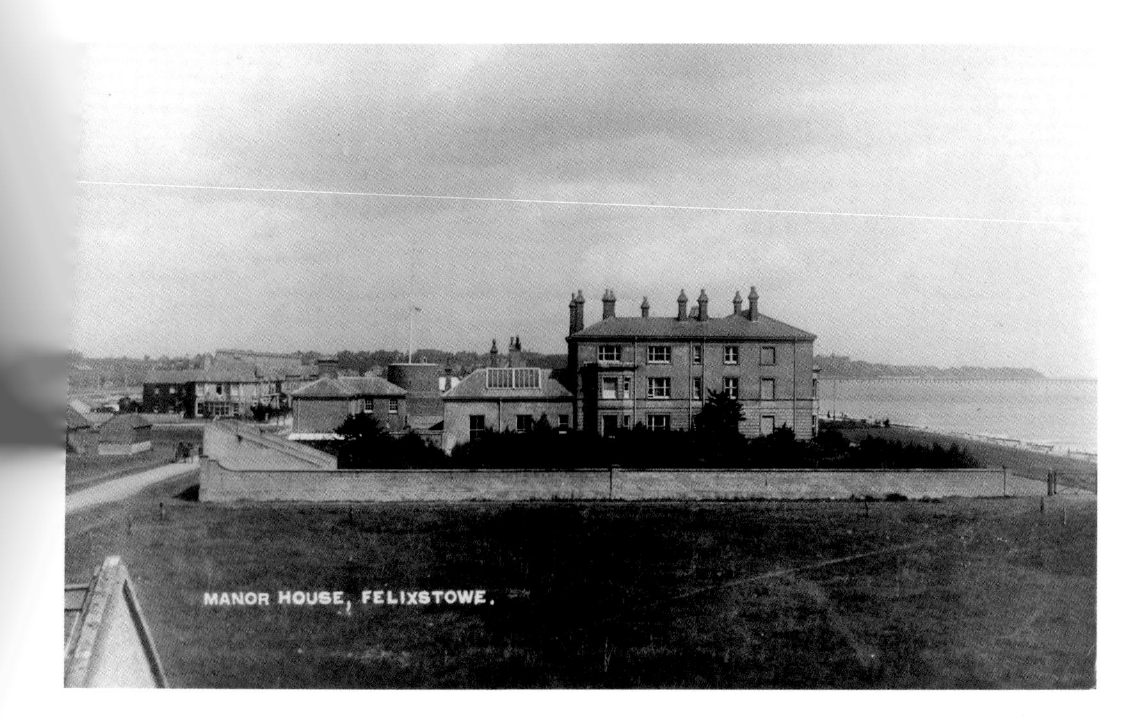

Manor House ***c.*** **1910**
Tomline's vision was to create a new resort along the southern seafront. In 1877 he built the Manor House Hotel and Manor Terrace which can be seen in the background. The Hotel wasn't successful, because already Felixstowe was developing more along the cliffs around the Bath Hotel. In 1888 the Manor became Tomline's Felixstowe home. After his death in 1889 it became a golf club, then in 1900 a preparatory school. During the First World War it was requisitioned as a naval officer's billet. Now much reduced in height it is part of the Suffolk Sands caravan park.

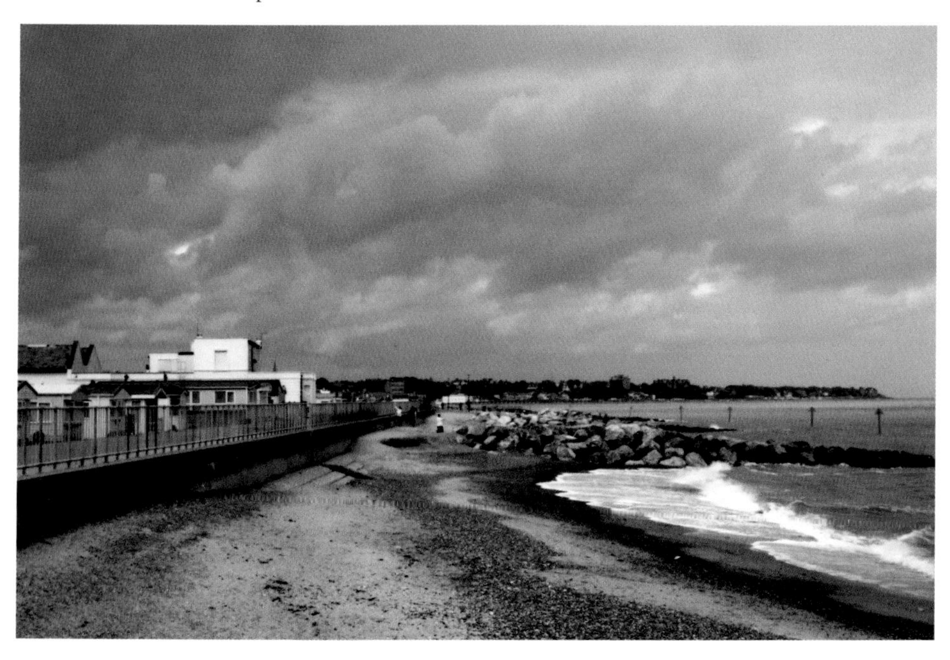

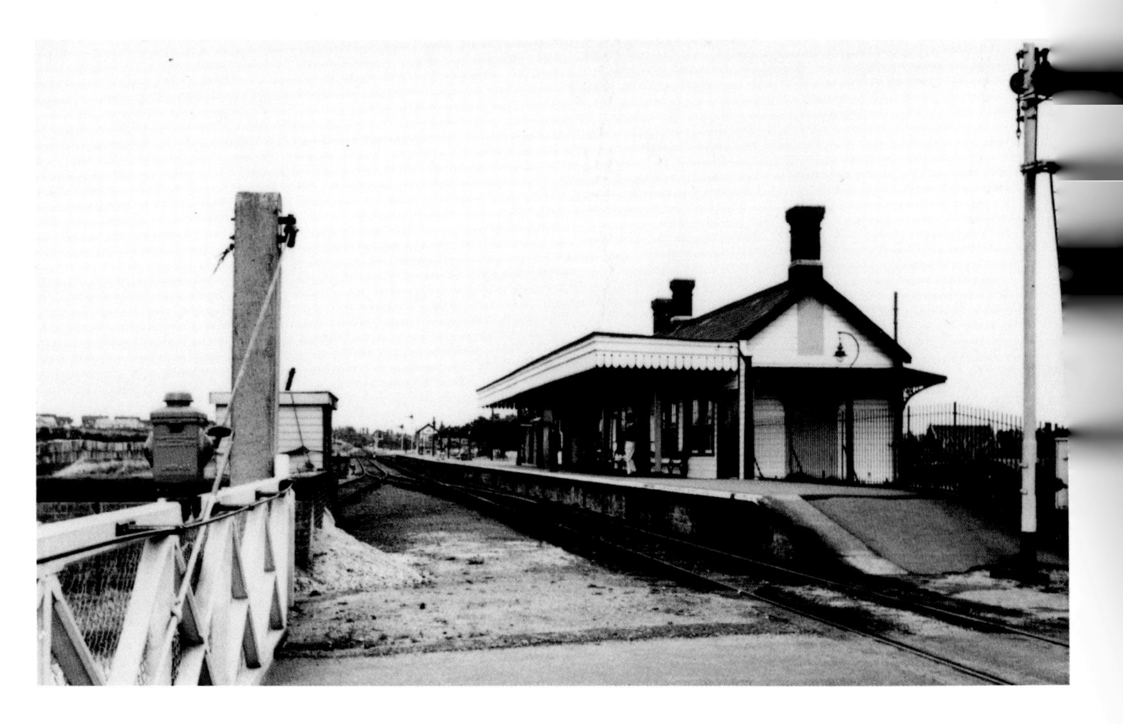

Beach Station

This station was opened in 1877 when Tomline's railway line from Ipswich reached the port. In 1887 the line was bought by the Great Eastern Railway. At first it was the town station, but when a new station was opened on Hamilton Road in 1898, it became known as the Beach Station. The Felixstowe Old Pier station closed in 1951 while this station remained open until 1967. Despite considerable local protests the building was eventually demolished in 2004.

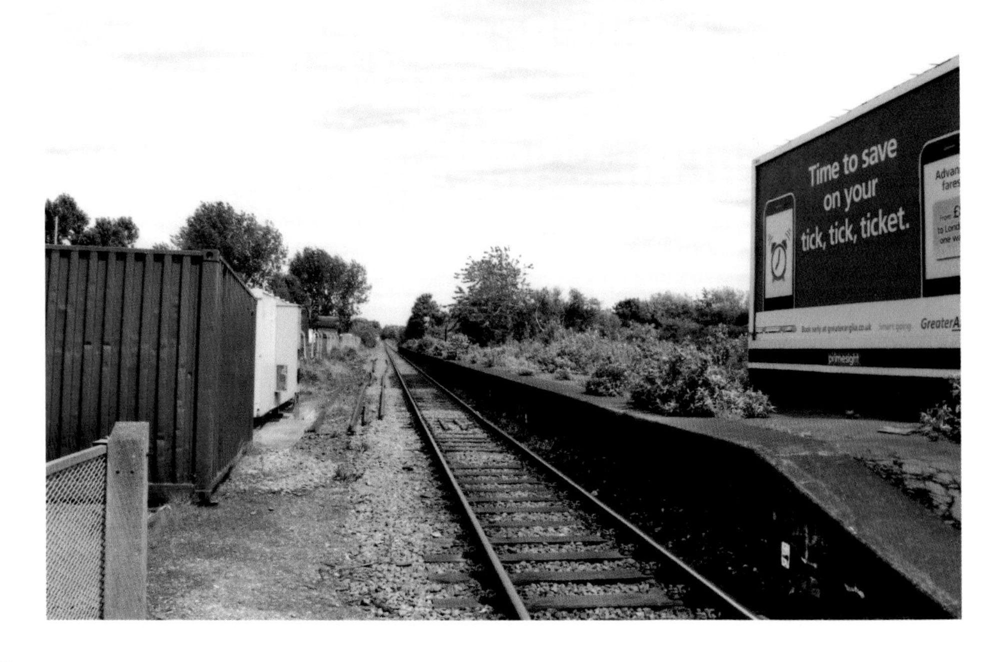

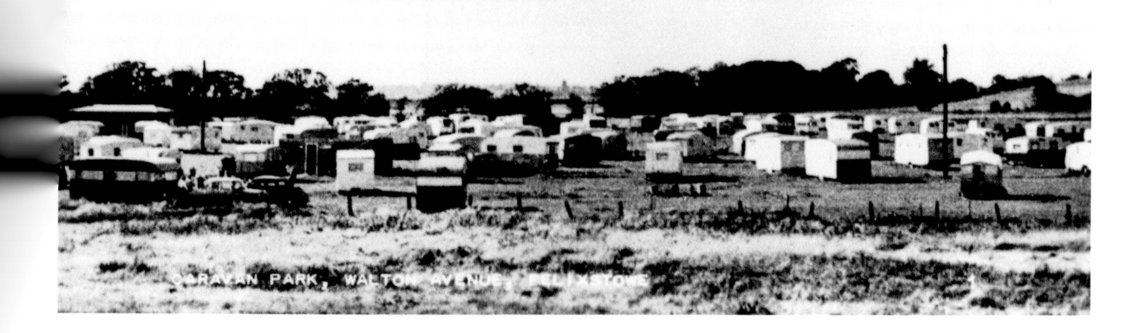

Caravan Park, Walton Avenue

Now known as the Felixstowe Beach Holiday Park, this caravan park benefitted from being next to the Beach station. Despite the closure of the station, in the age of the car it seems busier than ever. The early caravan parks were little more than fields with a basic wash and toilet block, a far cry from today. Part of the Hoseasons holiday business, it offers an indoor heated swimming pool, clubhouse, entertainment, amusements and an adventure playground for a family holiday.

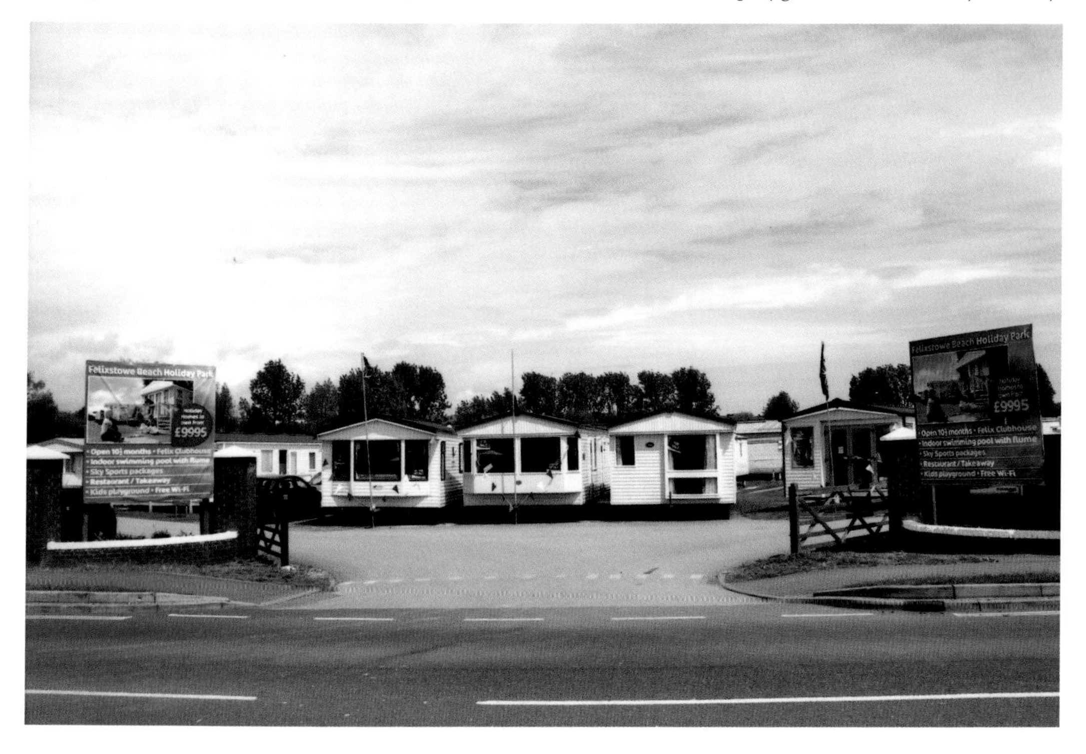

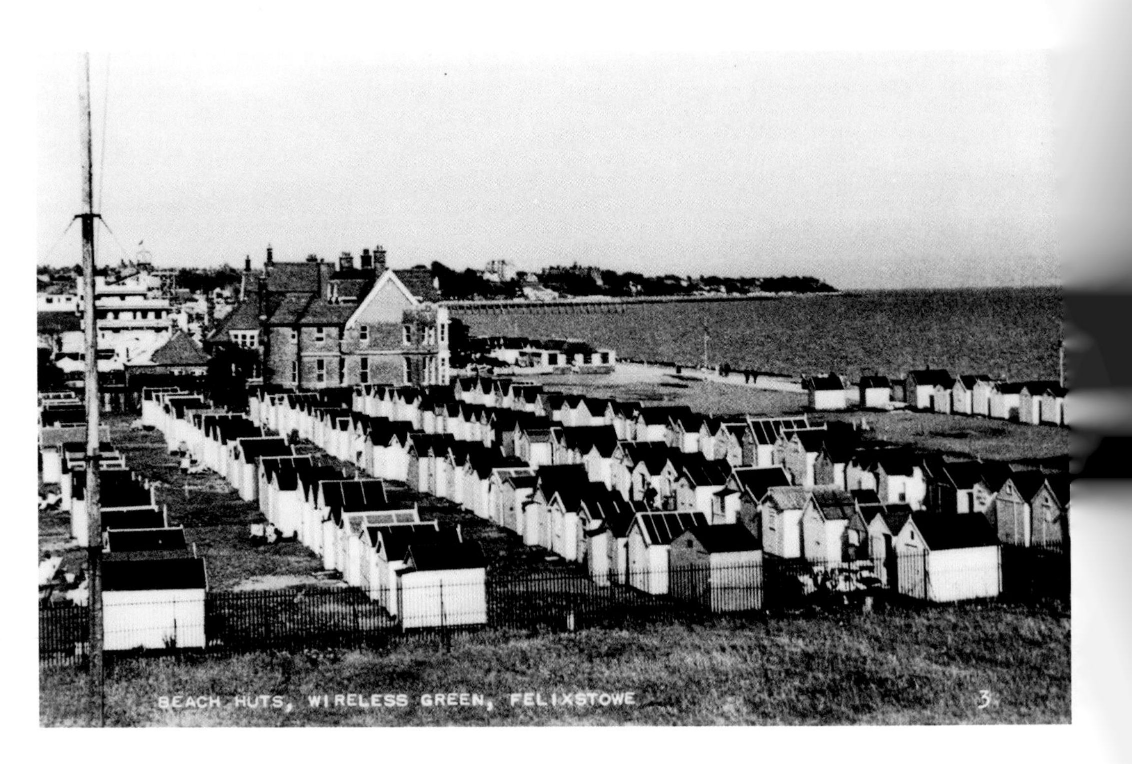

Beach Huts, Wireless Green *c.* 1950
Between the Manor House and the Herman de Stern Convalescent Home were these extraordinary rows of beach huts. The twenty-three houses of the Victorian Manor Terrace lie behind this site. Manor Terrace seems as far as Tomline's new resort reached. This site, though low lying and protected by a sea wall, and the area around the Martello Tower has been cleared and a housing redevelopment scheme has just begun. The Wireless Green reference is to the naval radio station that used to be at Martello Tower P.

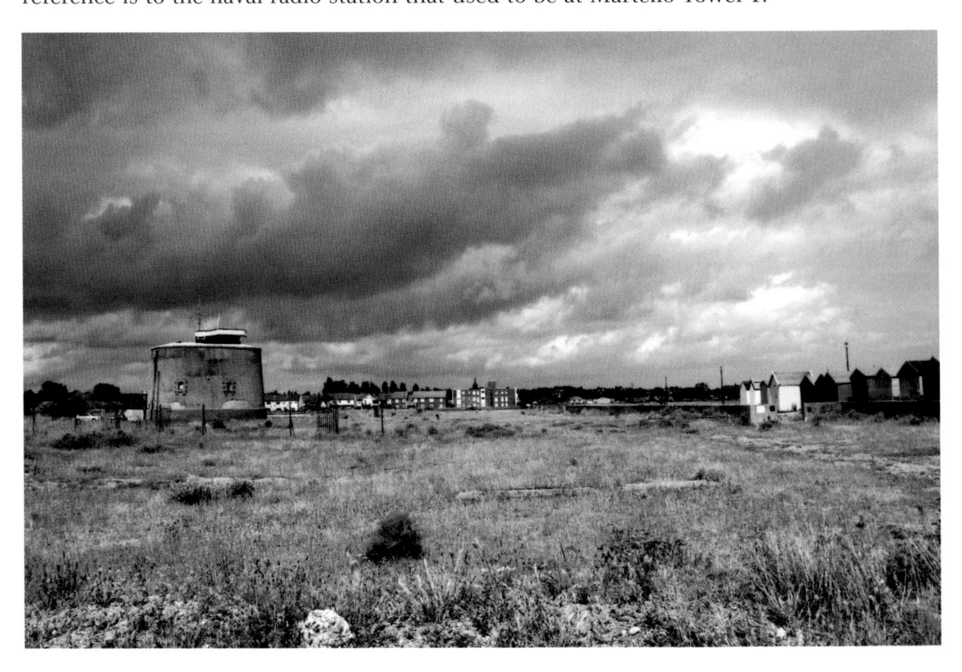

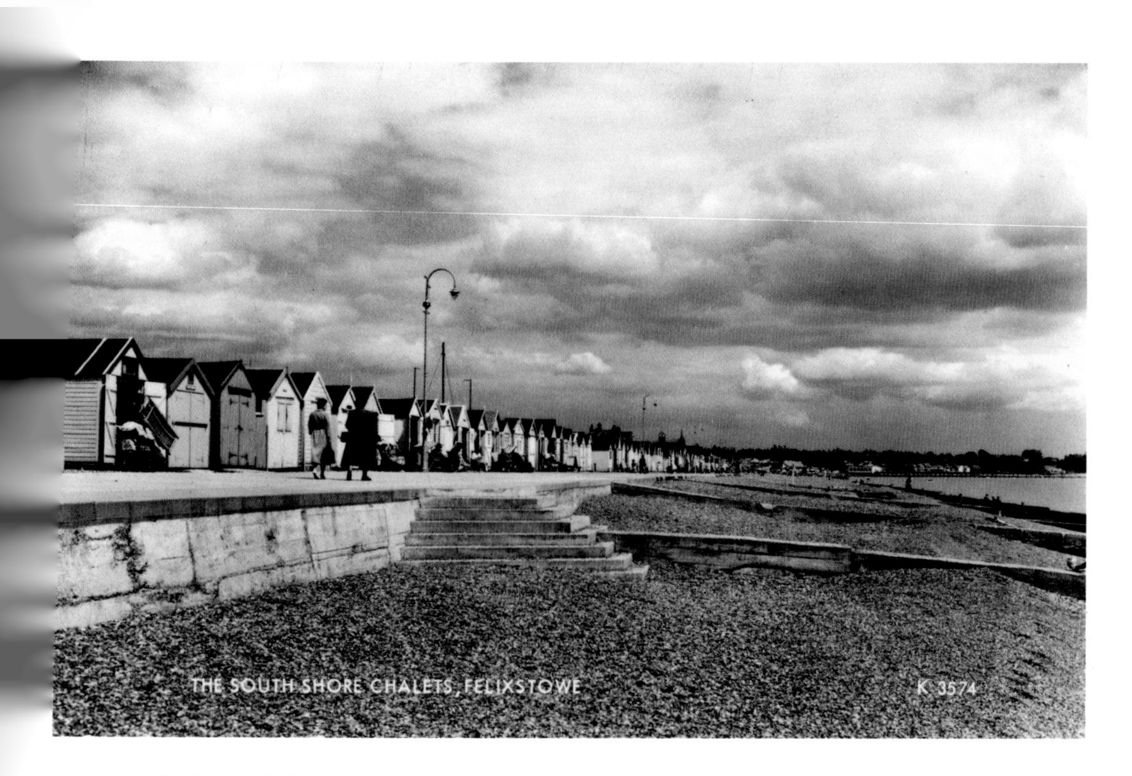

South Shore Chalets, 1950s

As with Southwold, the beach huts are a feature along the South Shore and along parts of the promenade. For many people this is their small castle by the sea and they are cherished and when sold fetch a high price.

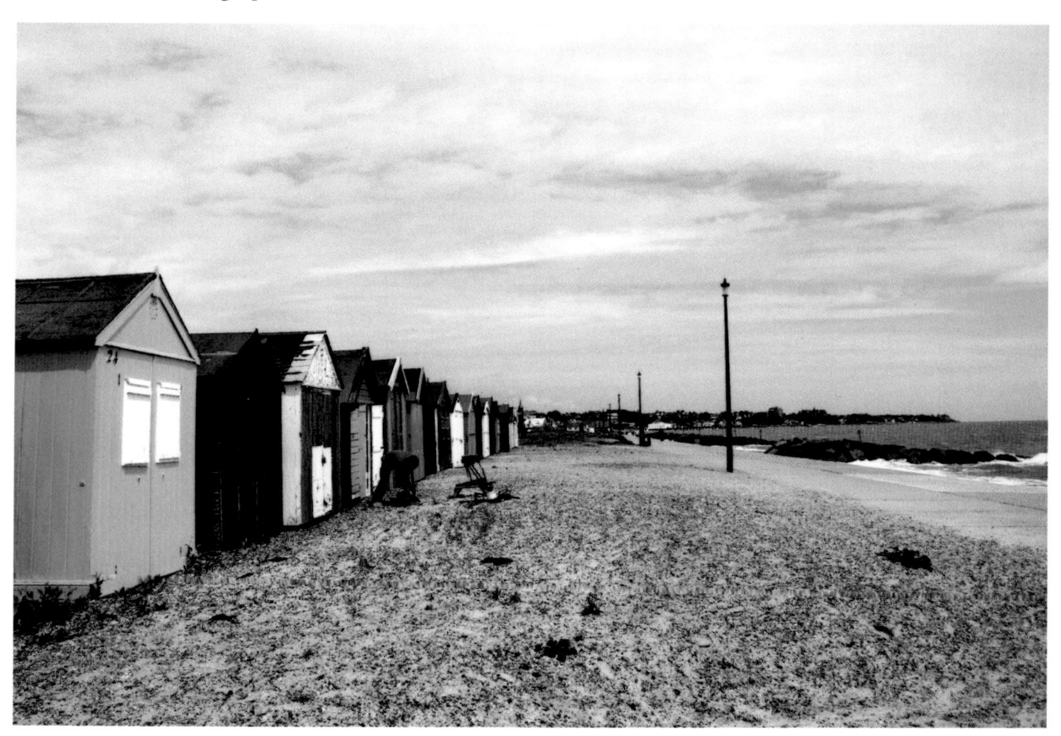

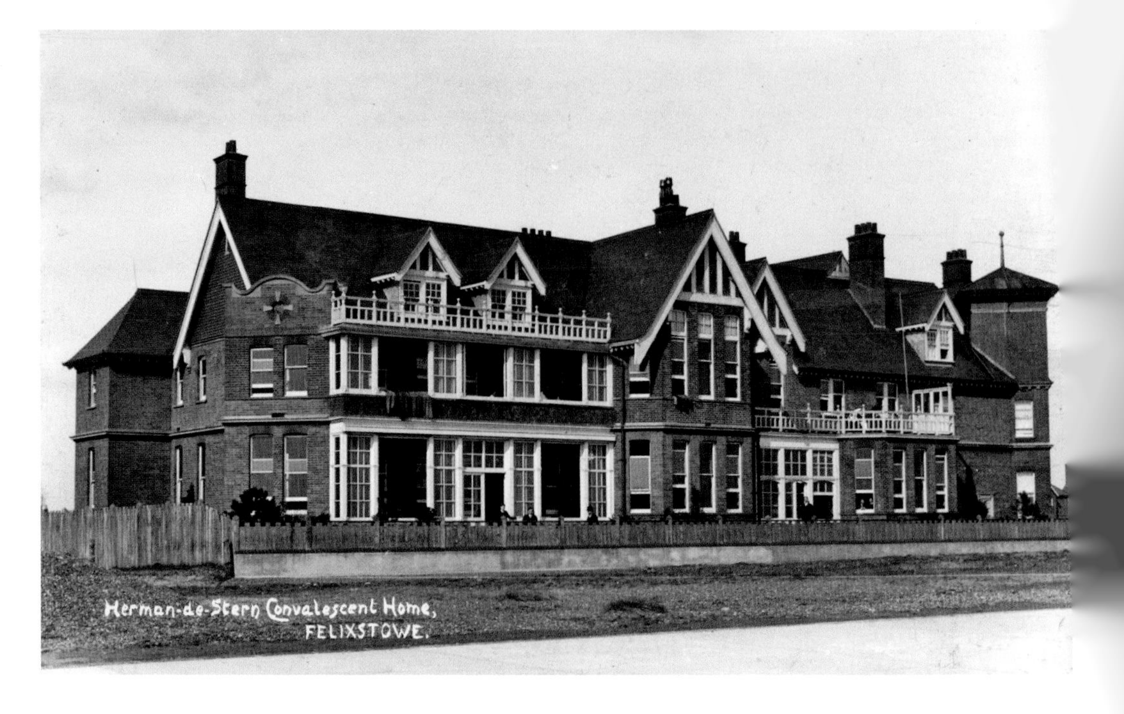

Herman de Stern Convalescent Home *c.* 1910
Baron de Stern (1815–1887) was a banker and one of the wealthiest men in Britain. This home for male patients of the London Hospital was built and endowed by his widow in his memory and opened in 1902. According to Alf in this early postcard: 'The Home is jolly fine and a fine journey down. Write soon.' During the First World War it became a military hospital. The building was eventually sold by the NHS in around 1980. In 2005 it was destroyed by fire. The boulder in the photograph below marks the completion of the Flood Alleviation Scheme in 2008.

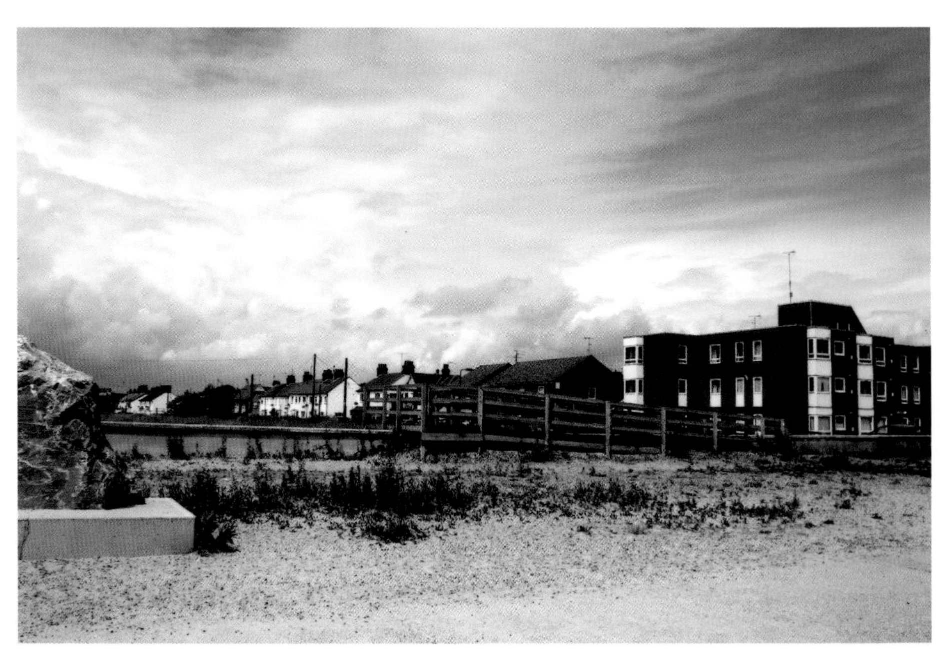

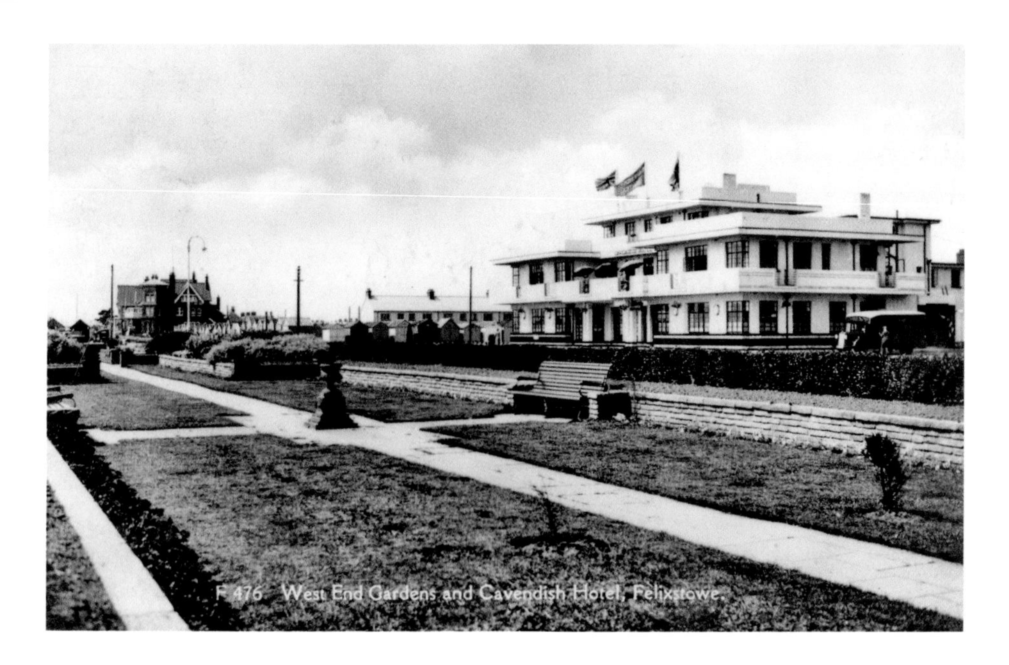

Cavendish Hotel ***c.*** **1938**

The splendid Cavendish on Sea Road opened in 1937. In its heyday in the 1950s it boasted 'Excellent cuisine, produce from own farm, ample garage accommodation, central heating and hot and cold water in all bedrooms.' In 1953 when the East Coast Floods hit Felixstowe and thirty-nine people died with hundreds being made homeless, the Cavendish opened as a rescue centre for two weeks. A popular music centre for young people in the '70s, in 1988 it was demolished and this prime seafront site remains undeveloped being used solely for a Sunday market.

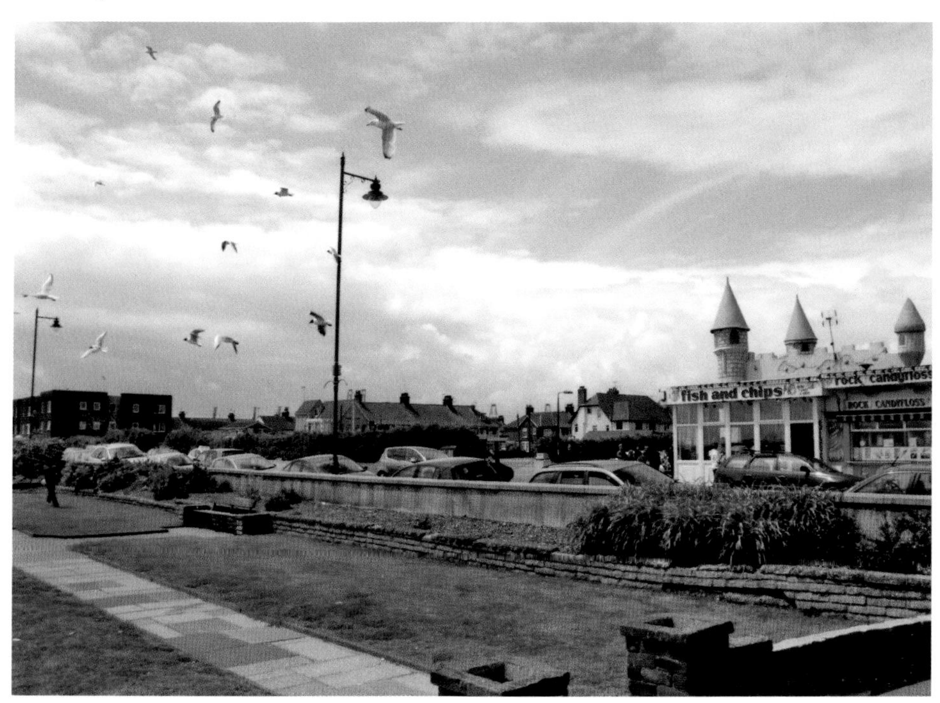

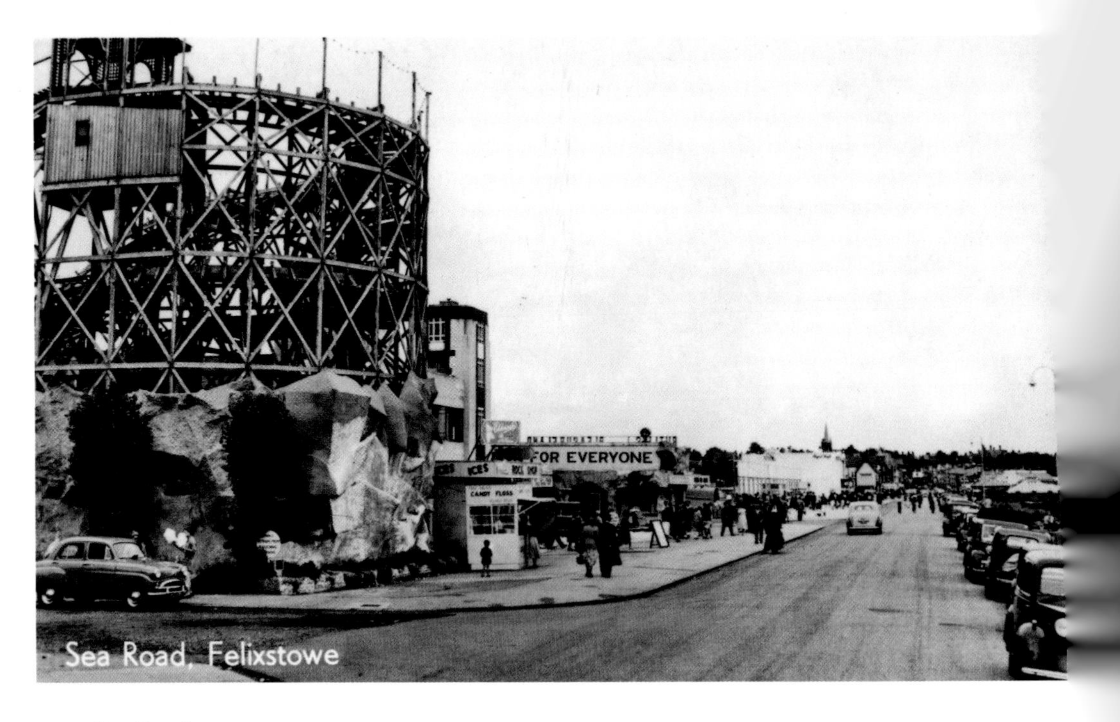

Sea Road *c*. 1955
Billy Butlin opened the amusement park here in 1932. A feature of the park was the wooden roller coaster, which was eventually demolished in 1976. Manning's have run the park since the end of the Second World War and have owned it since 1995. In the 1947 guide, Butlin's claimed the 'Longest Snack Bar in East Anglia'. There were Dodgems, Big Eli Wheel, Galloping Horses, Loop o' Planes, the Ghost Train and Caves of Love, while today there is a waltzer, children's rides, crazy golf, markets and events, indoor amusements and food outlets, with ambitious plans for future attractions.

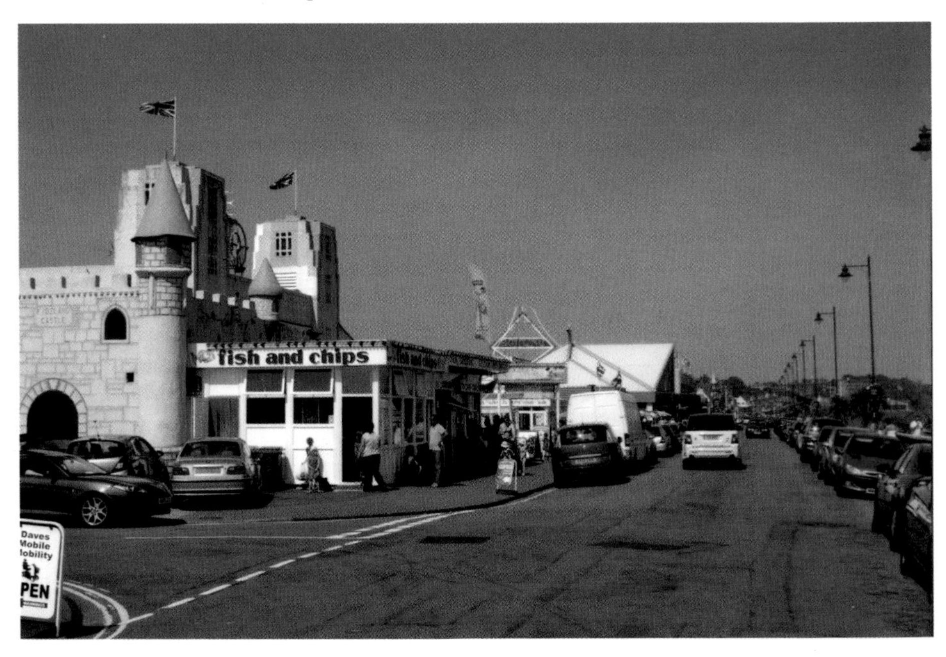

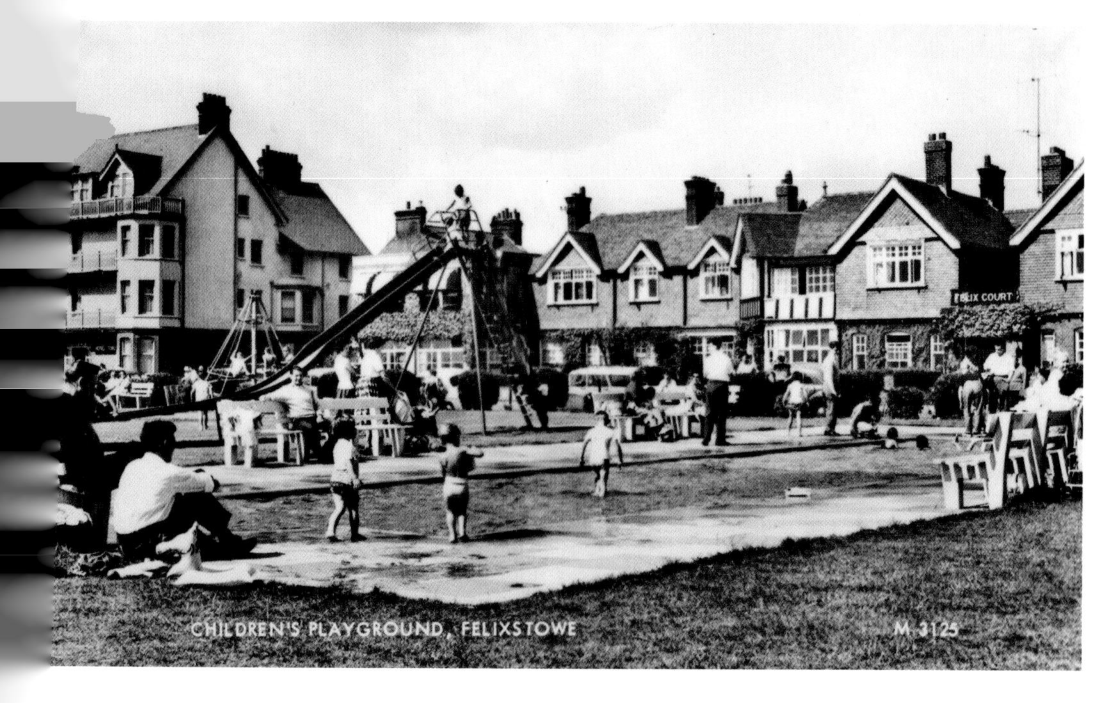

Children's Playground *c.* **1955**

A small children's play area and paddling pool was situated on the gardens opposite the Felix Court Hotel. The hotel closed in 1972 and part of it is now the Felsto Arms. The site of this small play area and paddling pool is now in a sorry state, which is a shame as families appreciate some inexpensive facilities while at the seaside. The donkey rides are based on this part of the green.

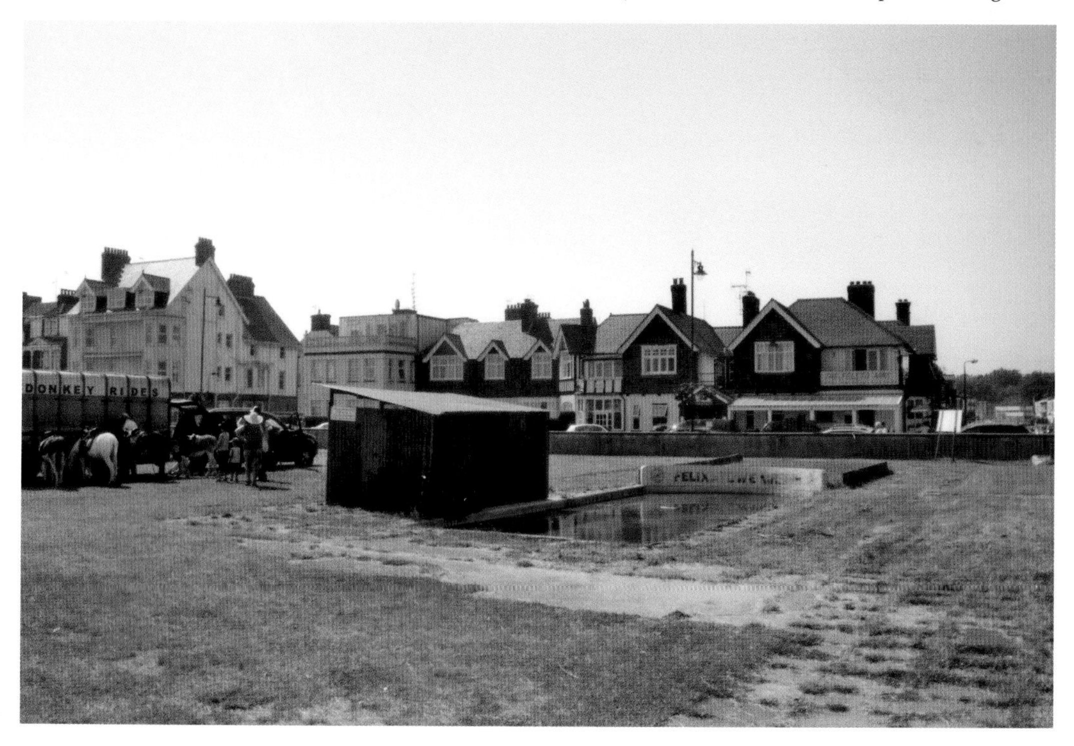

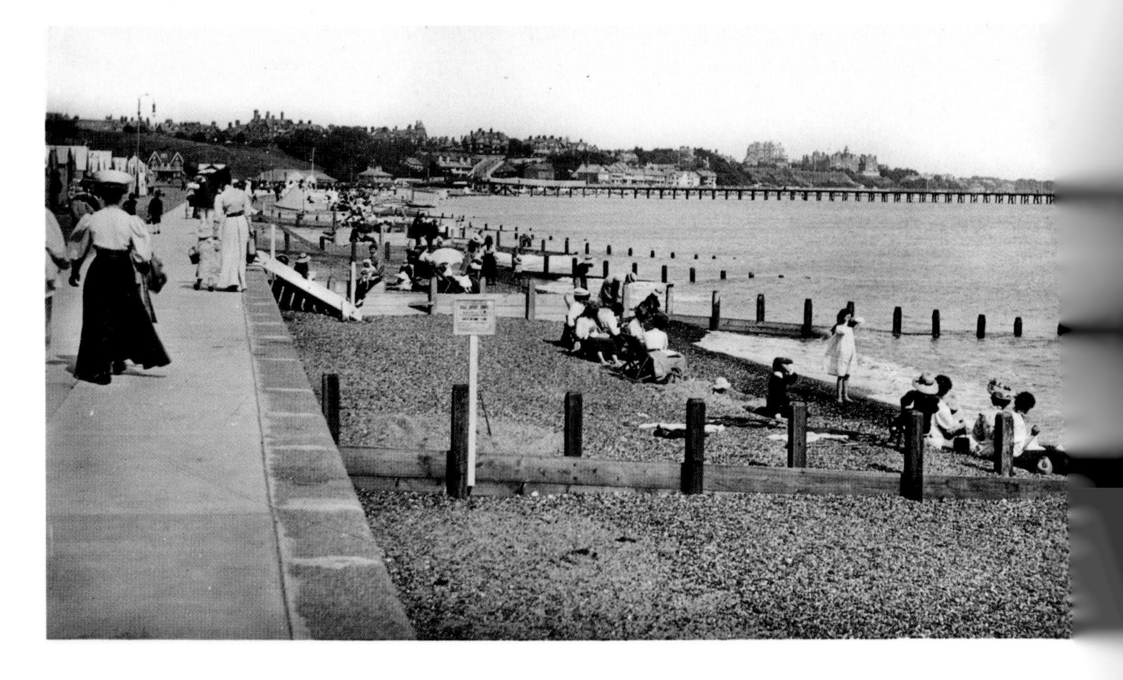

The Bay, Looking East 1908

A card sent to Dulwich in August 1908: 'We have had splendid weather up to the present, today is rather cloudy.' By 1904 a new two mile Promenade was in place showing how the resort was growing in popularity. The hotels were spreading along the Sea Road. Before the First World War, gardens were laid out between Sea Road and the promenade. The bathing machines are lined up to form a bathing station with changing facilities.

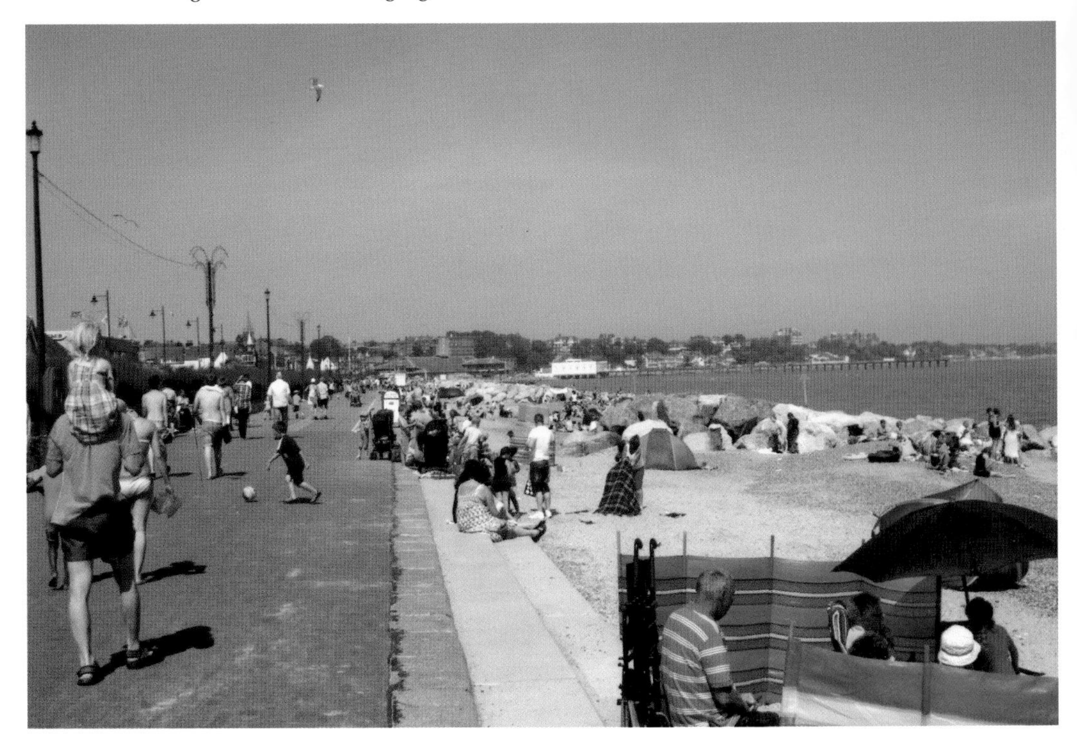

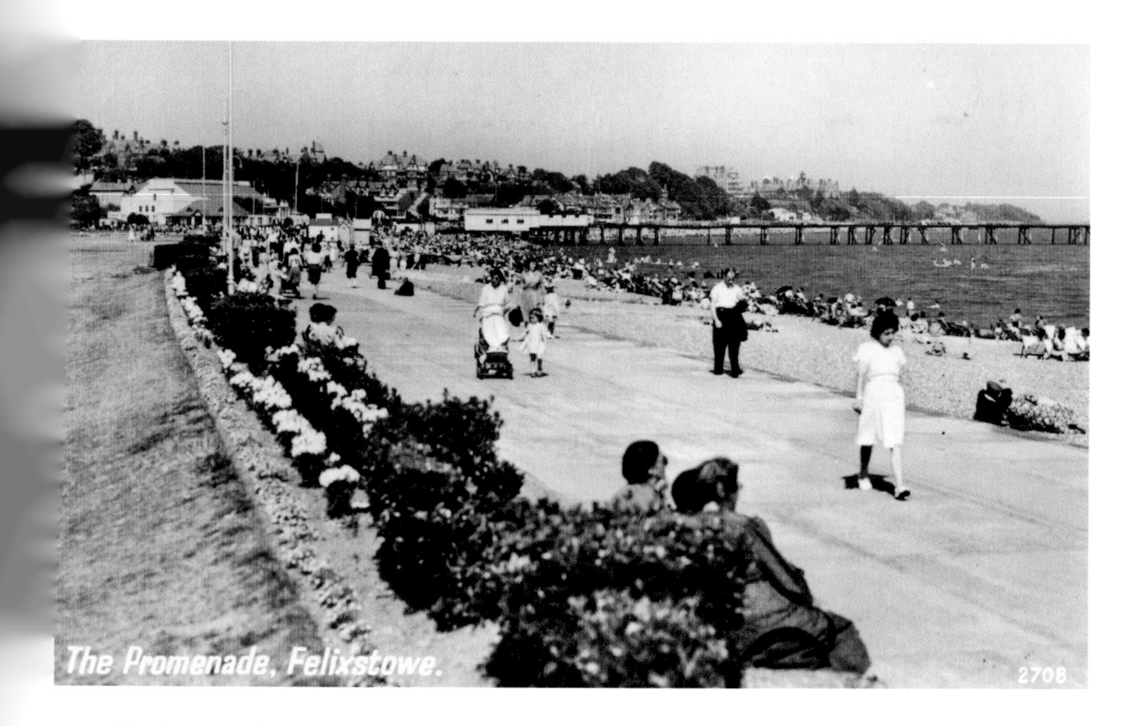

The Promenade *c.* 1950
Felixstowe was a front line town in both the First World War and the Second World War. In 1913 a naval air station was built next to the port. From 1924 to 1939 it was the home of the Marine Aircraft Experimental Establishment and holidaymakers got used to seeing the flying boats over the town. There were the naval connections already mentioned and the use of many hotels and houses as the First World War hospitals brought many recovered patients back to the resort in peace time.

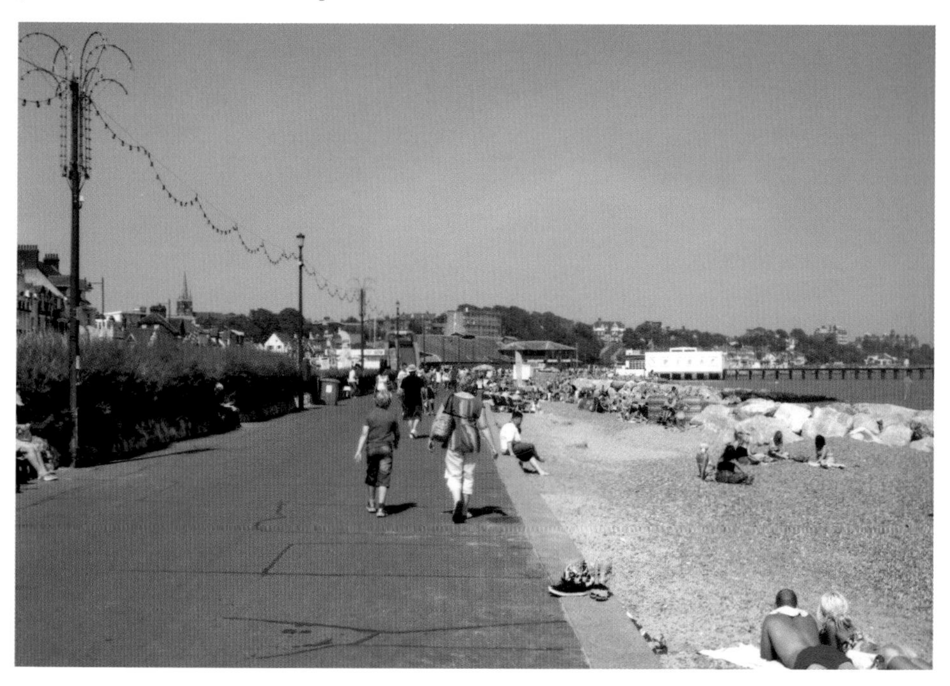

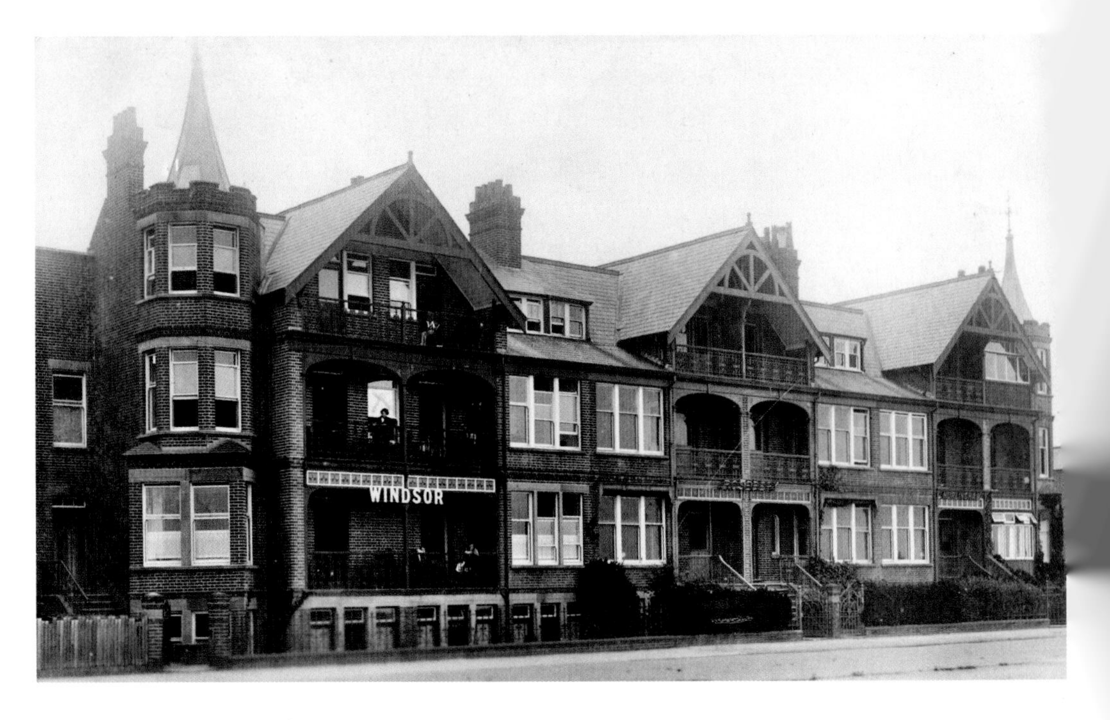

The Windsor Hotel *c.* 1920

The Windsor Hotel once occupied this distinctive turreted seafront building. By the time of the 1936 Guide it was known as the 'Bristol – Felixstowe's Popular Private Hotel' with accommodation for fifty guests and 'every modern convenience'. The right hand side of the building at that time was the Bracondale Private Hotel with forty bedrooms and the 'Best Position on the Sea Front'. By 1950 it was the Rosebery Private Hotel. Today it appears to be all apartments.

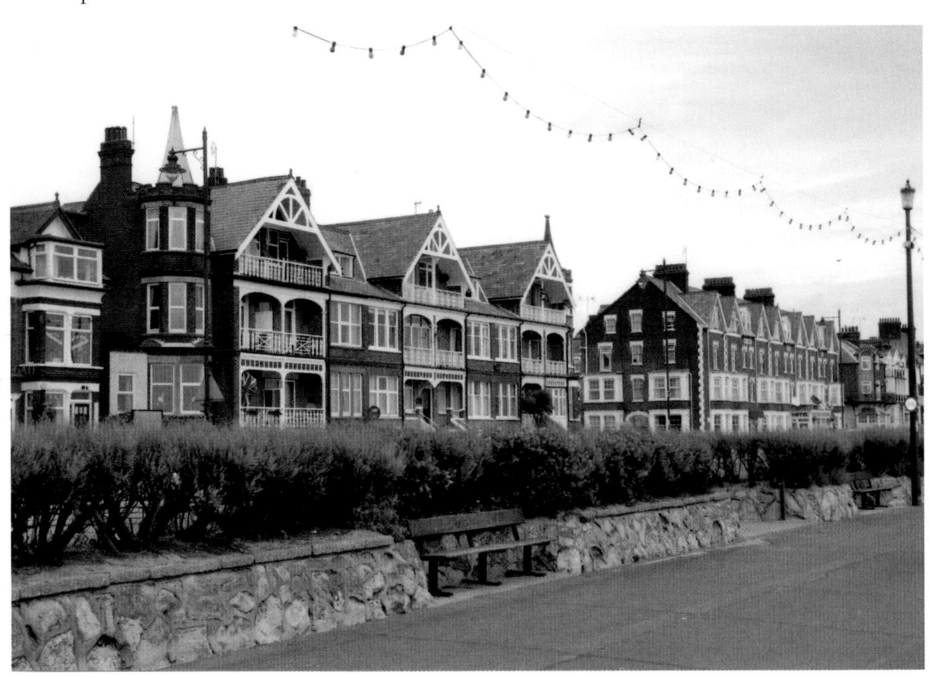

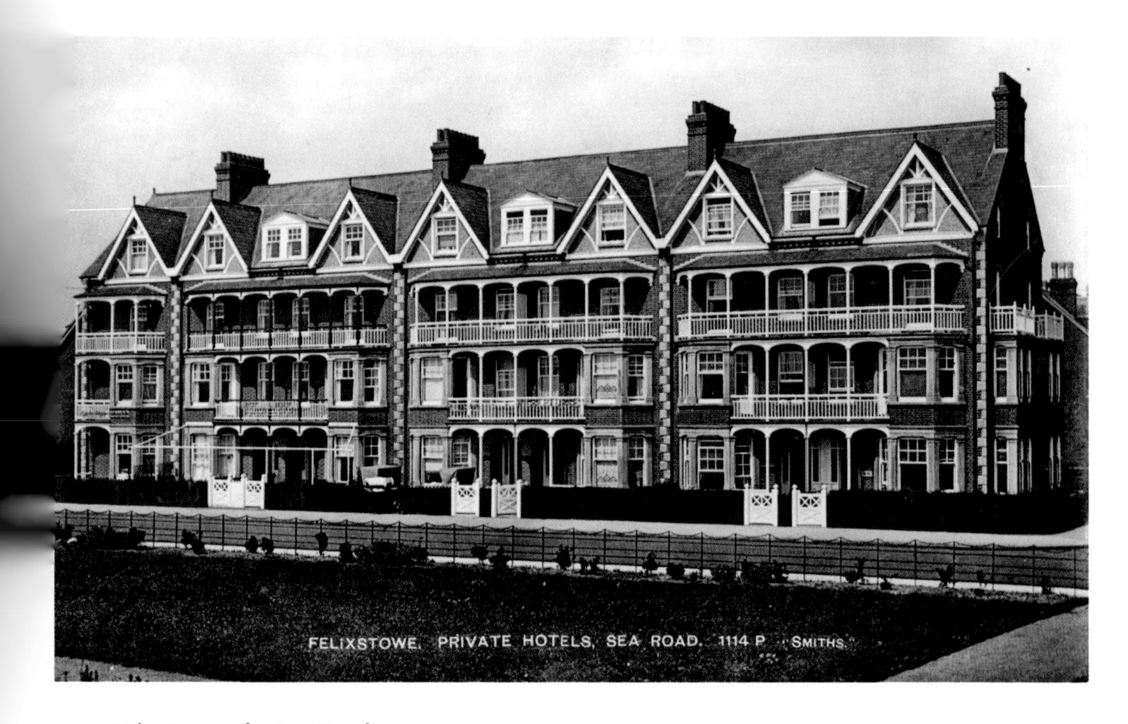

Private Hotels, Sea Road 1914

Also advertising itself in the 1930s as 'the best position on the sea front' with accommodation for over 100 guests, the Marlborough is still in business today. Whereas it was once one of many along Sea Road, it now claims to be 'the largest and only sea front hotel' in the resort. It has forty-nine *en suite* bedrooms and a lift. The original wooden balconies were removed when the hotel was modernised and extended in the late 1970s.

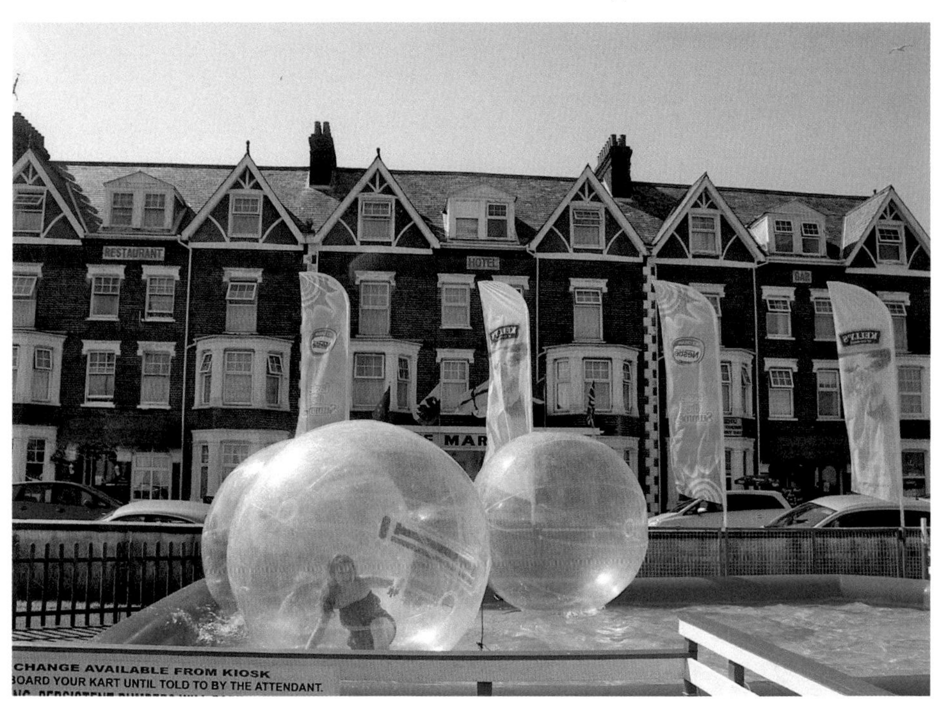

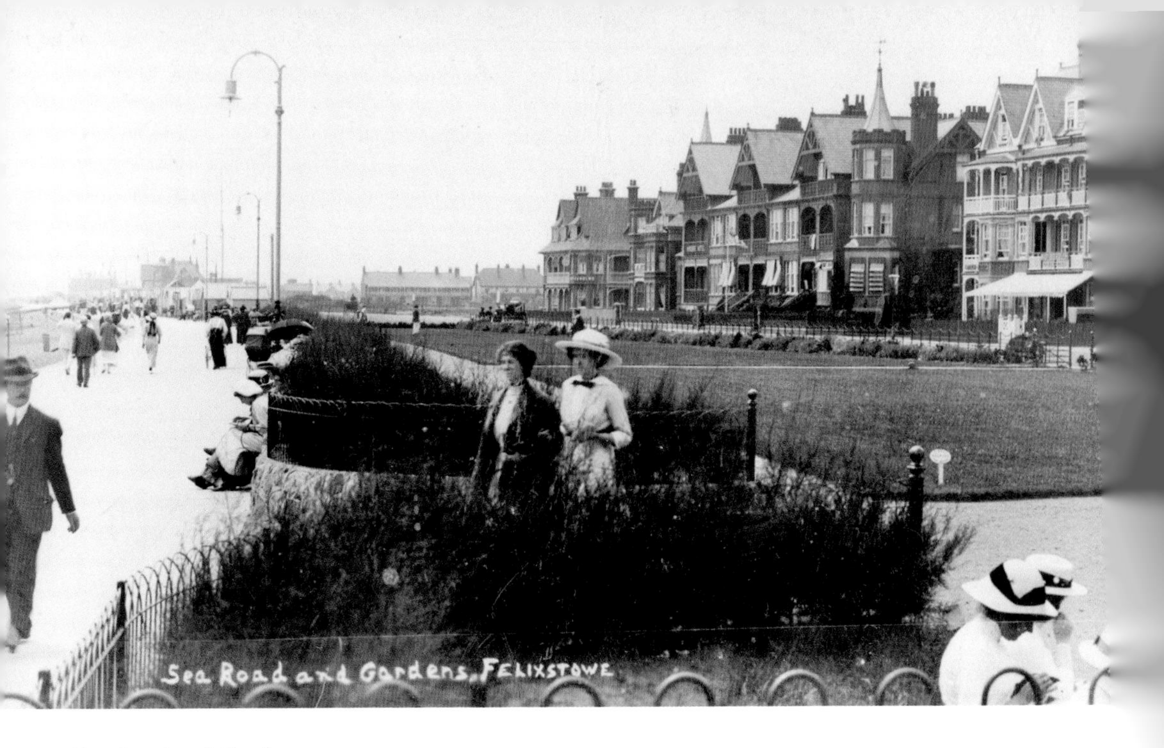

Sea Road and Gardens *c.* 1920

A part of Sea Road immediately recognisable today. In the 1930s Beecholme was a private hotel with central heating in public rooms, hot and cold water in all bedrooms, gas fires, and spring mattresses in all bedrooms. By 1950, Slumberland mattresses were part of the holiday experience offered; obviously a comfortable night's sleep was considered essential. Below is the same view from the other direction taken in the 1930s.

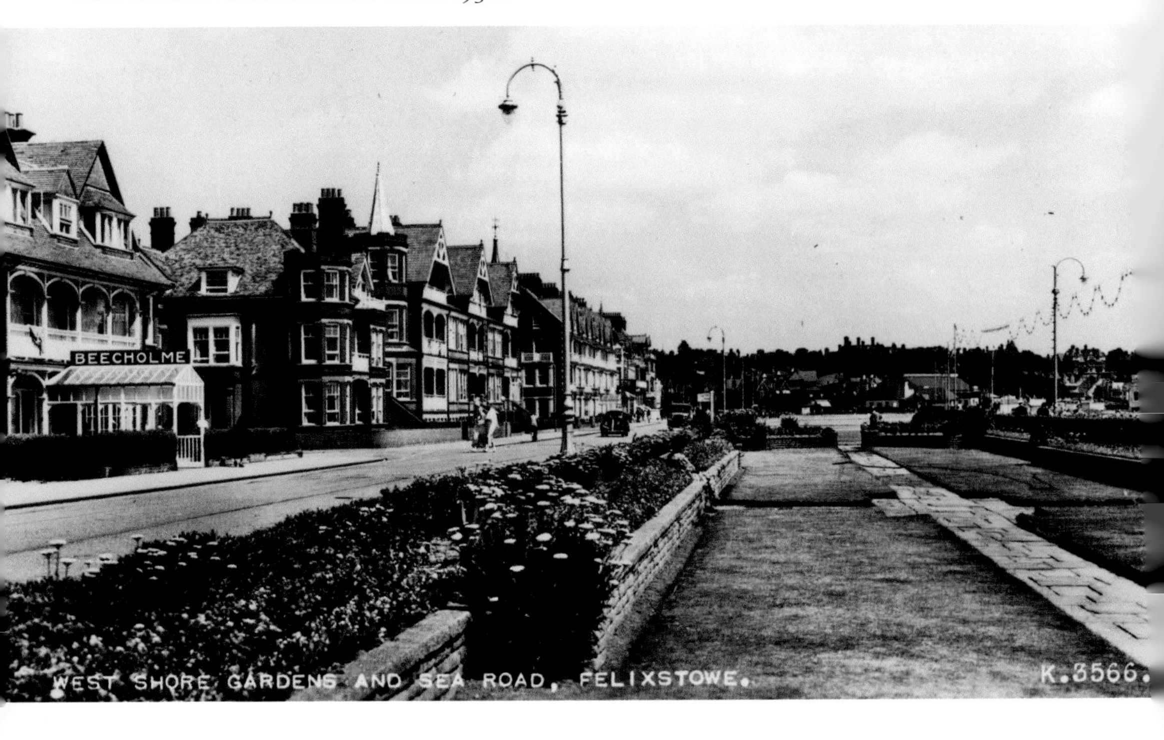

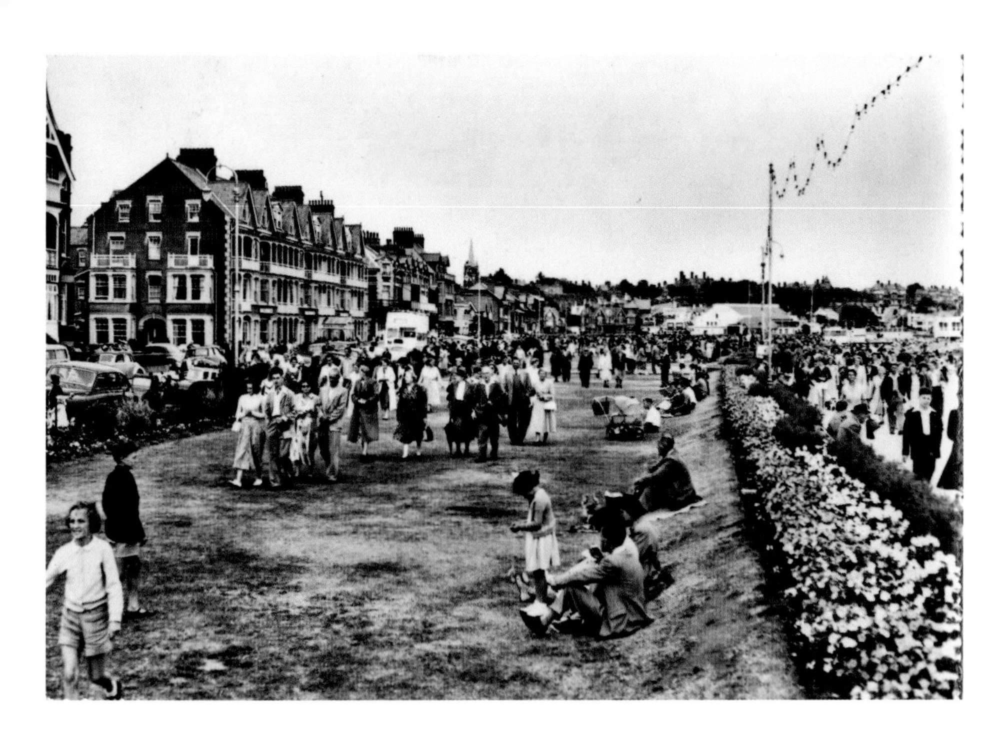

West End Lawns *c.* 1953
Surely a bank holiday when the resort would fill with day trippers? How the sea front businesses would like to see these days return. After a very wet start to the season everywhere this year, some scorching weather in late July that coincided with the school summer holidays brought the crowds flocking back; 'just like the riviera,' someone remarked to me.

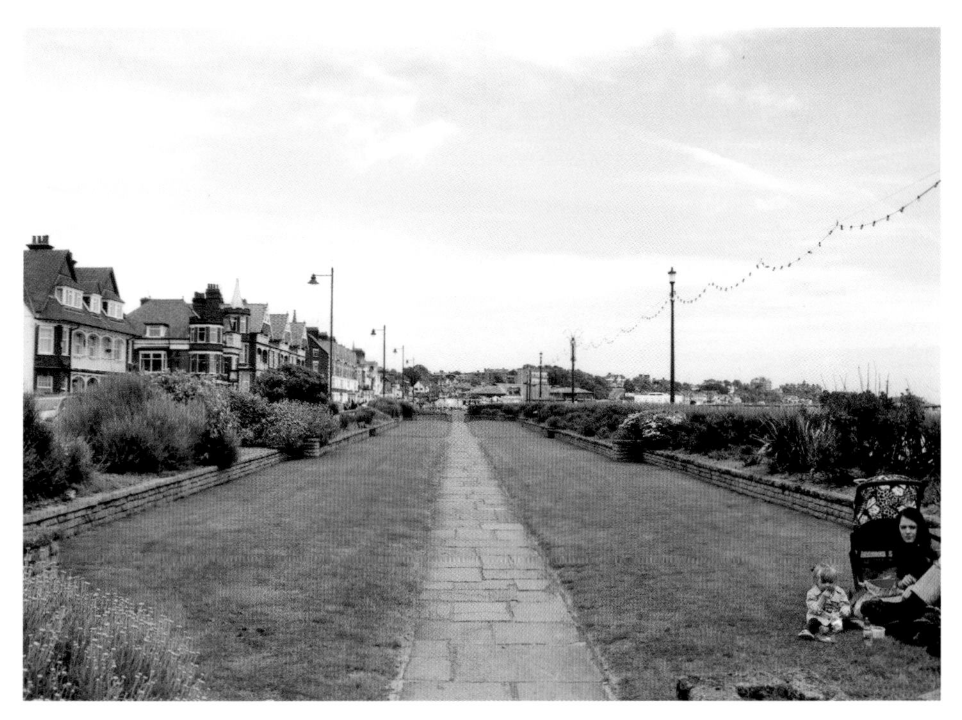

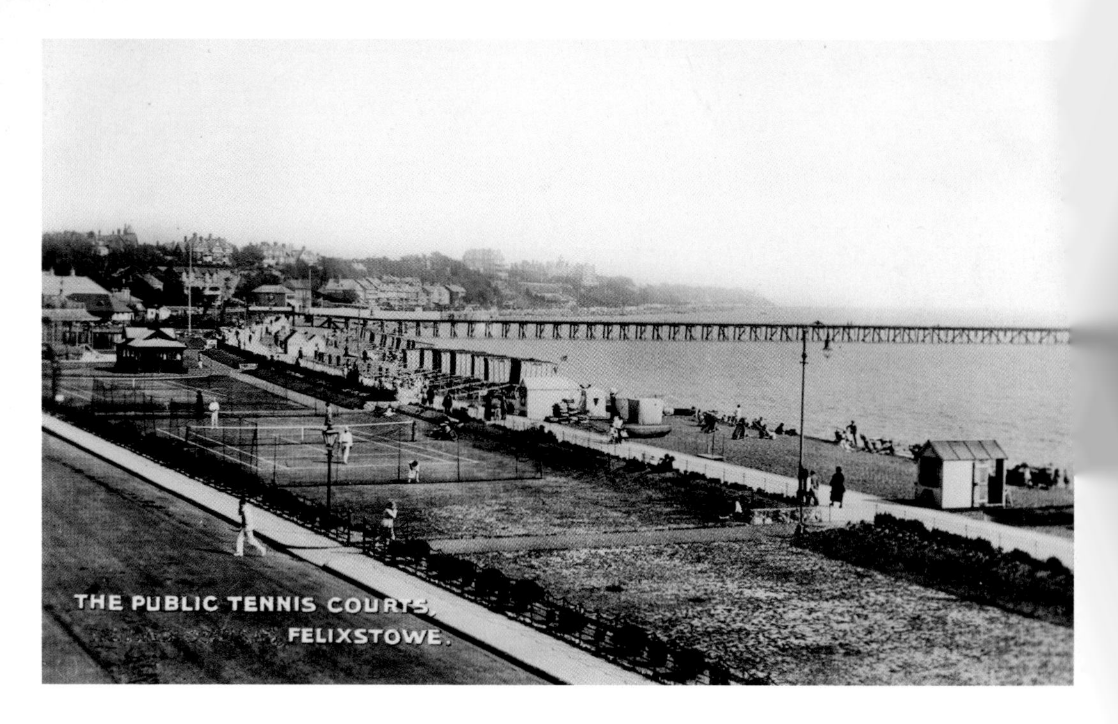

Public Tennis Courts *c.* 1920
Sea Road and the Gardens showing the bandstand and the model yacht pond and boating lake as they were laid out just before the First World War. Tennis was a popular way of making friends on holiday and some of the larger hotels, like the Felix had their own courts. The Felixstowe Lawn Tennis Club, founded in 1884, had the use of the twenty Felix grass courts close to the Bath Hotel and the East of England Tennis Championships are still held annually there. By the mid 1930s this area was a putting green.

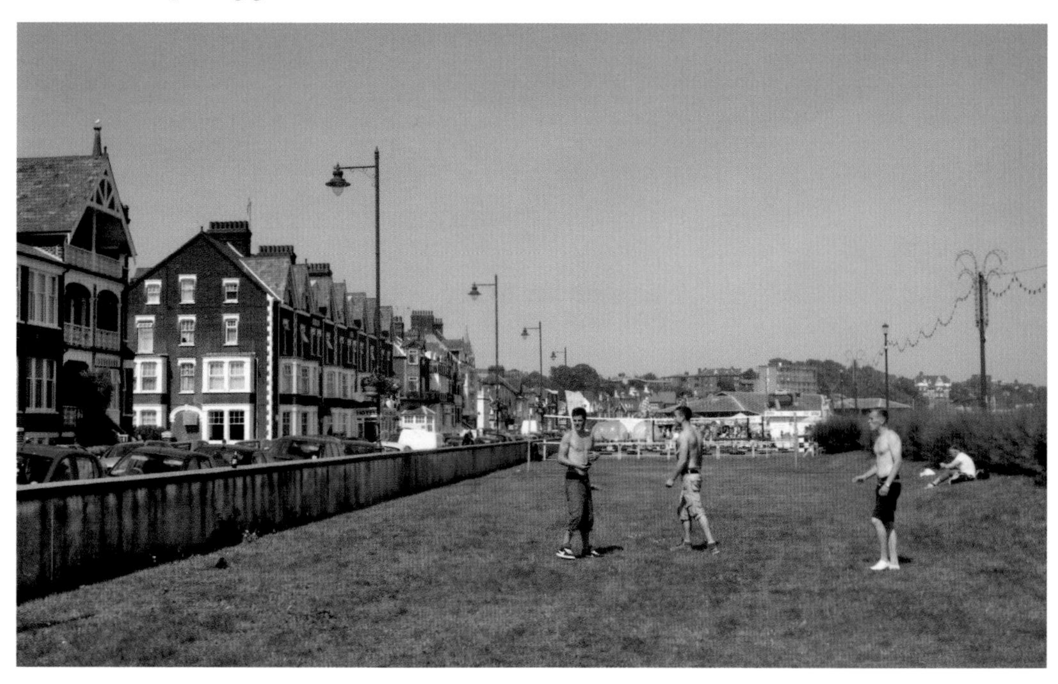

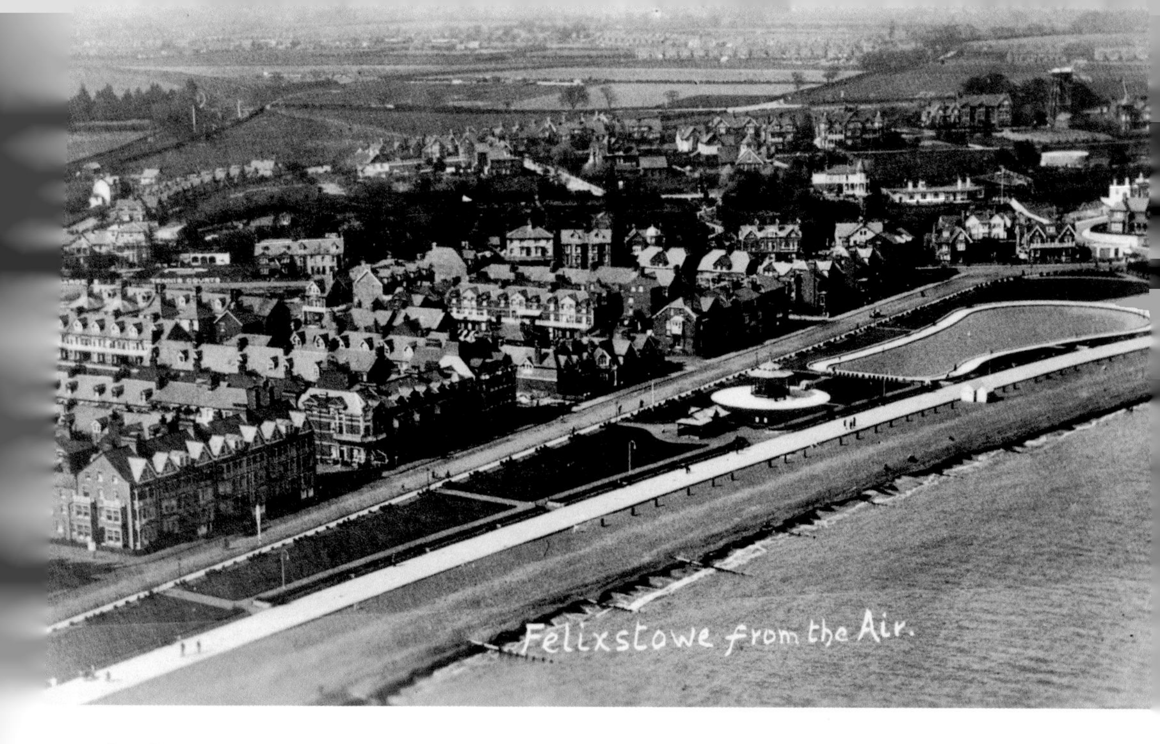

Sea Front ***c.*** **1930**

A classic sea front layout with spacious gardens, a broad promenade and room for a bandstand, boating lake, bowling green and at times, as in the previous photograph, tennis courts. It is all very genteel and part of a fashionable resort as Felixstowe always saw itself. In recent years the new sea defences have meant the building of a concrete sea wall between the road and the gardens.

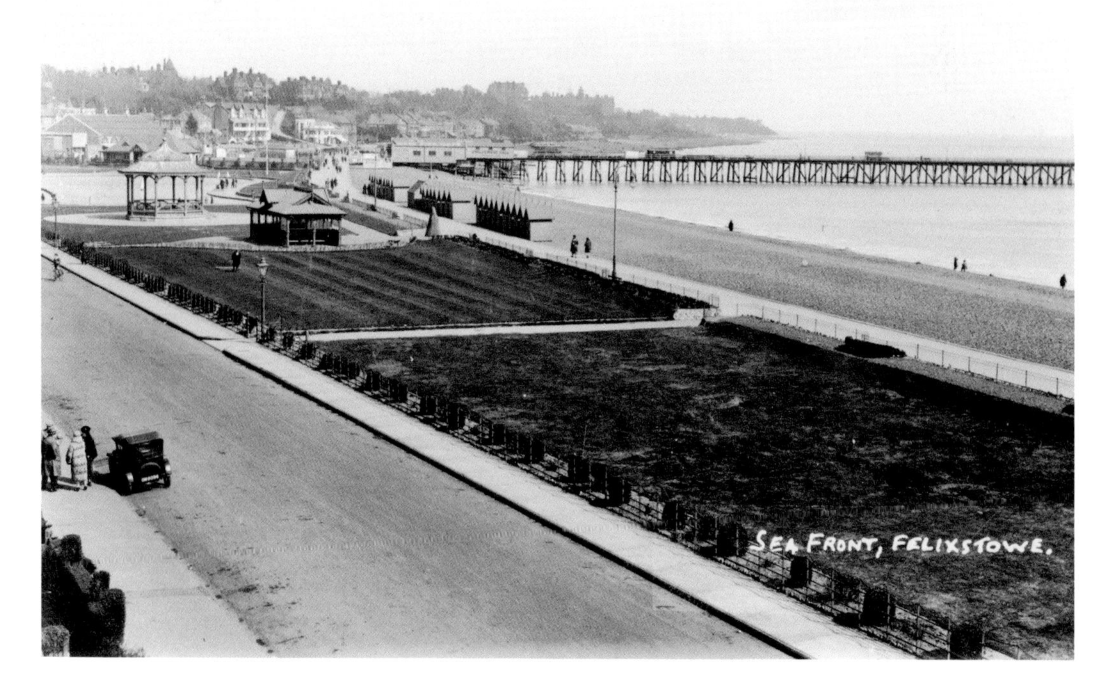

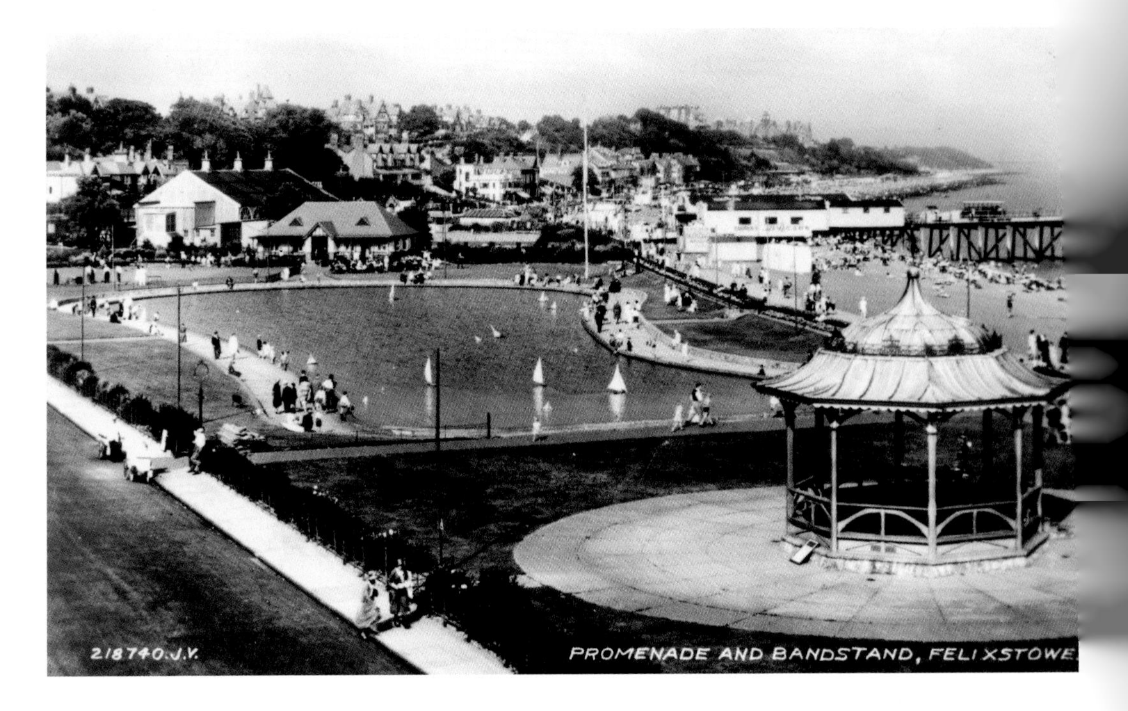

Promenade & Bandstand *c.* 1933
'Staying here a few days, lovely place' – isn't it just, with broad promenades, gardens, a boating lake and a chance to listen to the band, what more could you want from a holiday at the seaside? In the background is the first pavilion built in 1910 by Will C. Pepper to replace the tent in which his 'White Coons' performed. The Pier Pavilion was a popular concert hall and dance hall. In the photograph below the Pavilion has been greatly extended in 1938 and at the same time the bandstand was removed.

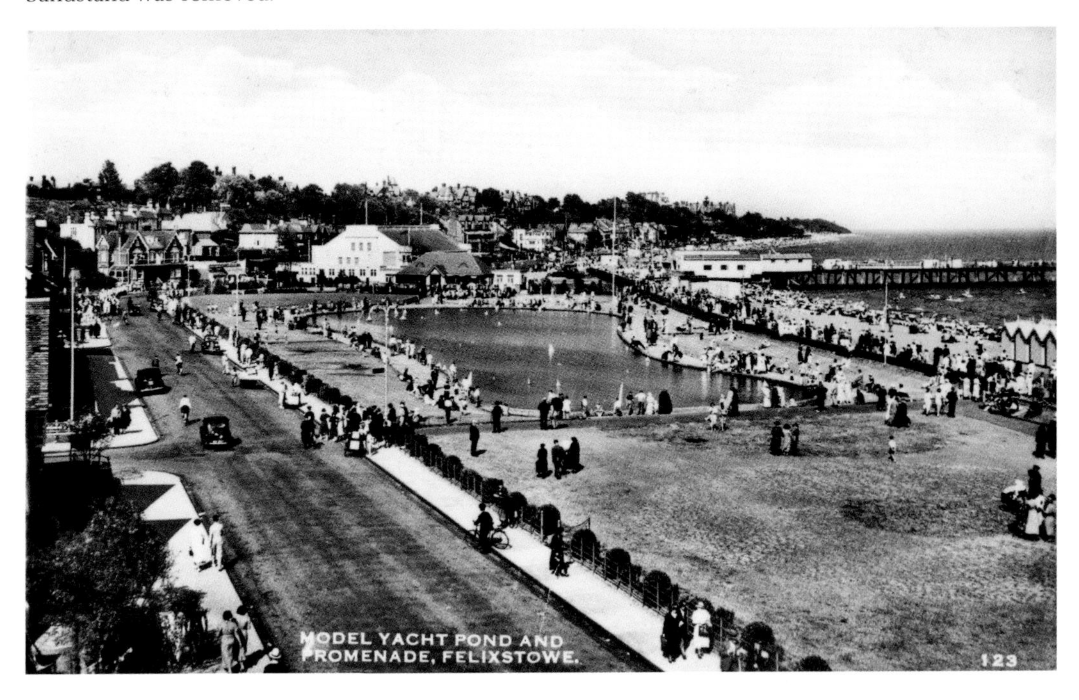

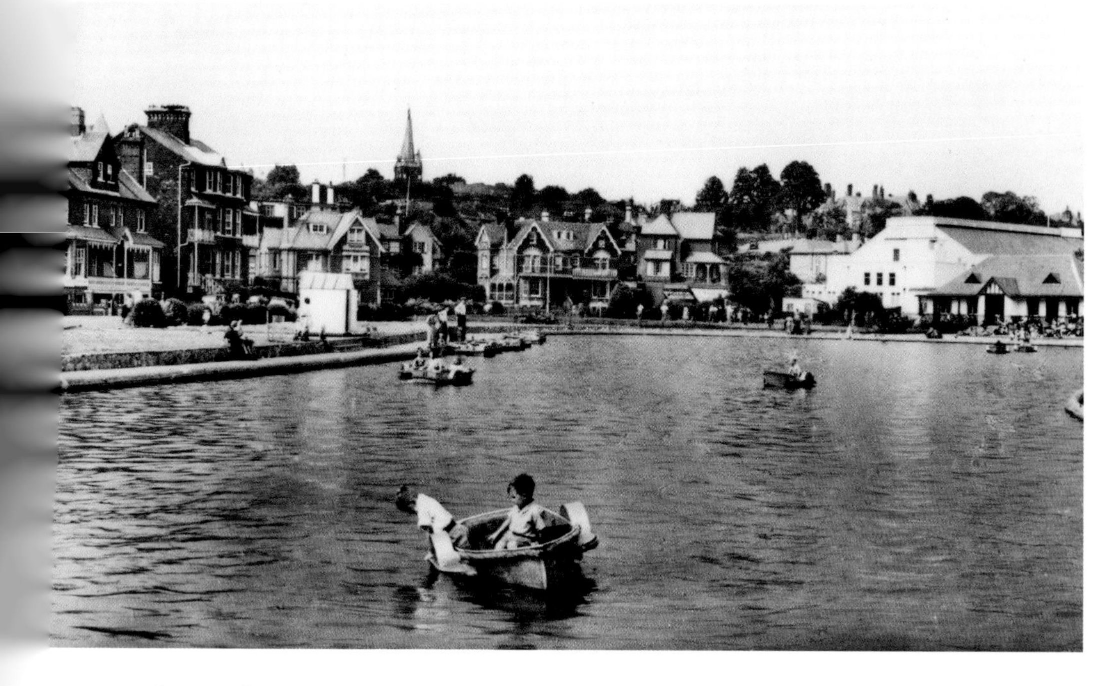

Boating Pond & Pier Pavilion *c.* 1955
Those wonderful small paddle boats are so much a part of a childhood holiday, but a real struggle to make any progress. No life jackets required here in the 1950s, but then the water was only about 2 feet 6 inches deep. The lake was subsequently reduced in size and part of it used as for small cars to race round. In 2010 a major leak as the lake was being prepared for the season caused its closure. Today's inflatable pool is not quite the same, but still good fun for young children.

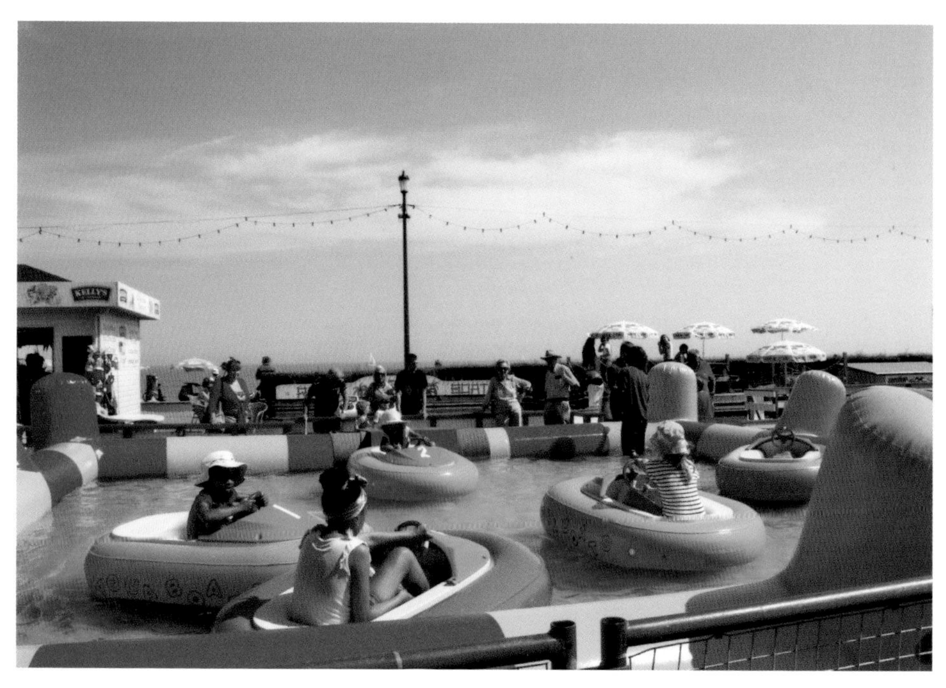

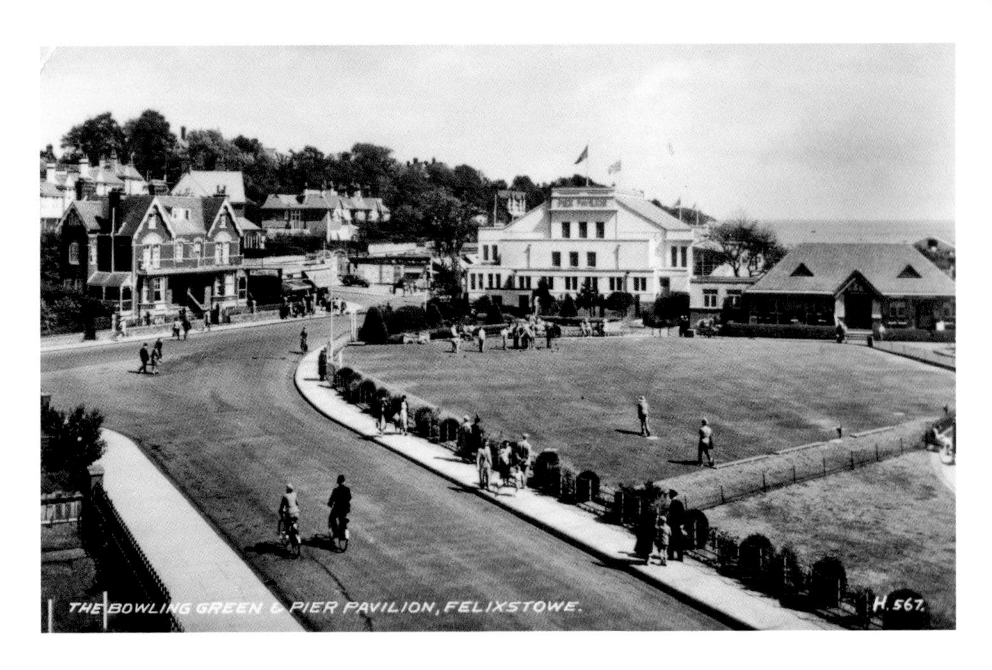

The Bowling Green & Pier Pavilion *c.* 1948

Felixstowe, which during the war had been a 'front line' town, was soon back in the holiday business. The Pier Pavilion was at the heart of its attraction. In 1947 it was advertised as 'The West End of the East Coast'. During July, August and September there were afternoon and Sunday orchestral concerts and every evening, except Saturdays John Barryman and Adele Wessely presented their super concert party, 'Evening Stars – The Show of Shows'. Saturday evenings were for dancing, with two bands. The old bowling green now provides car parking for the leisure centre.

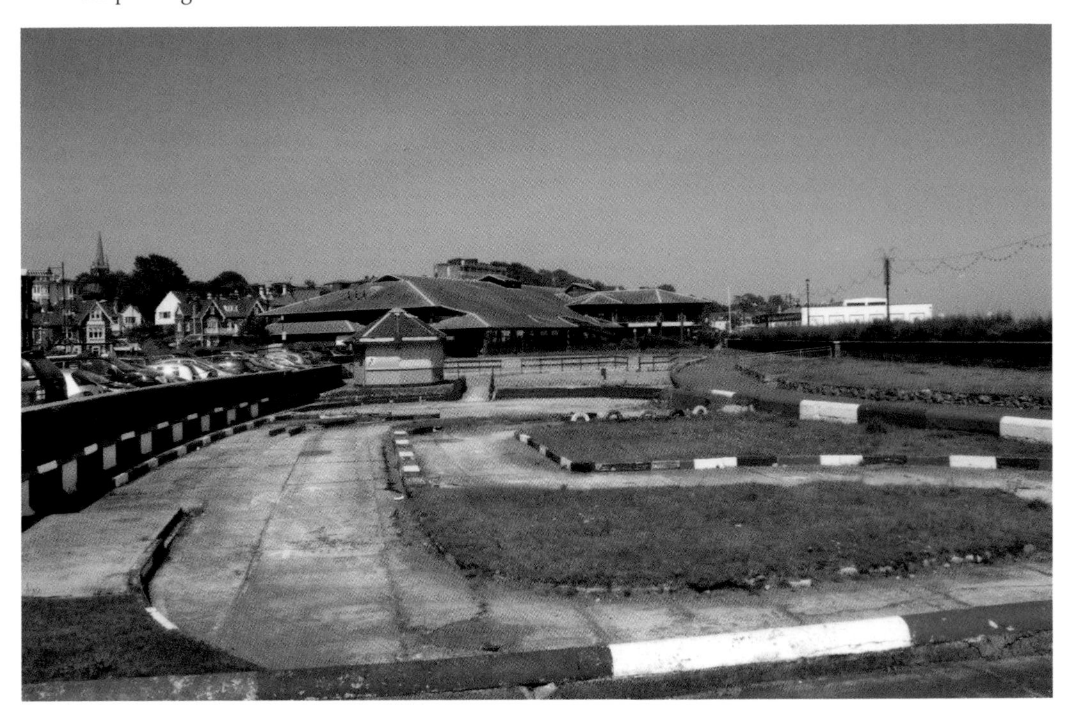

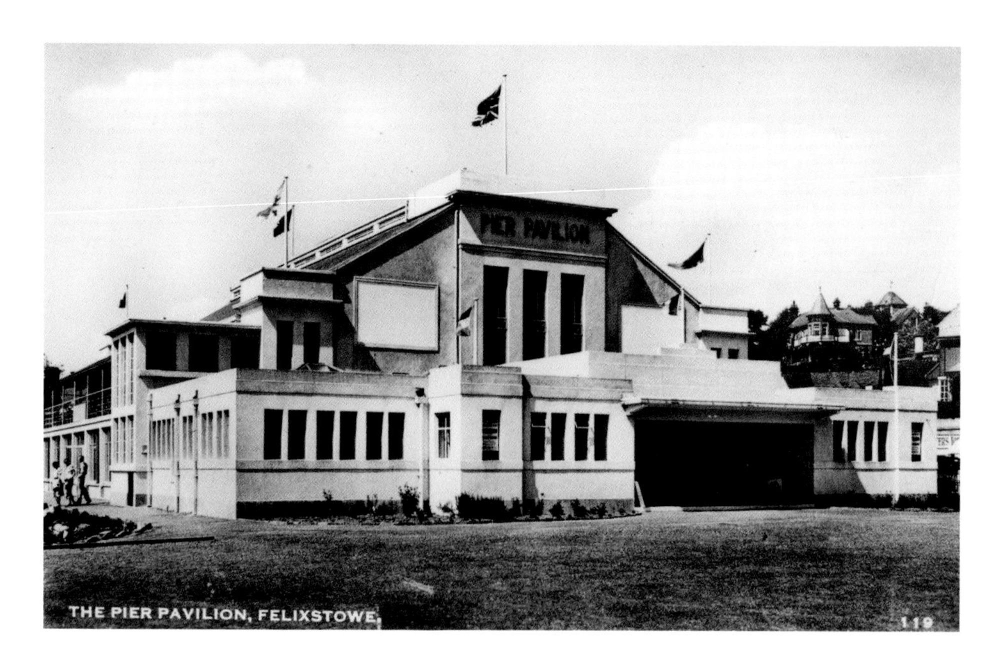

The Pier Pavilion *c.* 1948

In the 1960s and 1970s, season after season, the 'Fabulous Fingers of Handel at the £2,000 Hammond Organ' was a much loved regular at the Pier Pavilion. There were concerts in the morning and afternoon and 'entertainment for the whole family'. There was always a resident orchestra and in 1965 it was the Cyril Commins Orchestra entertaining every Saturday night throughout the year. In 1983, the pavilion was demolished and the next year the new leisure centre was built on the site with its indoor swimming pool, fitness suites and enormous dark roof.

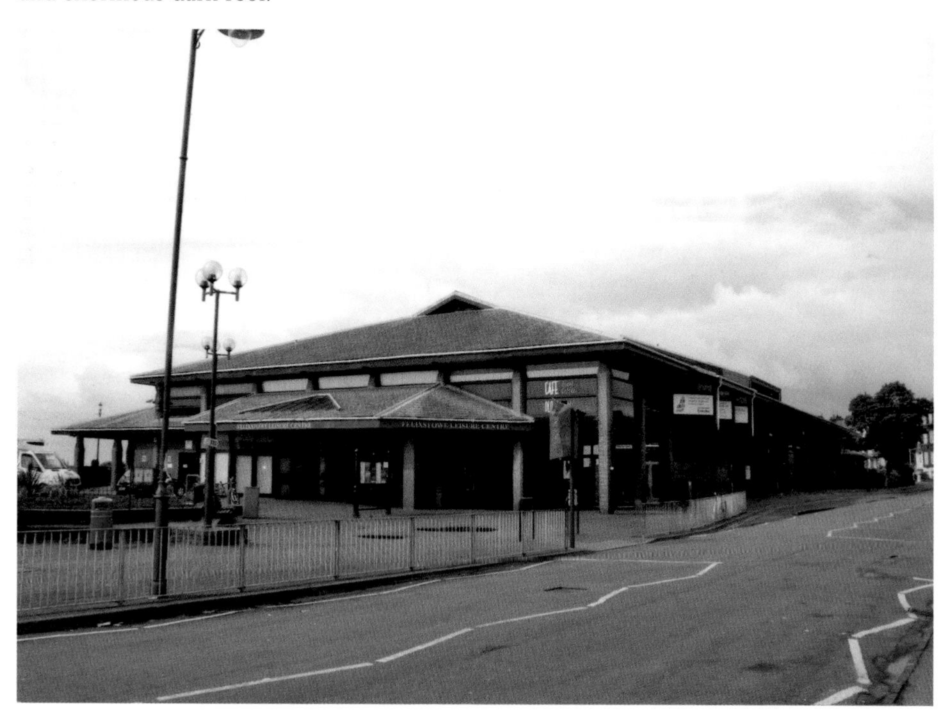

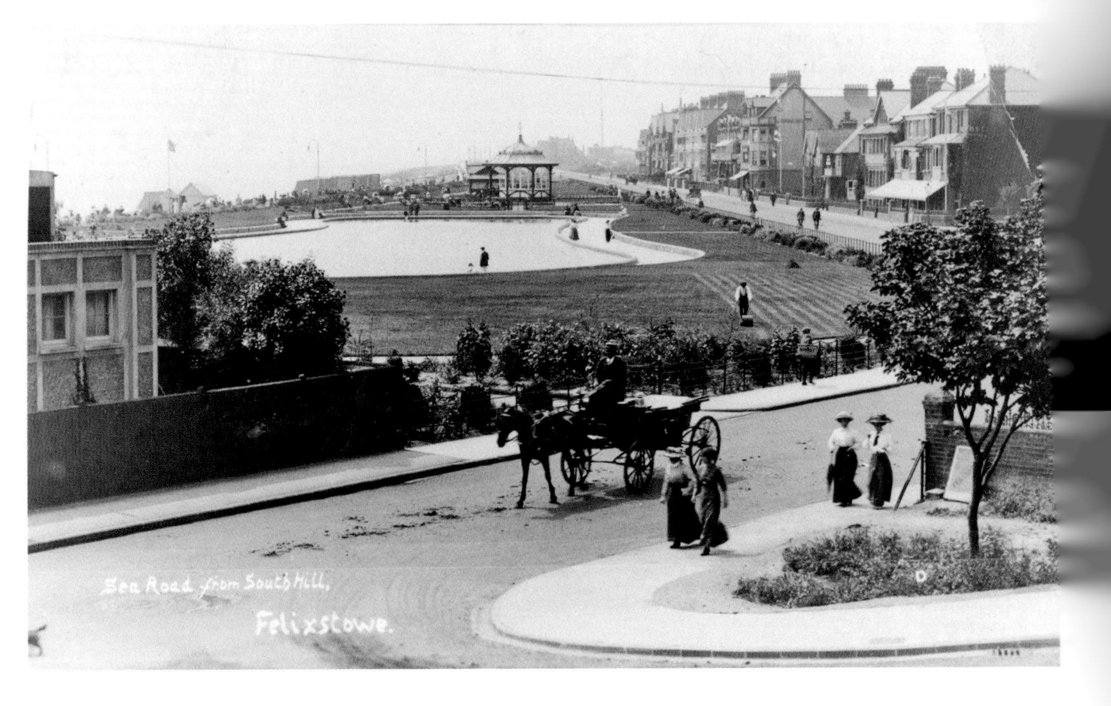

Sea Road & South Hill *c.* 1920
In the early days the view from South Hill took in the hotels along Sea Road, the boating lake and the sweep of the gardens. The Melrose Hotel can be seen on Sea Road and beyond that the Chatsworth. The bowling green is being mown by hand, a horse drawn carriage passes by and a delivery boy with his basket heads down the slope towards Sea Road. It is impossible to capture the same view today or the same unhurried charm.

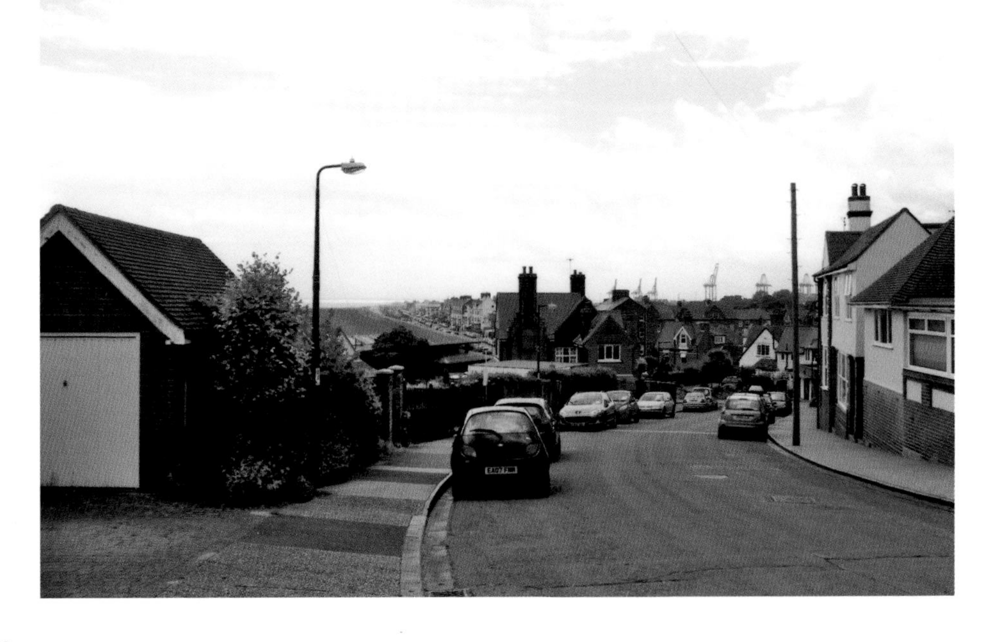

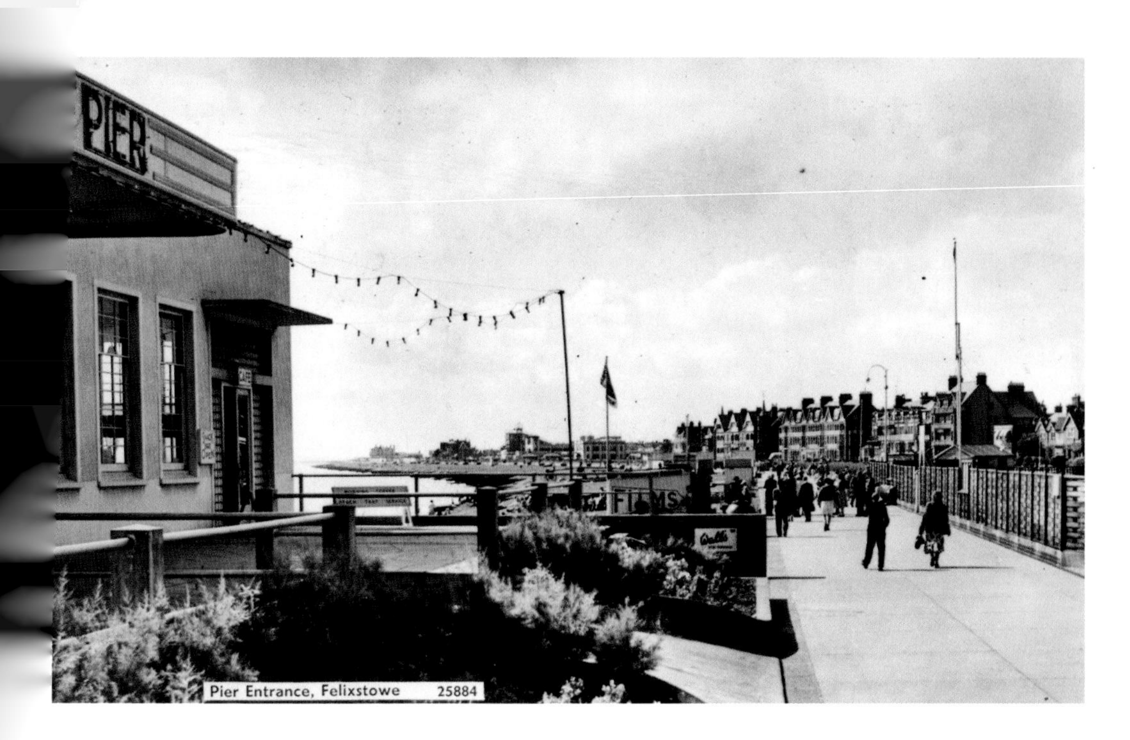

Pier Entrance 1950s

In the concert party days, the troupes would hope for a fine morning to bring the visitors – and then if it rained they would wish for good audiences sheltering from the wet. If there was demand the performers would entertain all day. Today the amusement arcades are there in all weathers, drawing in visitors for Bingo or machines that somehow manage to swallow up all the spare pennies and more. If plans by owner Pier Amusements Ltd go ahead, a new pier entertainment, retail and restaurant complex with an observation tower and outdoor promenade will transform this site.

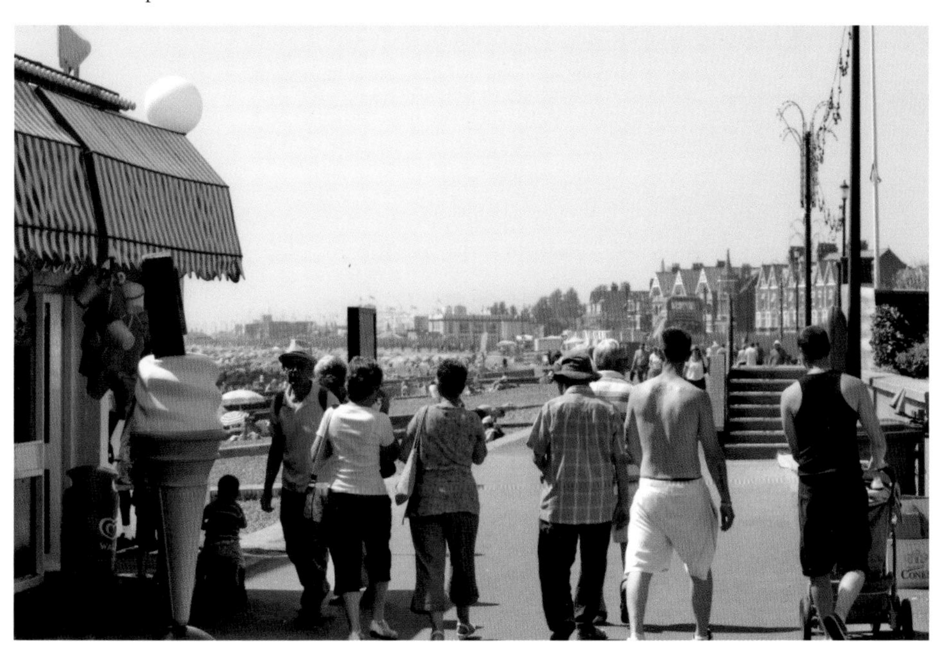

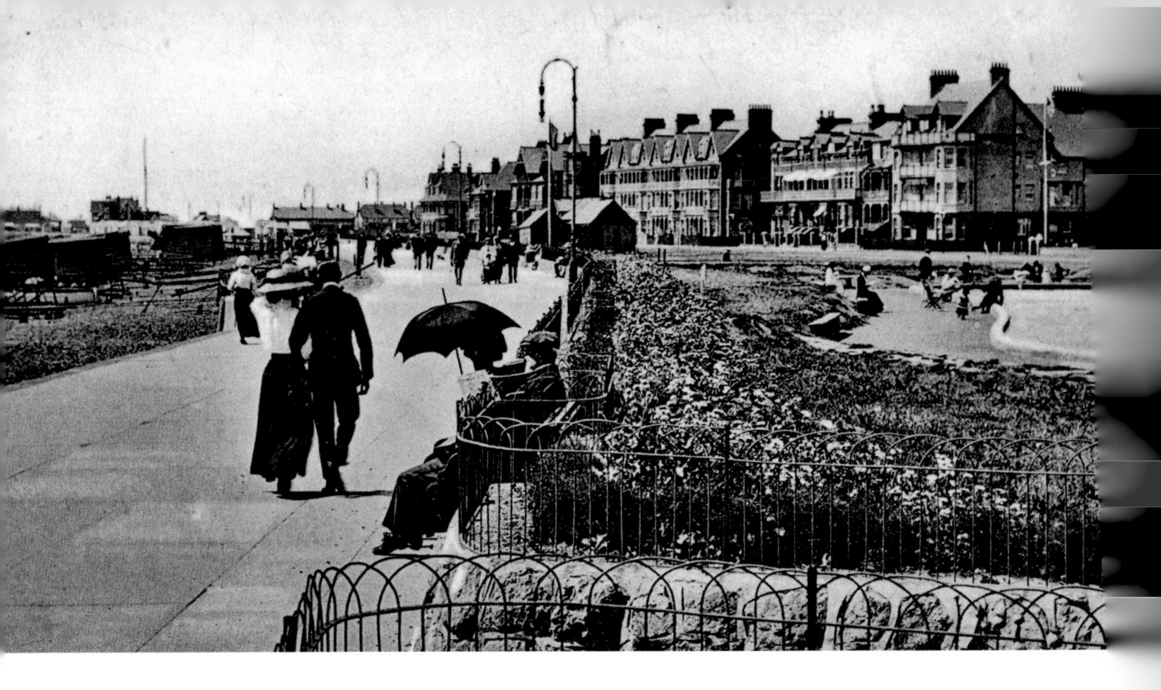

The Promenade *c.* 1910

What used to be an enjoyable promenade walk alongside the boating lake on the one side and the beach and sea, now a hundred years on has the gloomy leisure centre and disused lake, with funfair attractions at the start; much of it seeming temporary and stopgap. The need for a comprehensive regeneration, which could come with the new plans for the pier, is obvious.

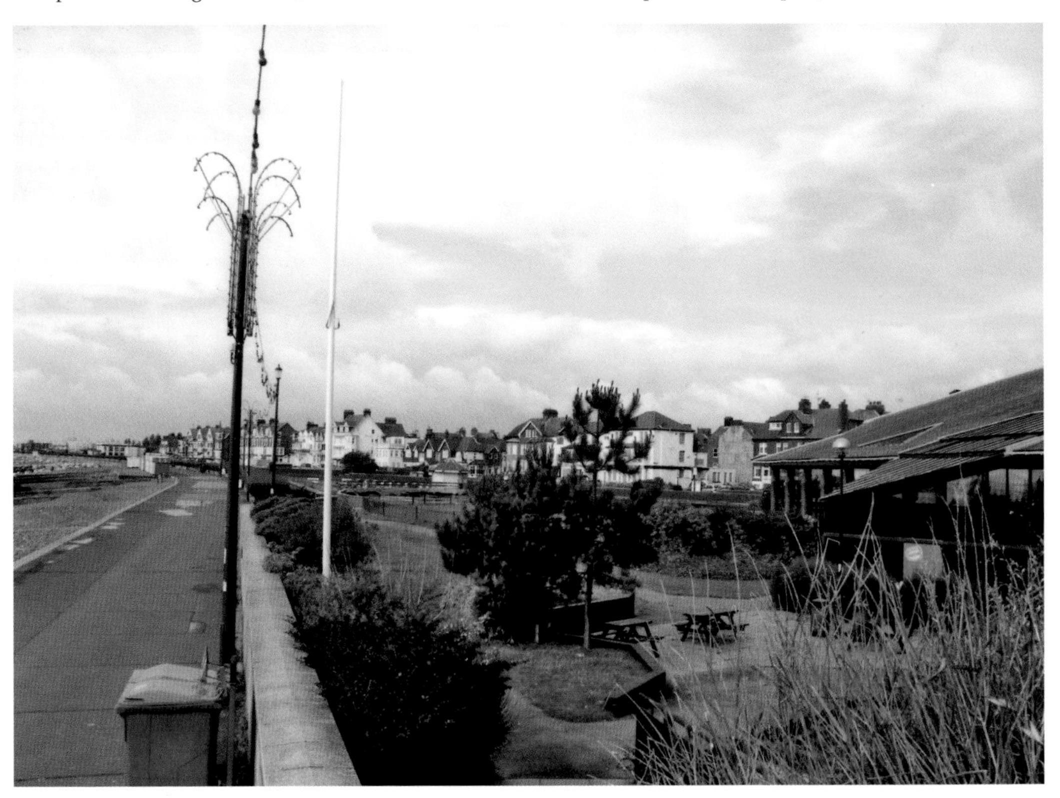

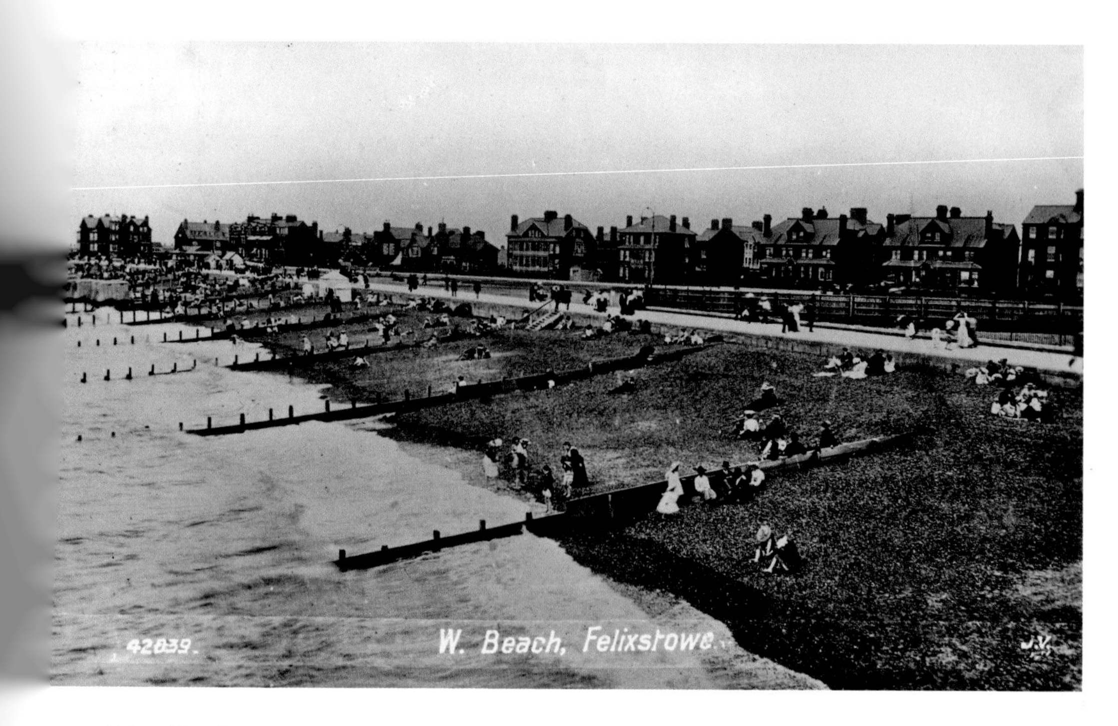

West Beach *c.* **1912**

The old rotting wooden groynes have been replaced by the boulder groynes. Felixstowe has been, and is, the scene of major sea defence works. A few days of sun and the beach soon fills up, particularly with children and young adults playing, paddling, swimming or just soaking up the sun. A locally made Peter's ice cream is a must, of course. There is a timeless pleasure in enjoying the sand and sea.

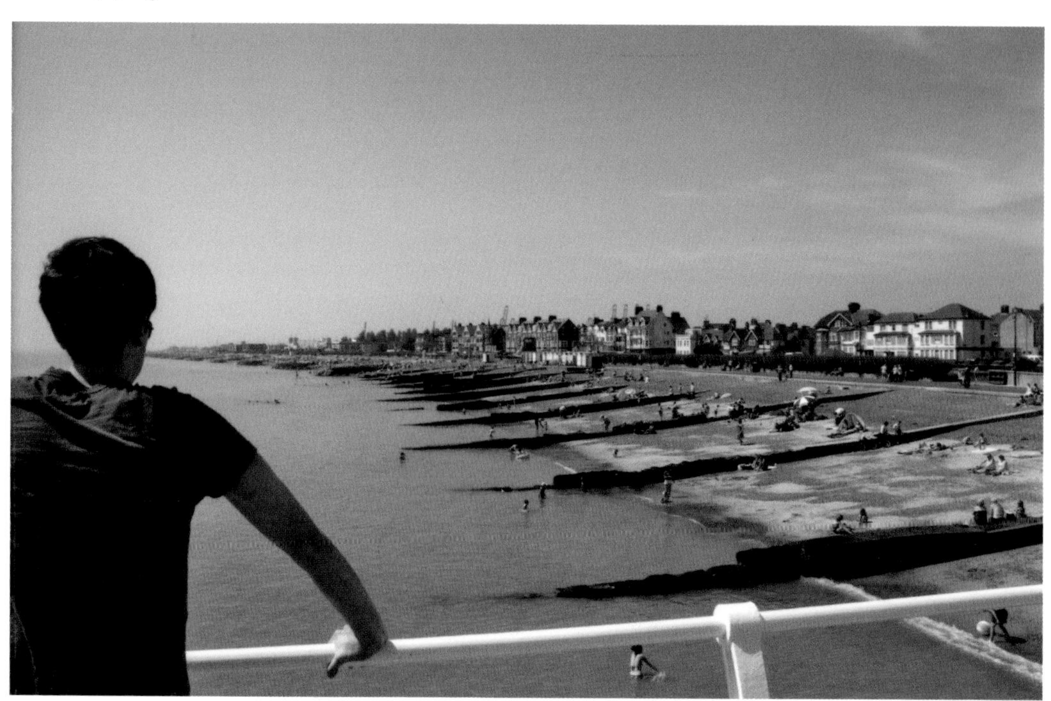

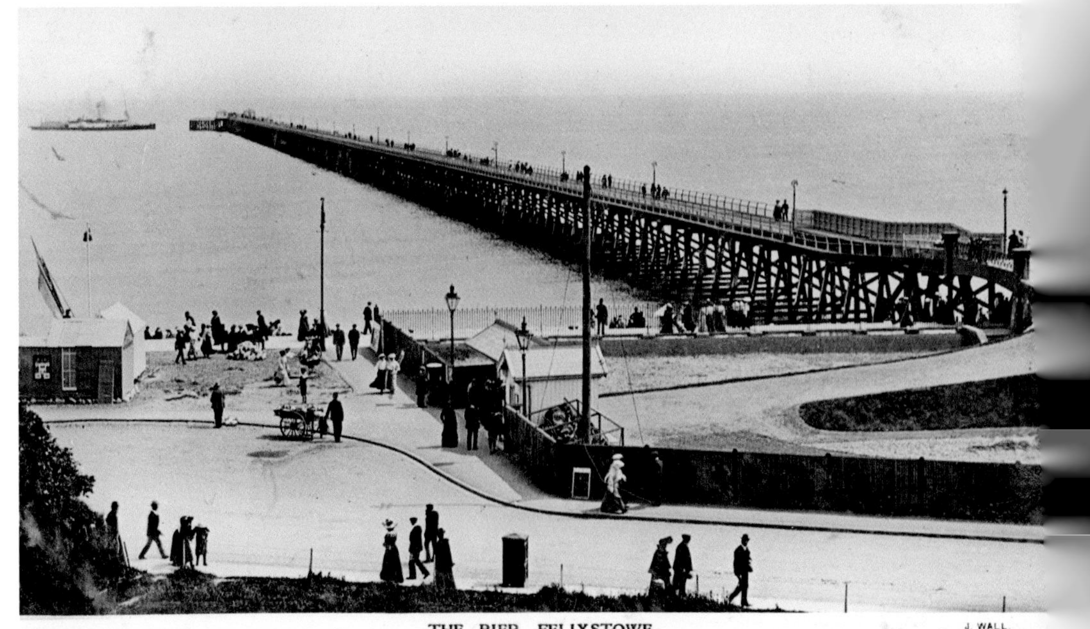

THE PIER, FELIXSTOWE.

J. WALL FELIXSTOWE

The Town Pier *c.* **1915**
In 1905 the Coast Development Corporation opened the new pier. At half a mile long it was the third longest in the country and connected with the Belle Steamers that operated around the east coast. In its early days it was a practical structure with an electric tramway to take passengers to and from the pier head. There was a bridge over the pier gardens, known as the pullover. This disappeared in the mid 1920s when the shore end developed as an entertainment centre.

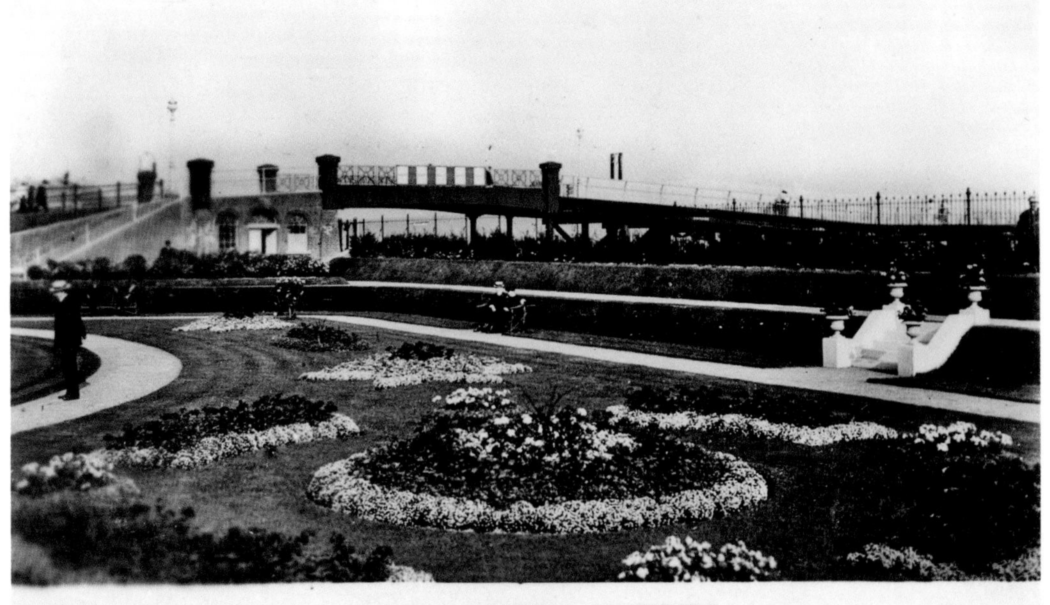

S 1299 THE PIER GARDENS, FELIXSTOWE.

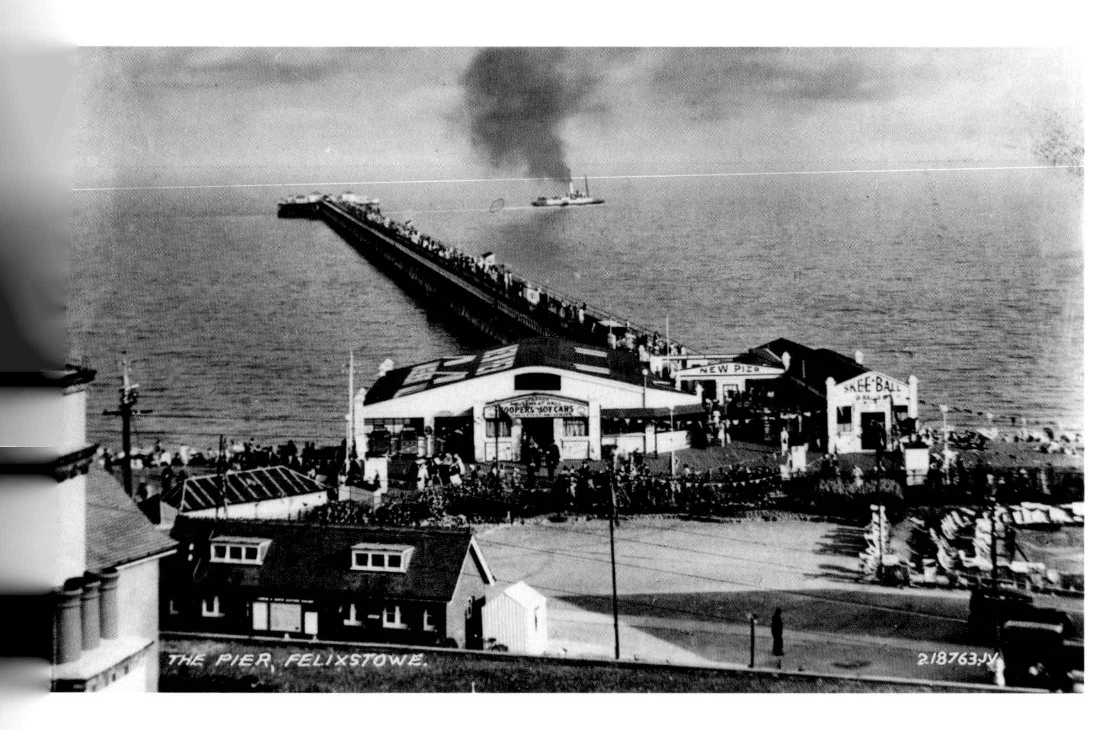

The Pier *c.* **1936**

The Belle Steamers ended their service after the First World War as the railways were carrying more passengers. Until September 1939 the 'Queen of Southend' ran a regular service to London. Coopers Joy Cars and Skee Ball are the principal attractions offered at the shore end. The Second World War ended the tramway and, like many other piers, this one was partially destroyed in case of invasion. It was never fully rebuilt and when re-opened, it was 450 feet in length. Much of the length of the pier was condemned as unsafe some ten years ago.

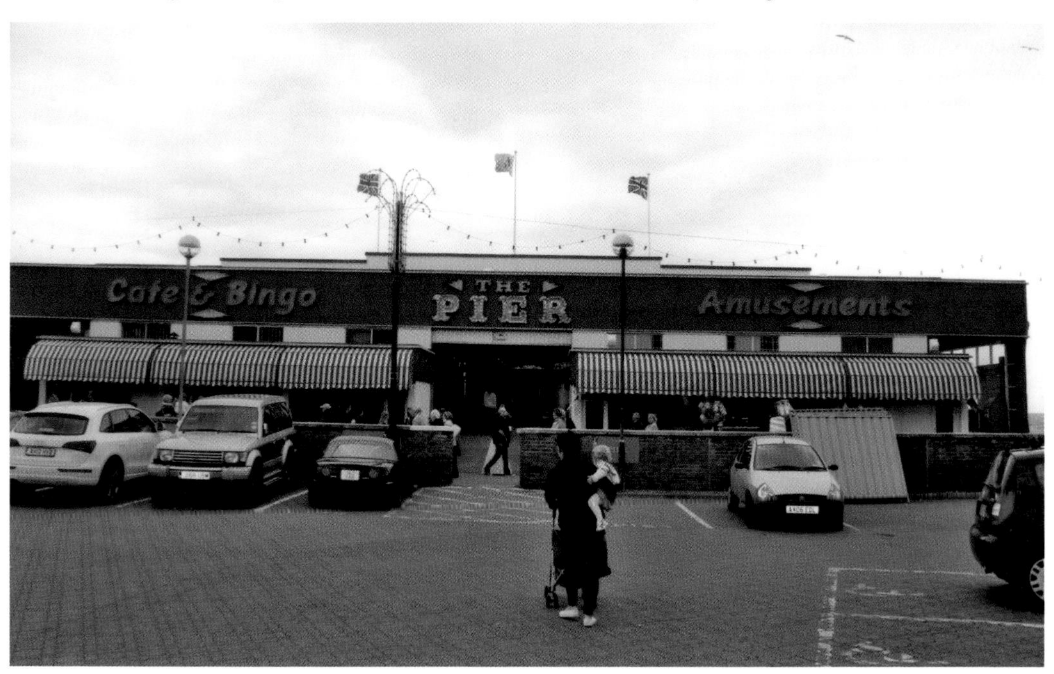

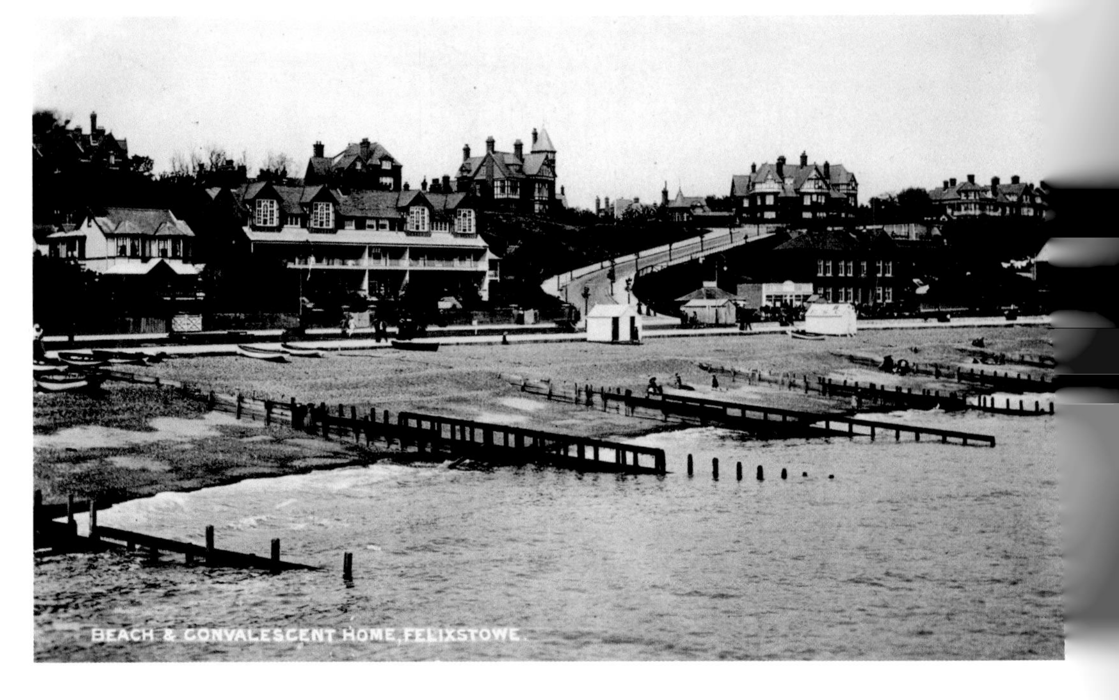

Beach & Convalescent Home *c.* 1908

The much publicised benefits of seawater and being dipped in it, led to many convalescent homes being built at coastal resorts. The Suffolk Convalescent Home, opened in around 1864, was in a prominent position and by the early years of the twentieth century it had been almost totally rebuilt. The *Ward Lock Guide* for 1921 described it: 'by the bounty of Mr J. D. Cobbold of Ipswich and others has had its usefulness and accommodation greatly increased... It is a well-managed institution for the sick poor among the artisan classes and is liberally supported locally'.

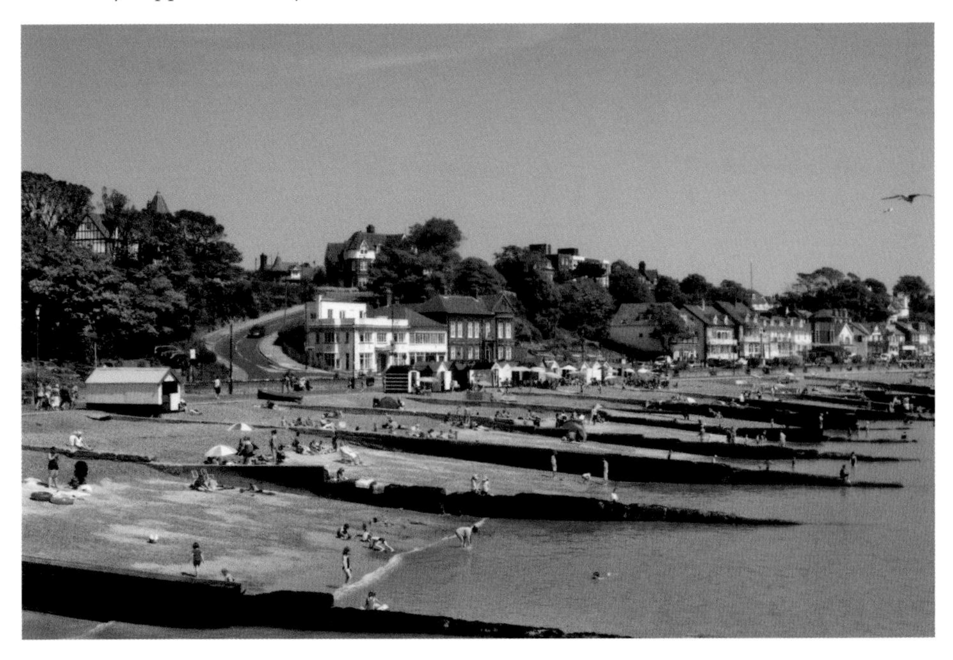

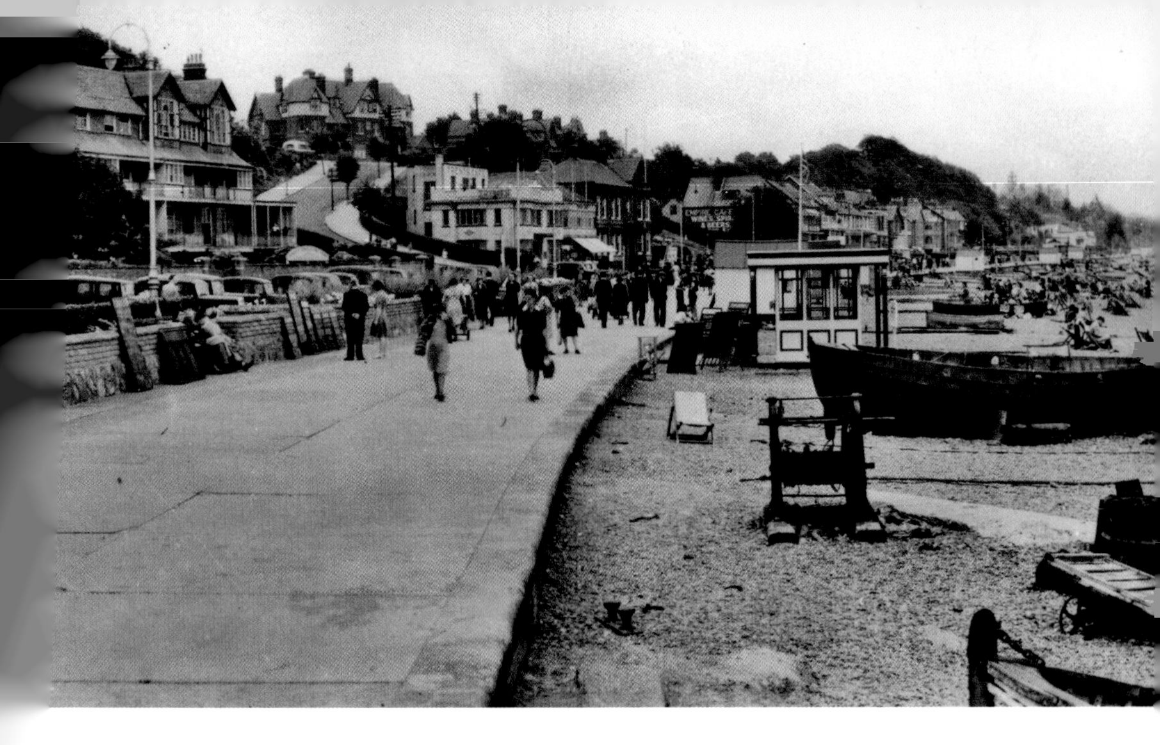

Promenade from the Pier ***c.*** **1935**
'Dear Teacher, I am very pleased to tell you that I am down at the Convalescent Home and I am feeling a little better. Give my love to the girls and tell them I am very happy down here,' said a message from Mabel to Ipswich in March 1908. Countless hundreds, like Mabel, would have benefitted from the home, perhaps seeing the sea for the first time. Modern research tells us that a lovely view is good for the health, so our ancestors knew. The home and the villa next door were demolished in 1967; the site is now a car park.

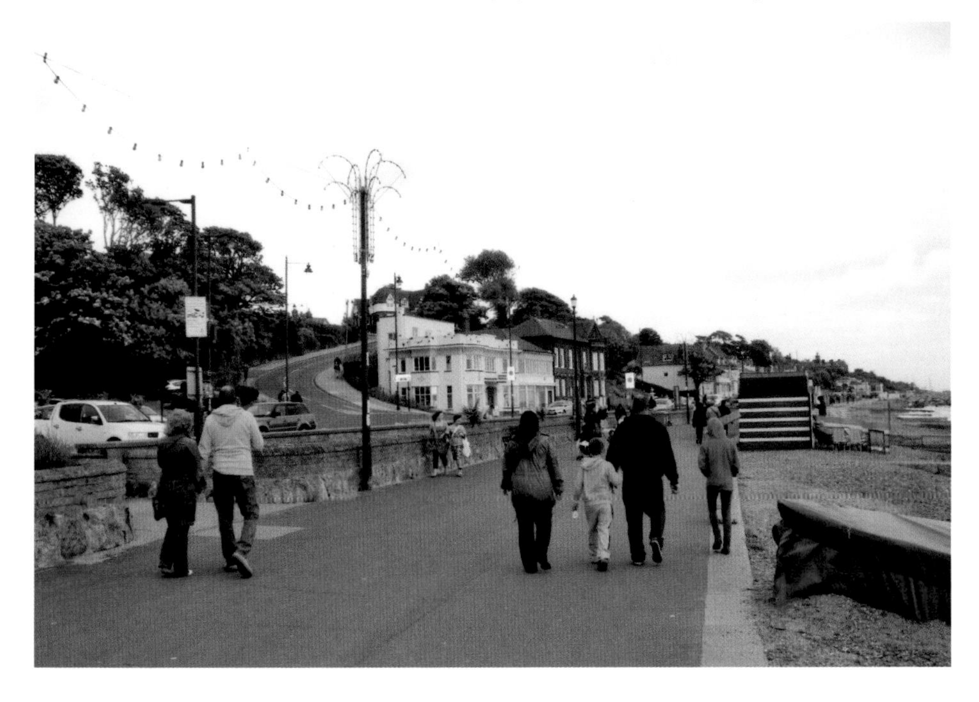

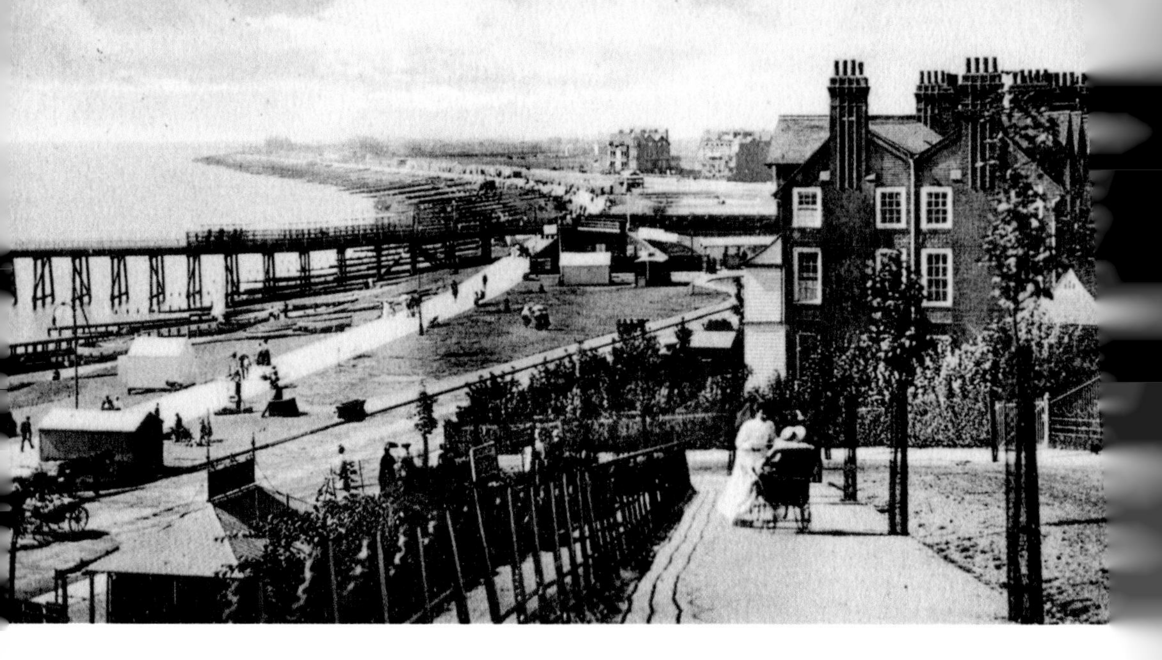

Felixstowe from Convalescent Hill *c.* 1909
A classic view of the resort looking across the new pier and the gardens towards Sea Road. The wooden hut with the sign board on its roof is W. G. Archer's Eastward Ho Estate Office, as Felixstowe is developing rapidly and the large hotels are beginning to fill the horizon. The side of the Convalescent Home is prominent.

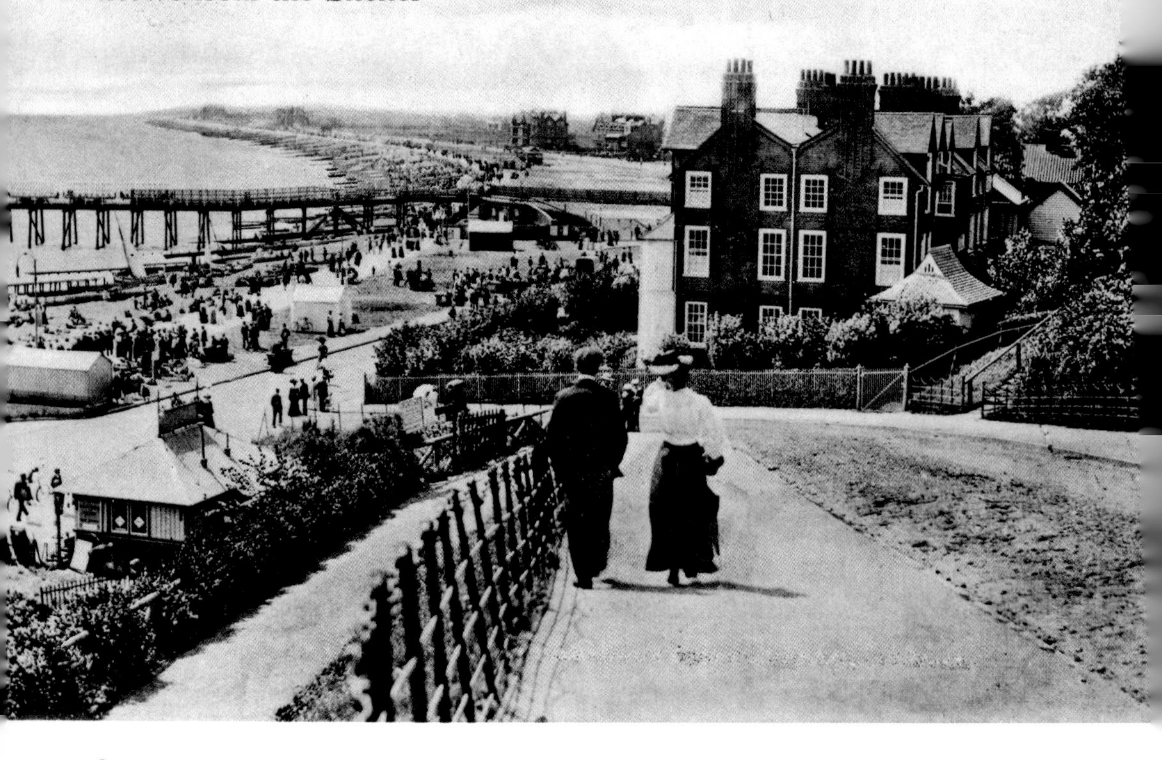

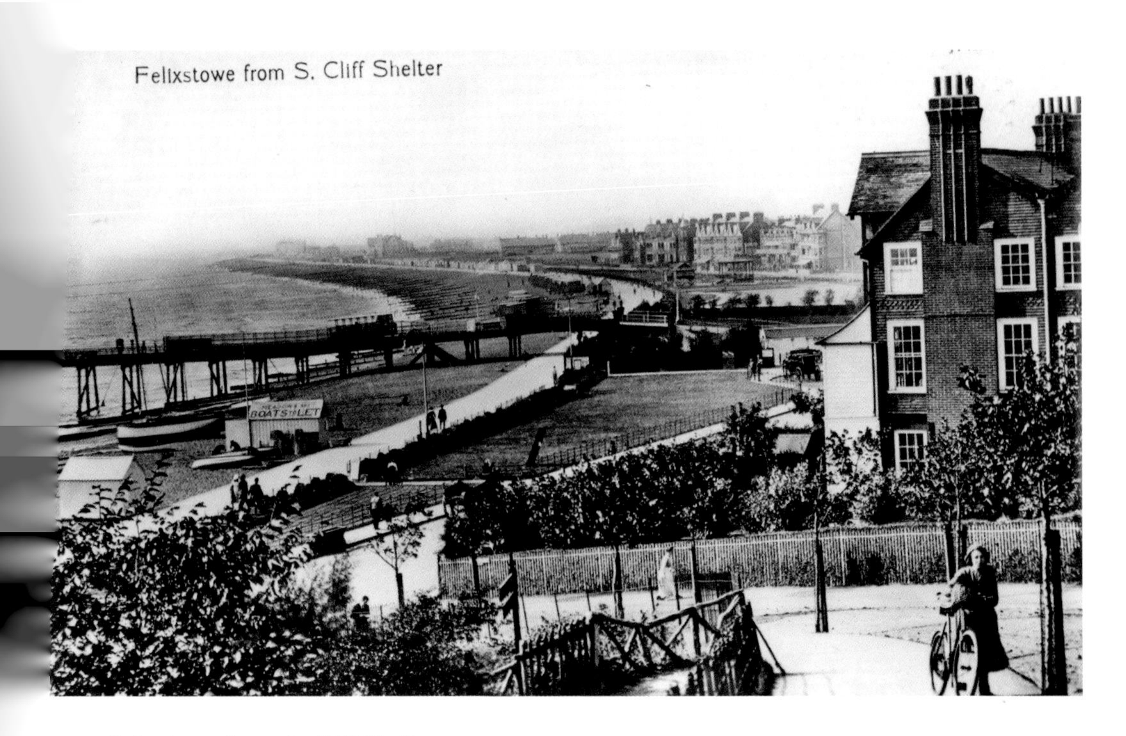

Felixstowe from S. Cliff Shelter *c.* 1917
The electric train can be seen on the pier, Sea Road has more hotels, and the hut on the beach is Meadow & Son, with boats to let. Part of the message on the postcard sent to Halifax reads: 'We had an air raid last night. They never reached anywhere near us.' In 1917 there were two bombing raids by aeroplanes flying from Belgium on the town mainly directed at the air station and army billets killing thirty people. The small car park on the site of the Convalescent Home seems rather a wasted opportunity.

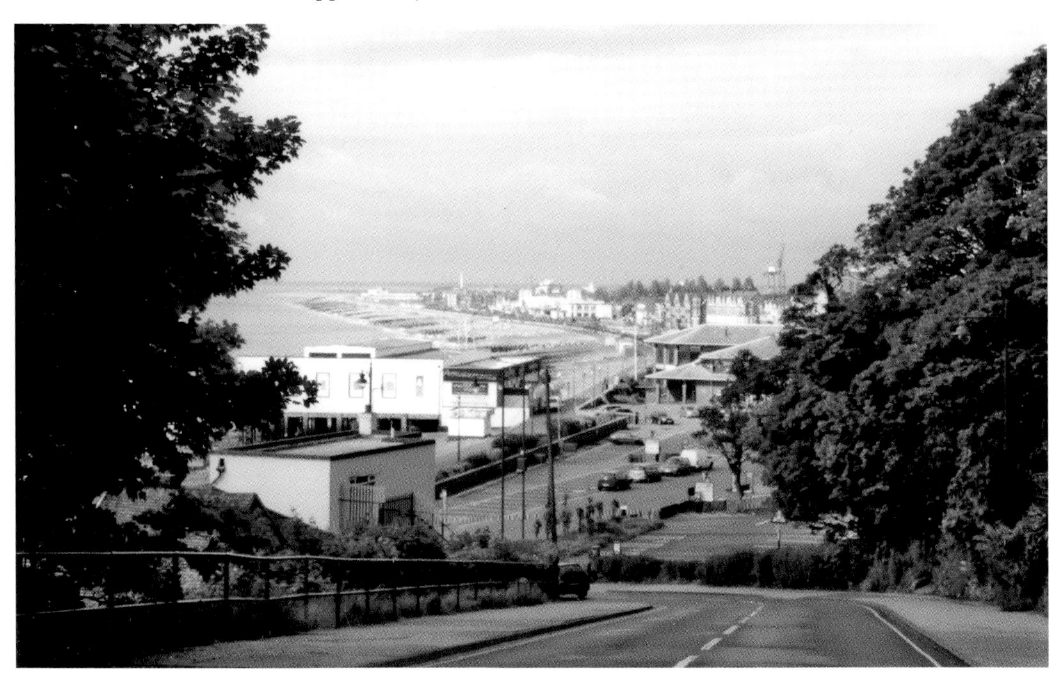

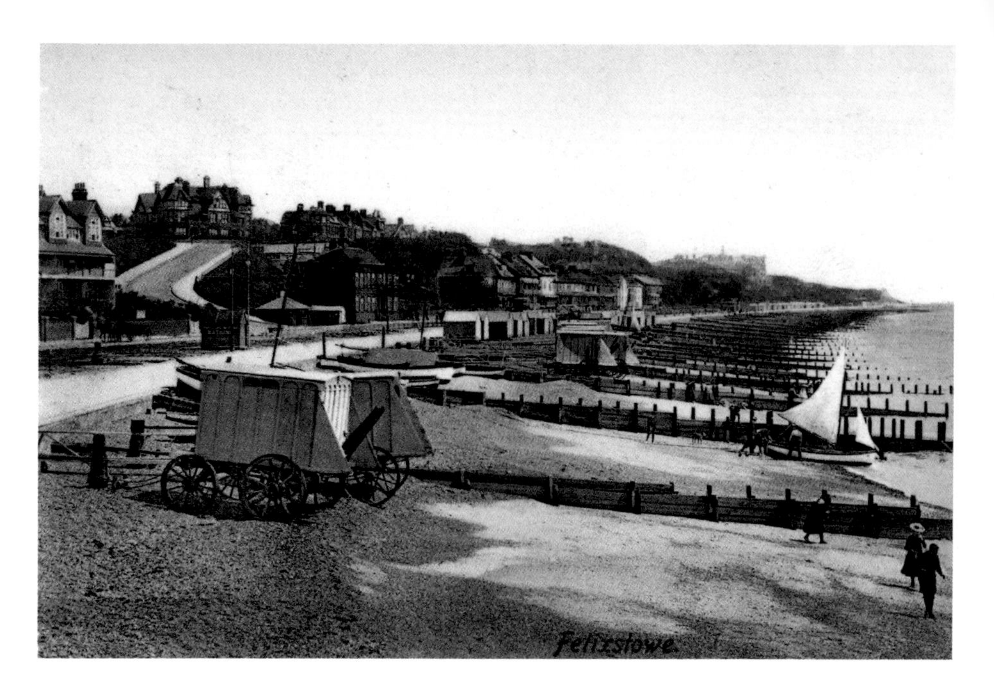

Felixstowe *c* .1904
Magnificent bathing machines that would be winched up and down the pebbly beach are prominent with the ladder that could be lowered so the bather could enter the water. The Cliff Hotel has not been built. At the height of the season this beach would be packed with trippers and boats. (*Below*) Parade and Beach *c.* 1912: 'Dear Nursie, I came down that steep hill in my cart to the parade. I have put an x where my house is. I went to have my hair cut today by a lady, yesterday I went to church, Your loving Betty.'

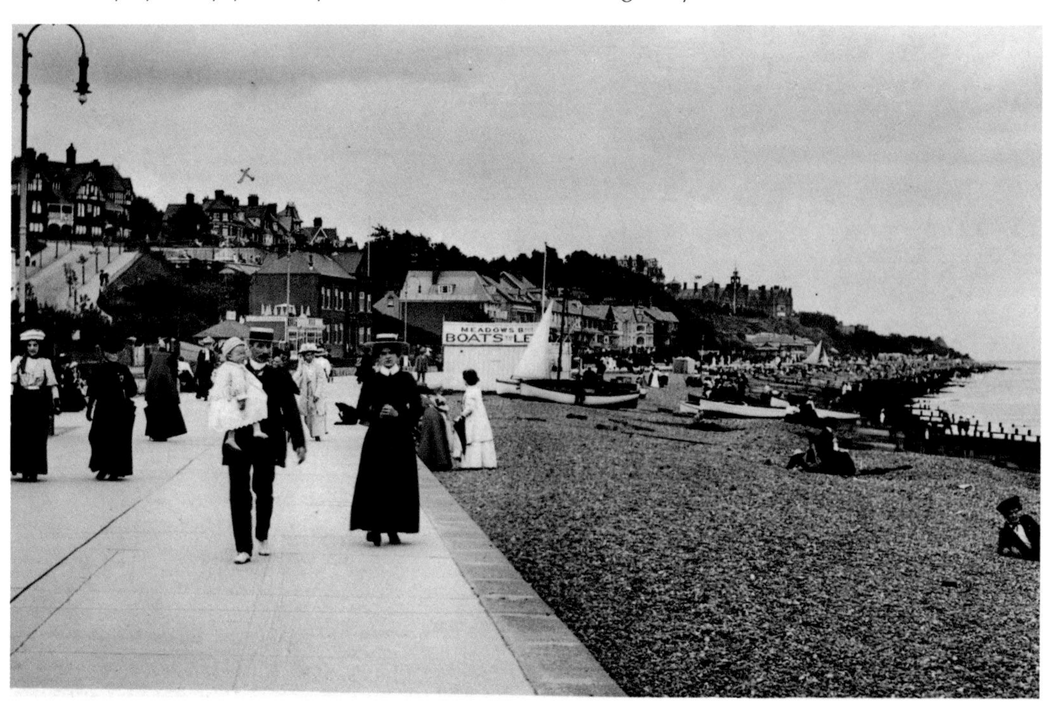

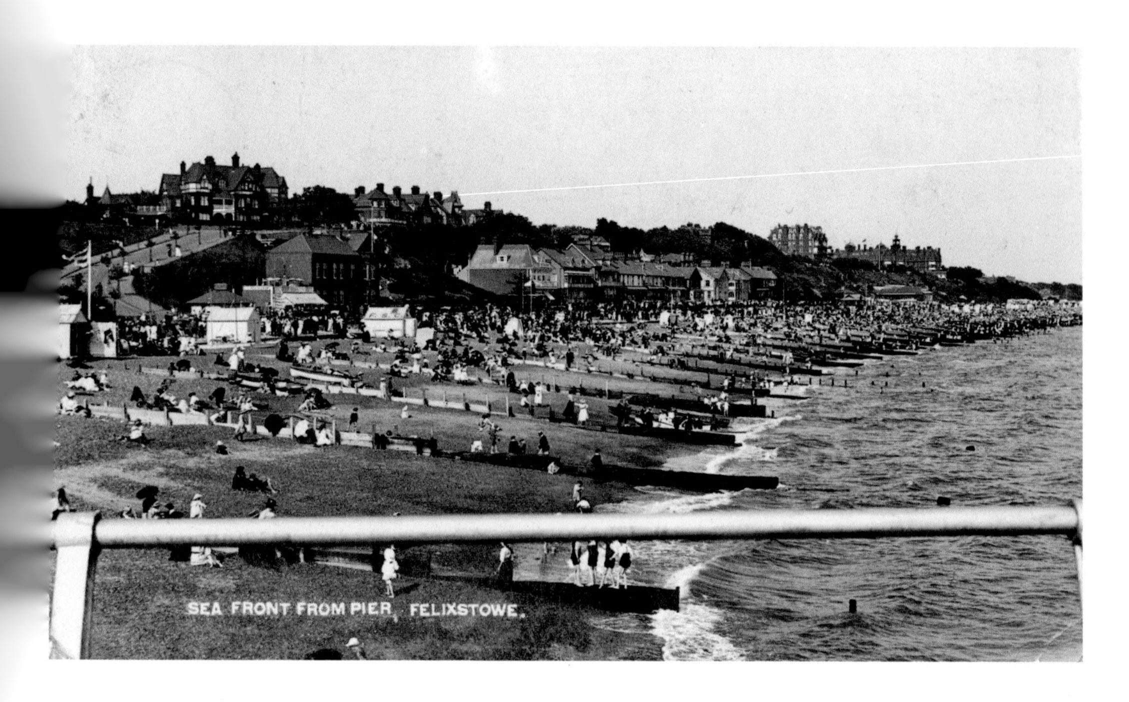

Sea Front from Pier ***c.*** **1914**

The first Trent's Café can be seen at the foot of Convalescent Hill next to the town hall. In front of it one of the white huts has the Felixstowe Swimming Club initials painted on its roof. Opposite the pier the large Millars Restaurant was established by this time. This is my favourite view of Felixstowe from the boardwalk, the last accessible part of the pier, capturing the seafront villas and the magnificent Edwardian buildings on the cliff top.

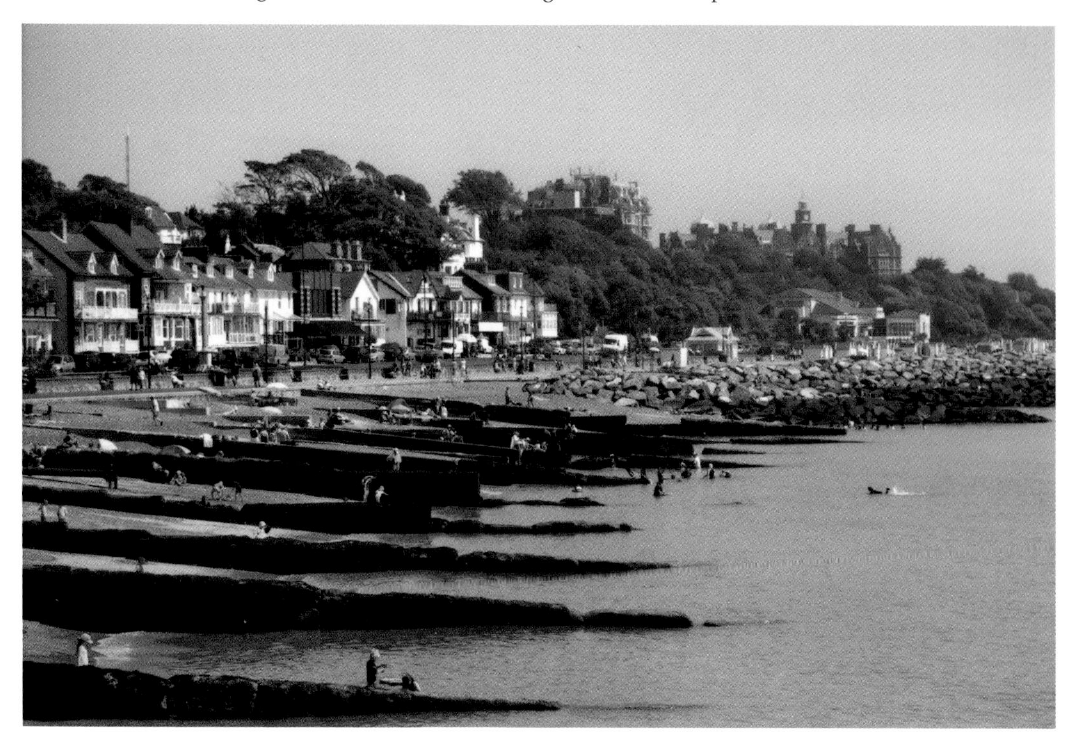

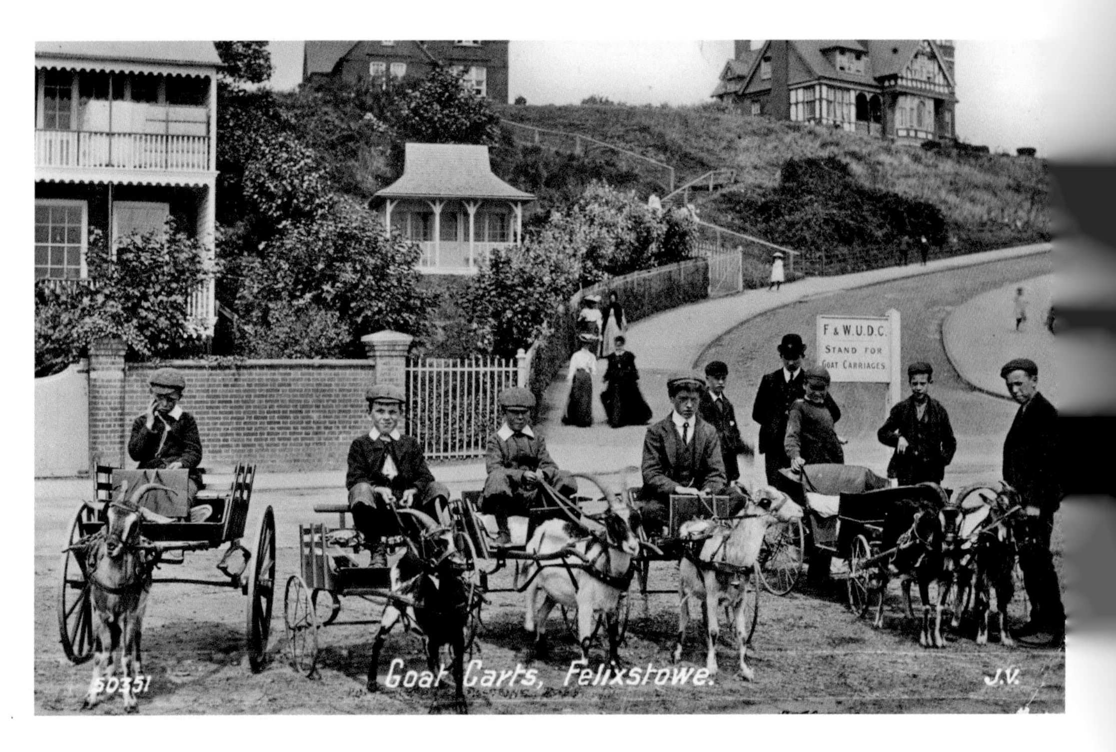

Goat Carts ***c.*** **1908**

'Daddy says wouldn't Roy enjoy a goat ride?' This is the official Felixstowe & Walton Urban District Council Stand for goat carts at the foot of Convalescent Hill. No goat carts today, but perhaps a ride on the small train running along the promenade instead?

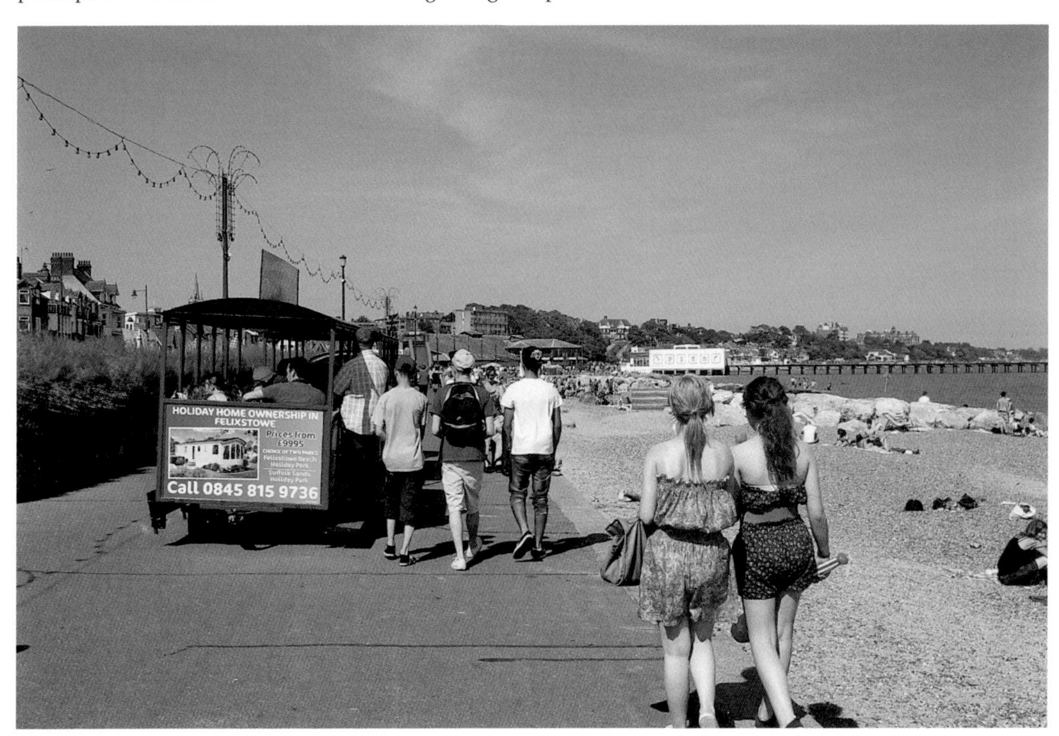

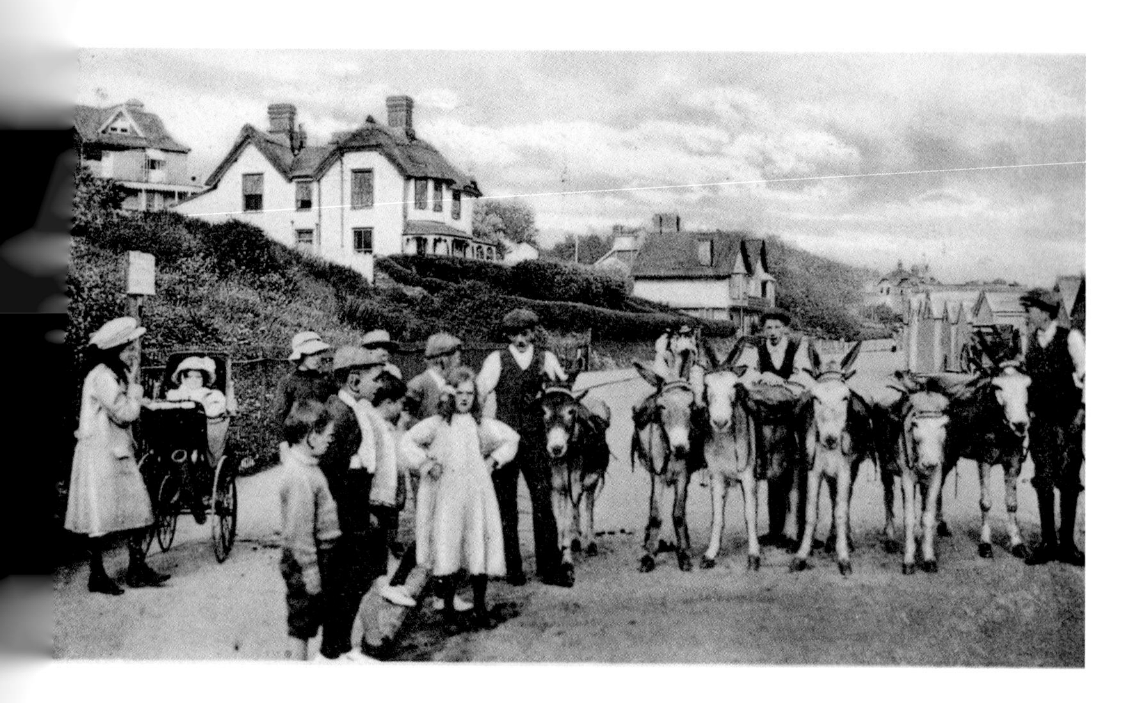

The Donkey's Parade *c.* **1910**

It is recorded that when the Empress of Germany stayed at Felixstowe in 1891 her children amused themselves with Jack Rattle and his donkeys. So much part of the traditional seaside, it was reassuring to see donkey rides on the gardens along Sea Road.

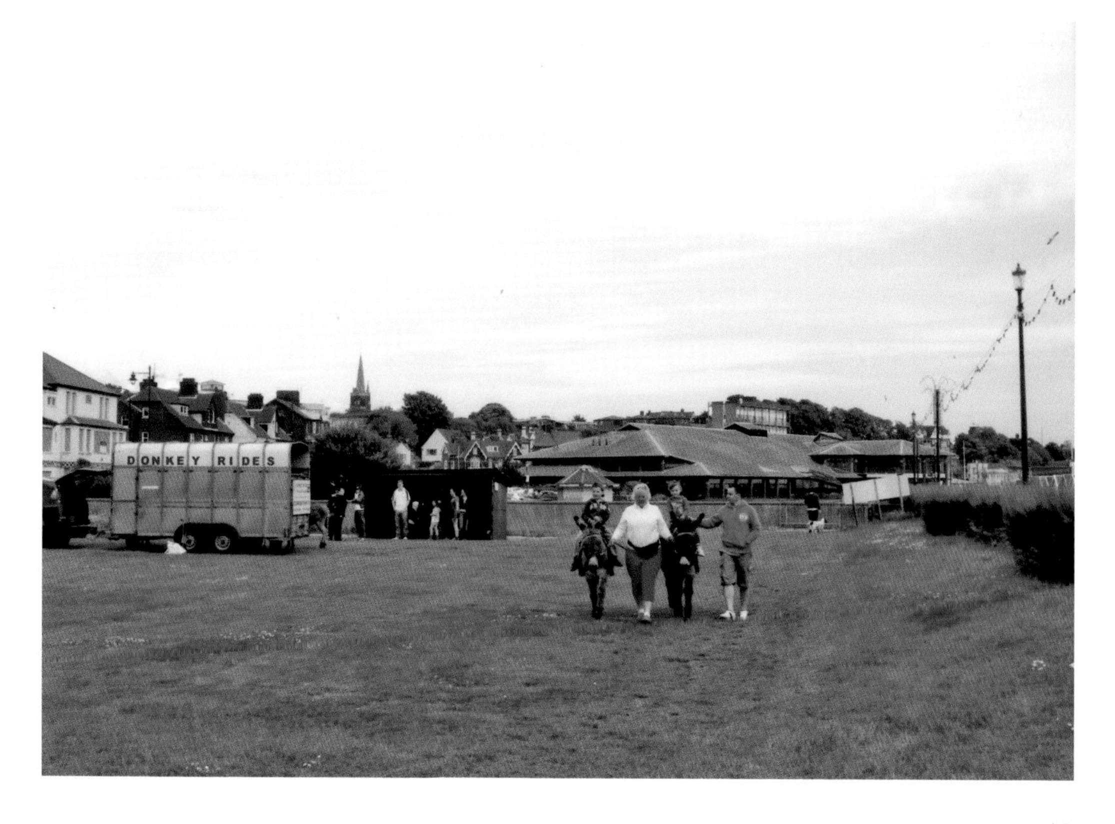

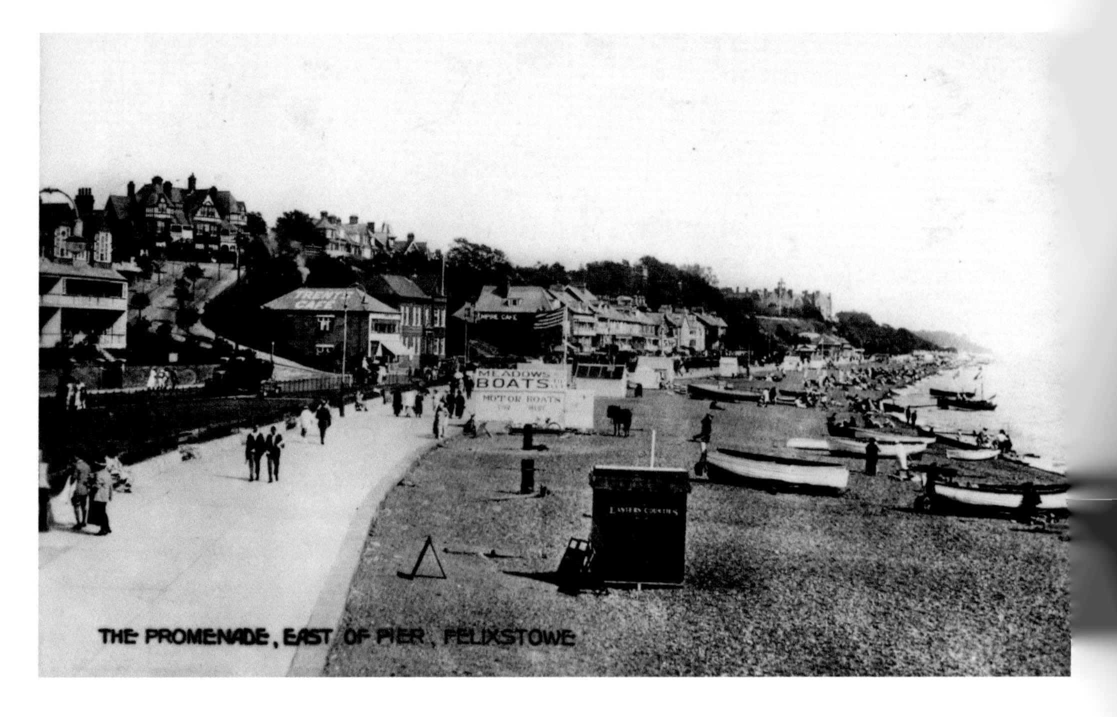

The Promenade, *c.* 1924

A practical postcard sent to Catford, London and a reminder that cards were delivered quickly and efficiently. 'Just to let you know we shall arrive home about 8 o'clock. We are bringing the meat with us. Please get 1lb Spanish onions. At present it is simply pouring with rain. I am very sorry I have made a mistake in your name, but we can't waste a postcard, Love from all, Gladys.' Below from July 1933: '...it is very hot to go about much, but it is nice to be at the sea.' Between the years Trent's Café has been rebuilt.

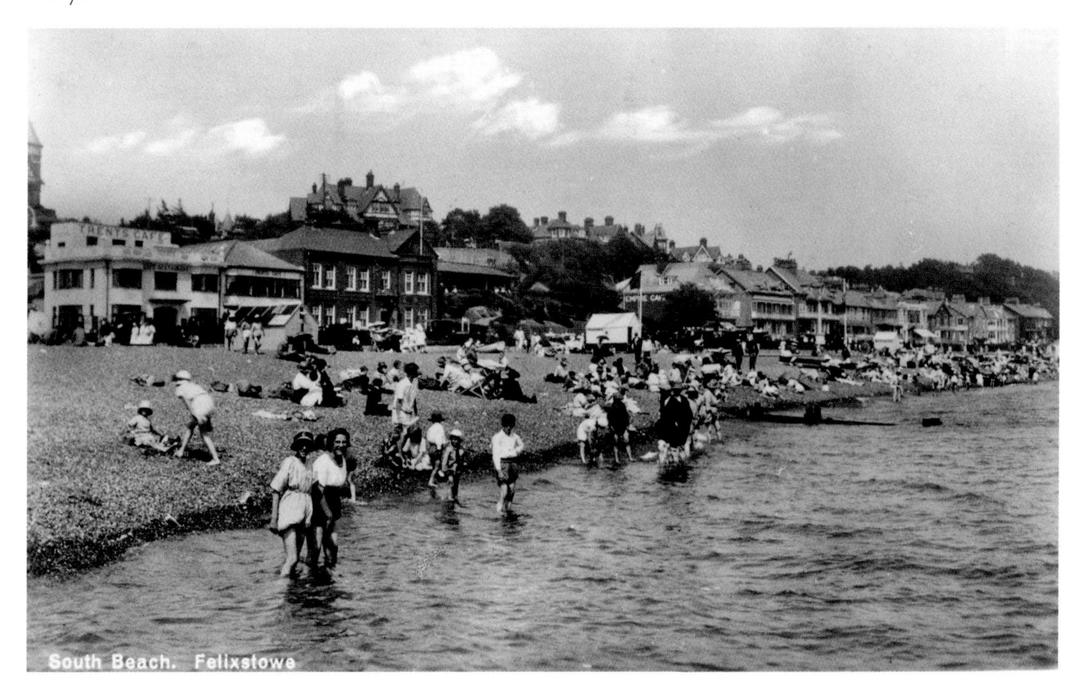

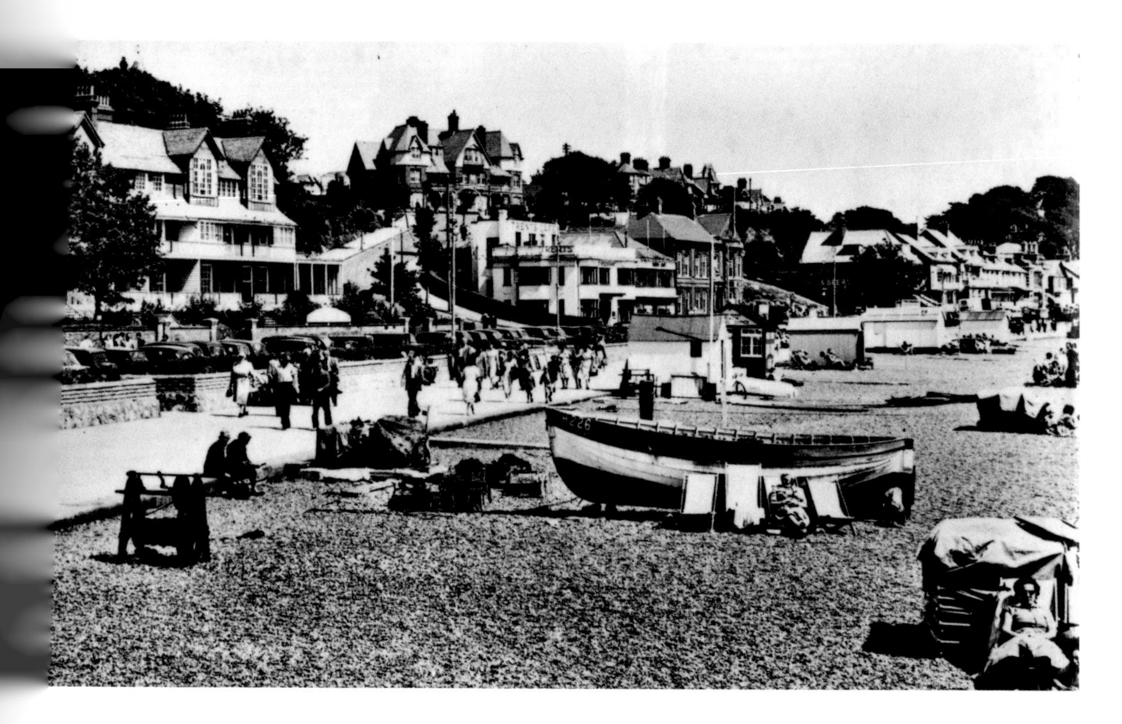

Central Sea Front, 1950s

By the 1950s Trent's Café boasted '200 feet of Windows overlooking the sea… the largest cafe-restaurant in Felixstowe seating 500.' It was competing with Millars, Cordy's Regal Café Restaurant, also with seating for 500 and the Empire Café, which also catered for parties and Cordy's Alexandra Café. By the mid 1960s this fine art-deco building had become the Town Council's Information Bureau. Today's eating habits seem more centred on fast food than sitting down in a restaurant.

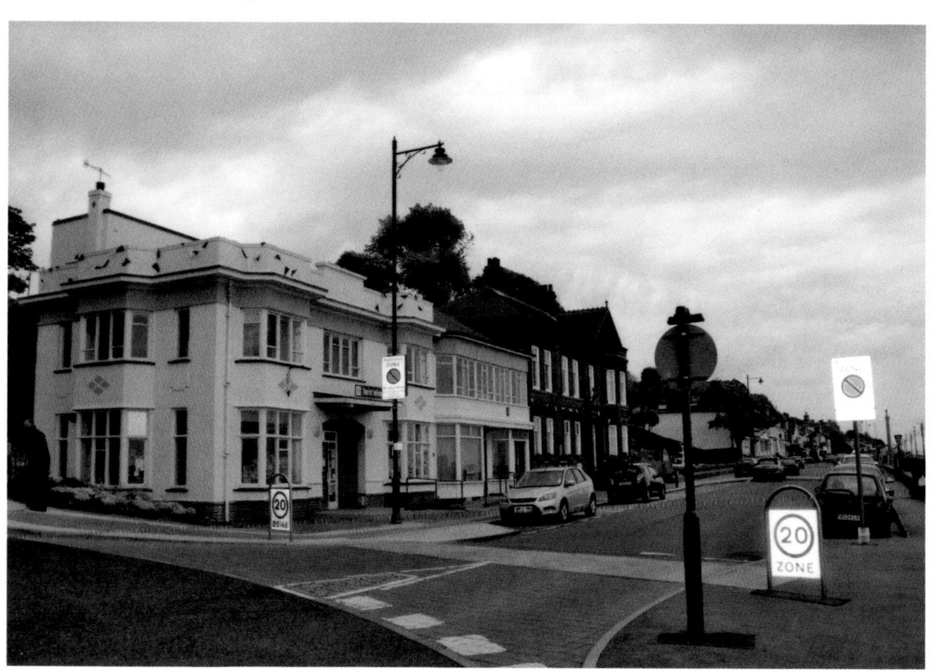

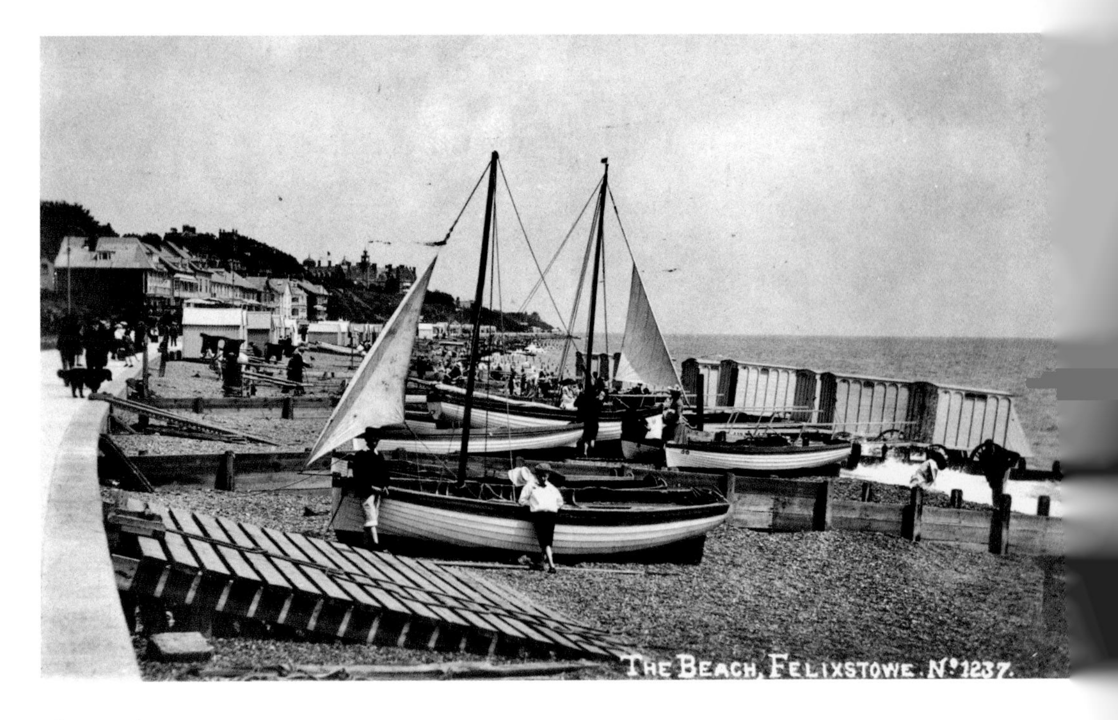

The Beach *c.* 1910

Although Colonel Tomline's vision of a new resort had faltered, Felixstowe around the Bath Hotel was prospering. In 1891 the Empress of Germany with her children and retinue of servants rented South Beach Mansions and South Cottage. The Royal yacht, *Hohenzollern*, anchored in the bay. In 1892 Felixstowe was described as a 'pleasant and rapidly spreading village,' while by 1911 the population had risen to nearly 10,000. Below is the beach in the 1930s.

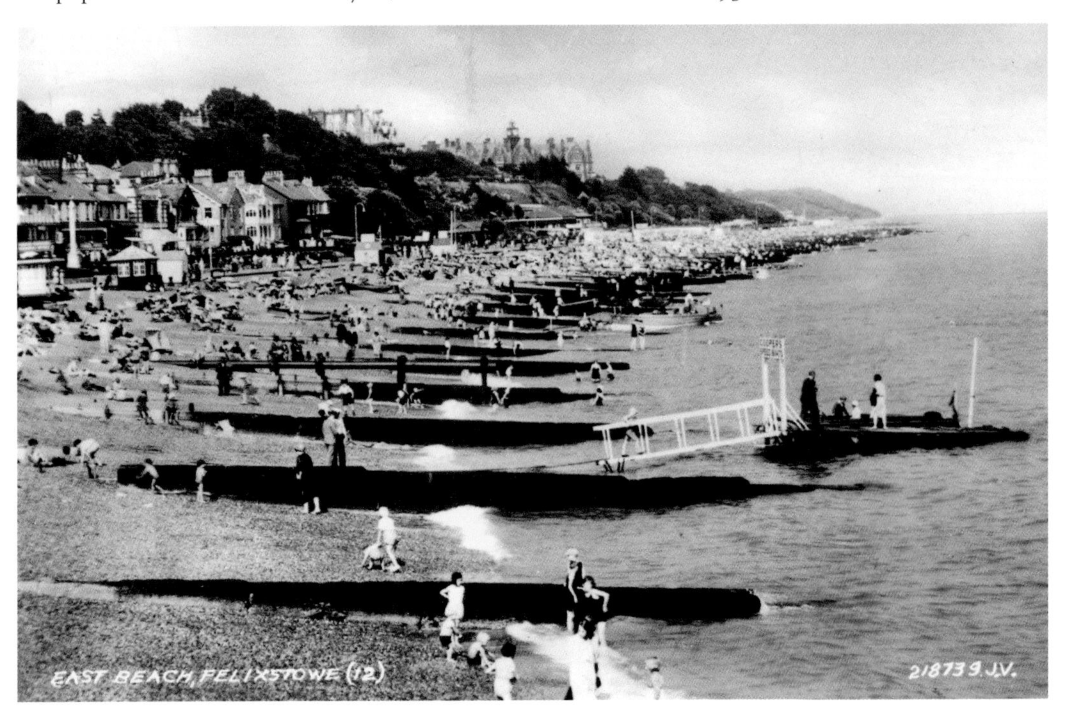

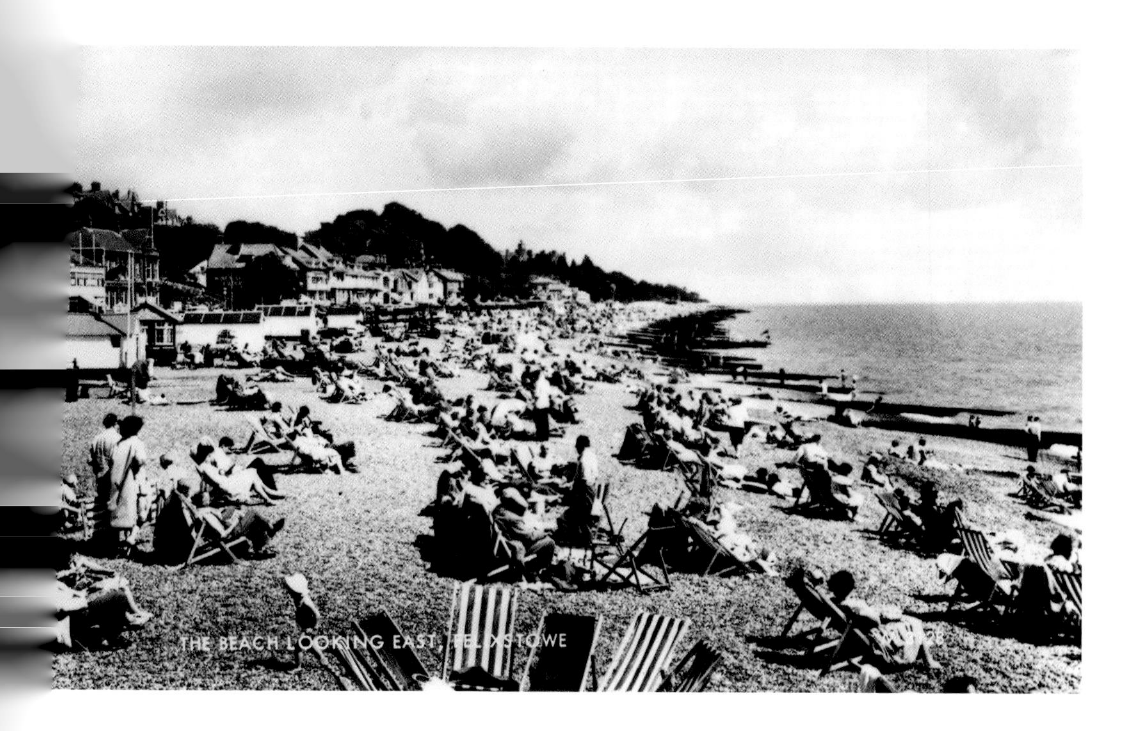

The Beach looking East, *c.* 1955
Fashionable Edwardian Felixstowe really developed as a popular resort between the wars and again in the 1950s. Despite the claims for being one of the sunniest places in England, the lure of cheap overseas holidays in the sun decimated the traditional holiday industry and scenes like this will probably never be seen again. Deckchair hire was obviously a booming business in the mid 1950s, but now it is something that has practically disappeared everywhere – today we can pop a couple of light folding chairs in the boot of the car.

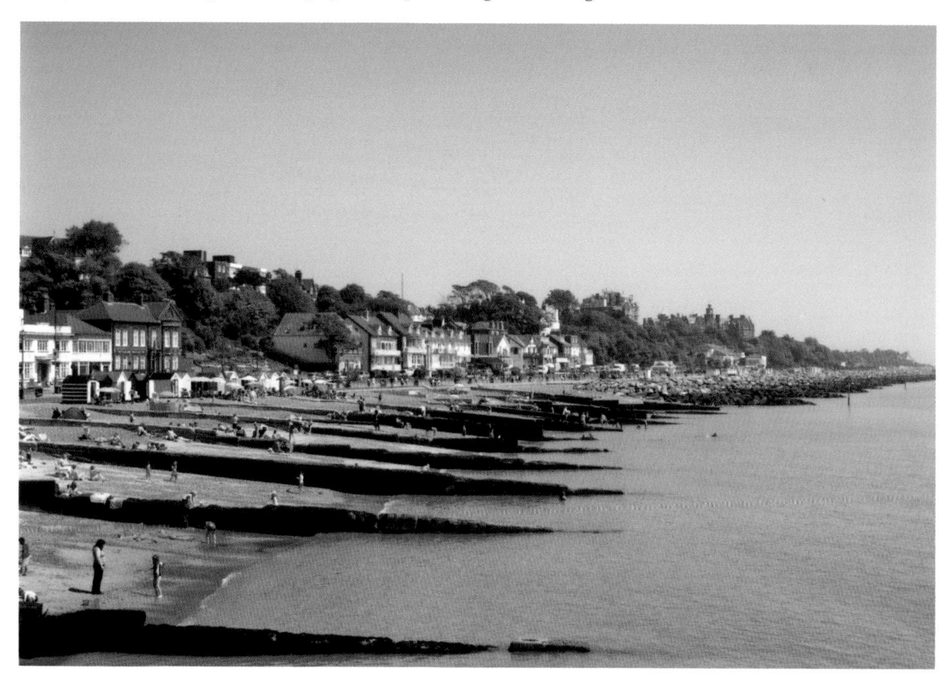

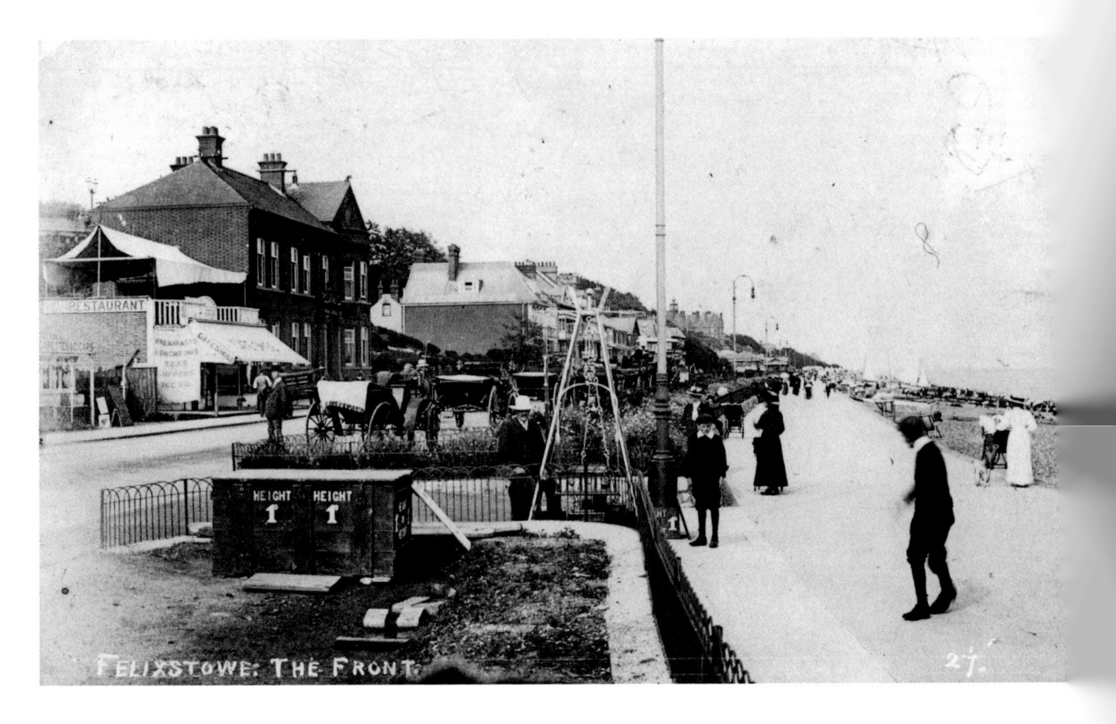

Felixstowe: The Front *c.* 1912
Horse drawn carriages line the road in front of the café and the town hall, which was built by the Local Board of Health in 1892 on a site given by Mr E. G. Pretyman, the Lord of the Manor, who was the heir of Colonel Tomline. The foundation stone was laid by Mr Felix Cobbold. In 2008 the Town Council refurbished the building. Jockey scales were a feature of many sea fronts. My grandfather would insist on everyone being weighed at the start of a holiday and at the end to see how much they had benefitted from the fresh air and food.

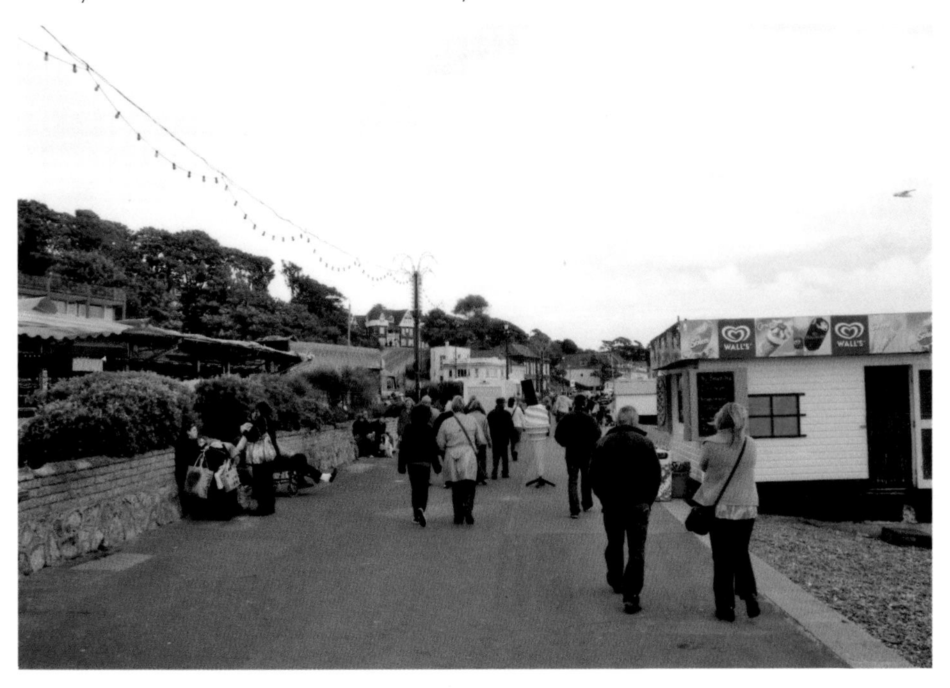

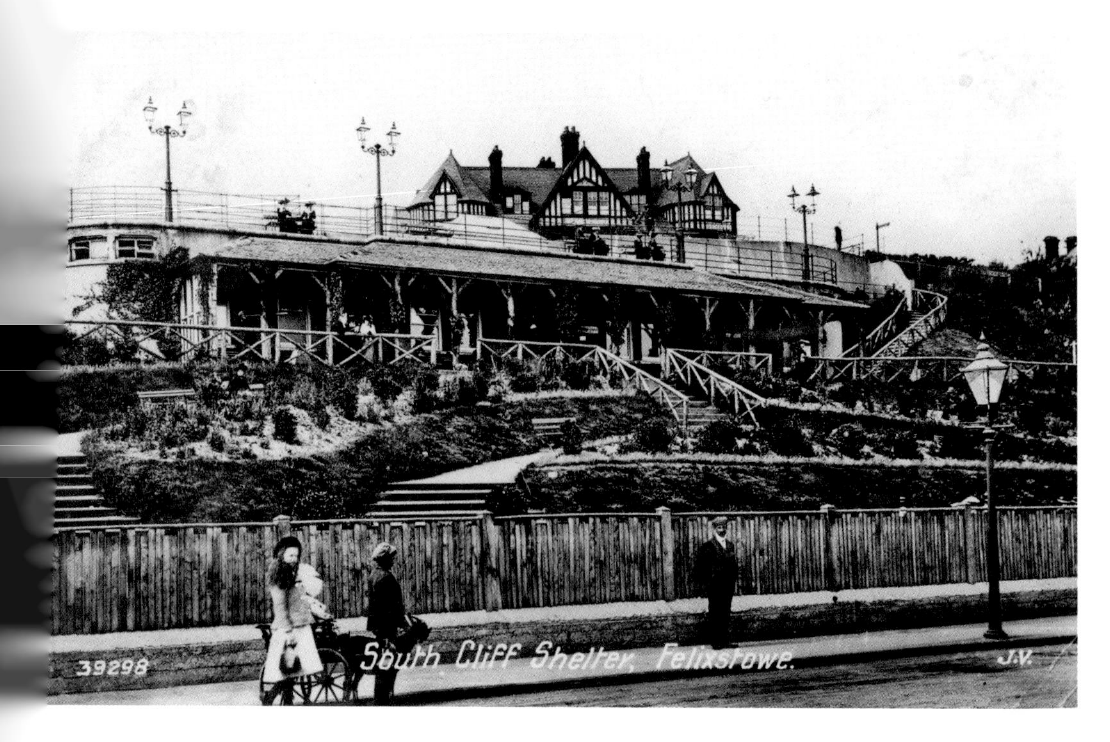

South Cliff Shelter *c.* **1909**

In 1894 the Local Board was replaced by the Felixstowe and Walton Urban District Council and one of the first major improvements for residents and visitors was the building of the South Shelter in Wolsey Gardens, next to the town hall. There were cloakrooms and toilets and a central hall with refreshments. In 1983 the shelter was removed having fallen into disrepair, but there are now plans for a modern structure as part of a £2.7 million pound renovation of the sea front gardens.

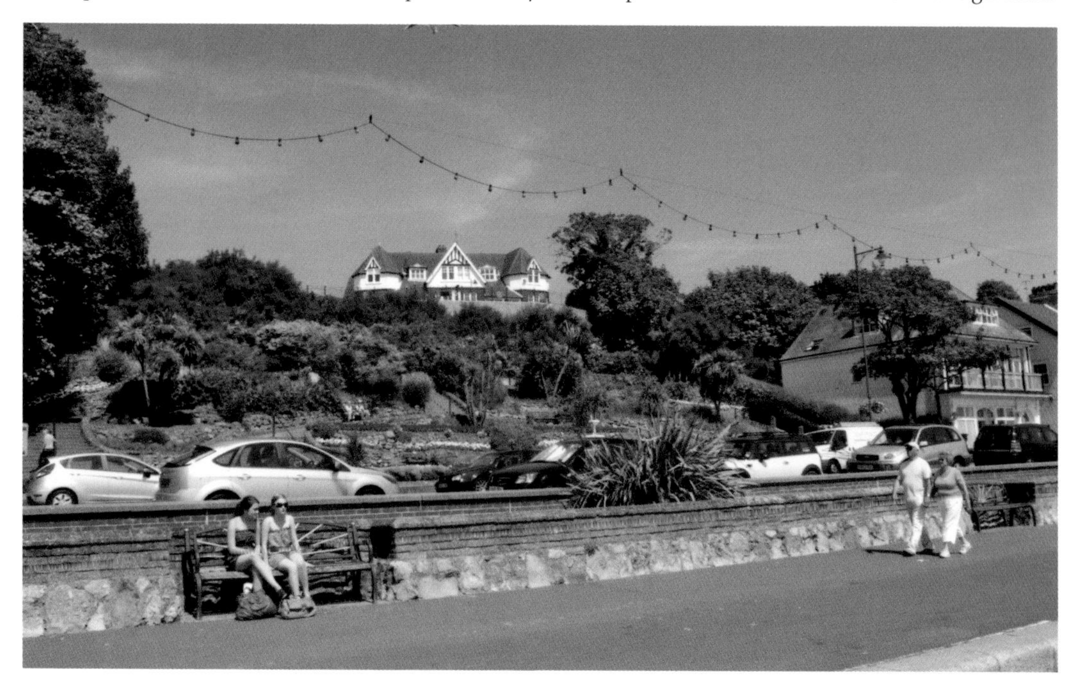

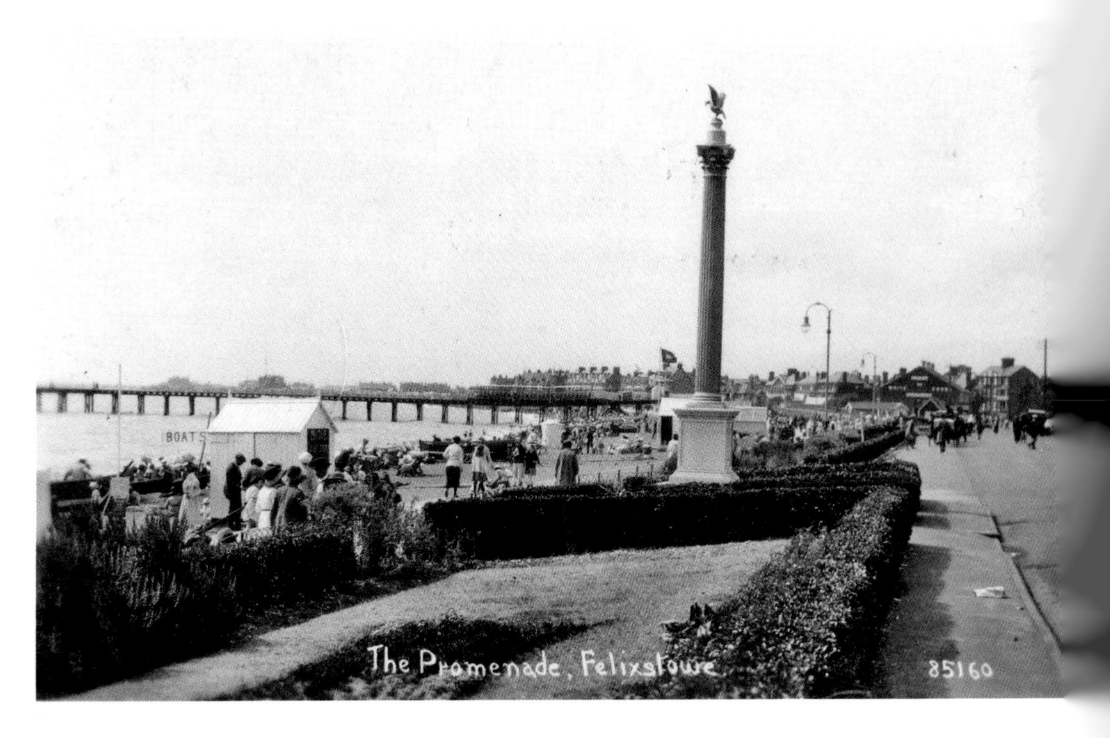

The Promenade *c.* 1920

An appropriate setting for the town's war memorial – on the promenade looking out to sea. It was unveiled in August 1920 and recorded 163 names from the First World War, during which the town was a taken over by the military with many hotels and large house requisitioned. In the distance the Pier Pavilion is advertising Will C. Pepper's 'White Coons' Concert Party, who first appeared in a marquee at the resort in 1906 and played their last season in 1920.

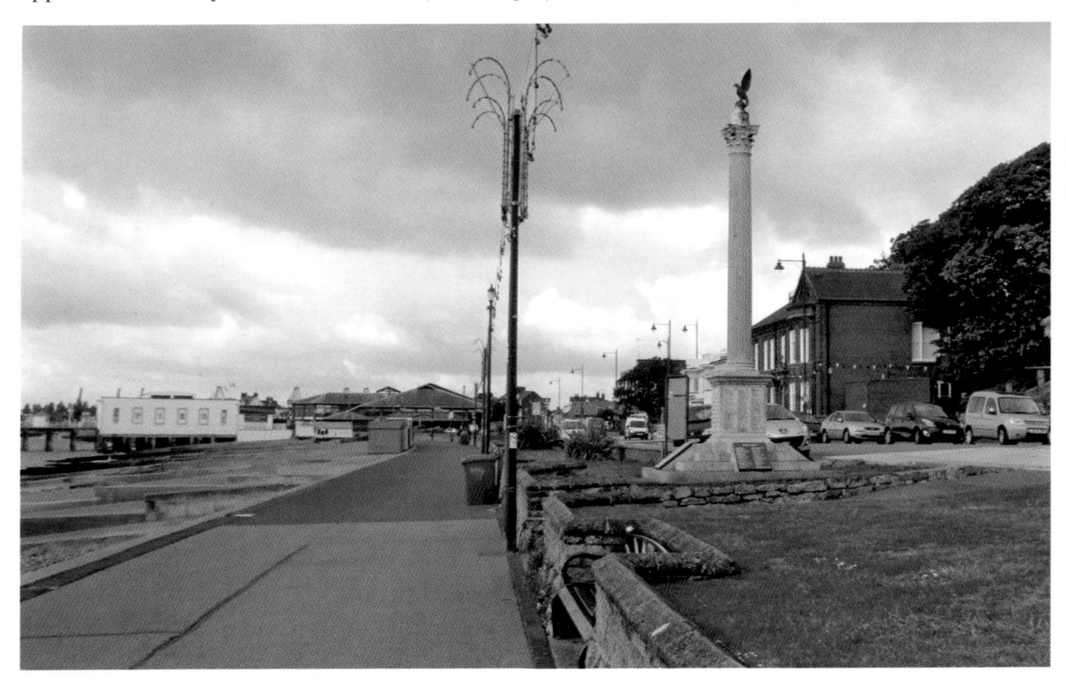

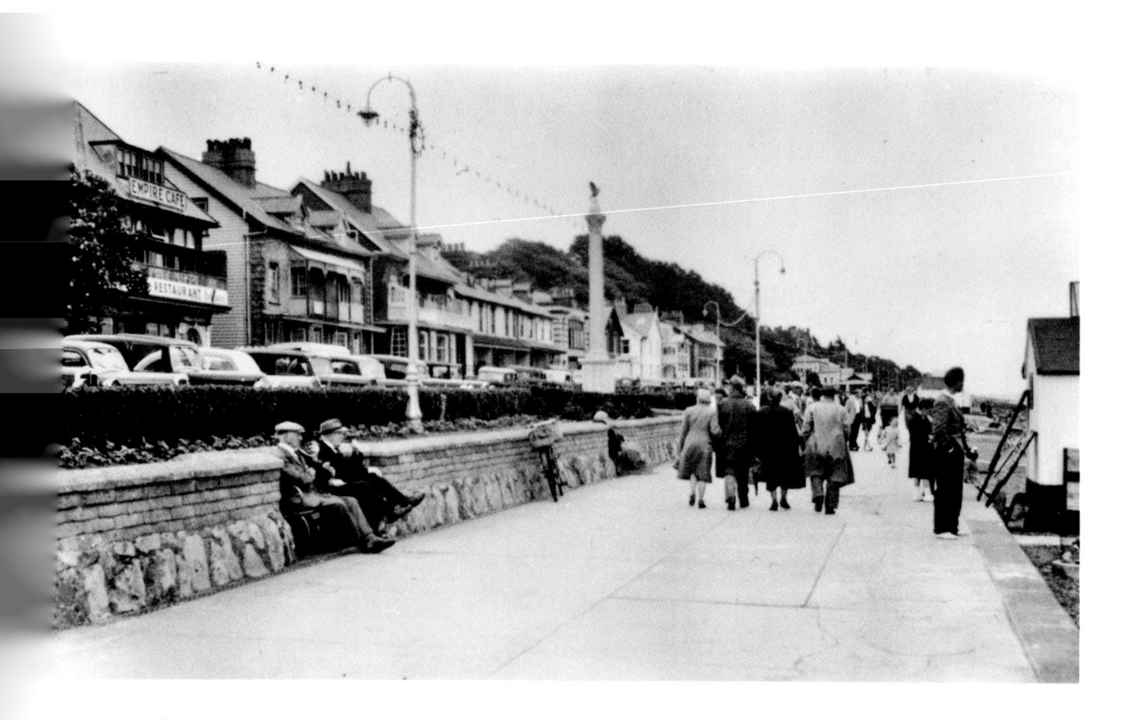

Parade & Memorial *c.* 1923

Despite the symbol of the dove of peace at the top of the Corinthian column, the Second World War saw another 111 names added to the memorial. Felixstowe was heavily fortified during the war with tank traps and barbed wire all along the front. Fearing invasion the pier, like others along the east coast, was blown in two in 1940 by Royal Engineers.

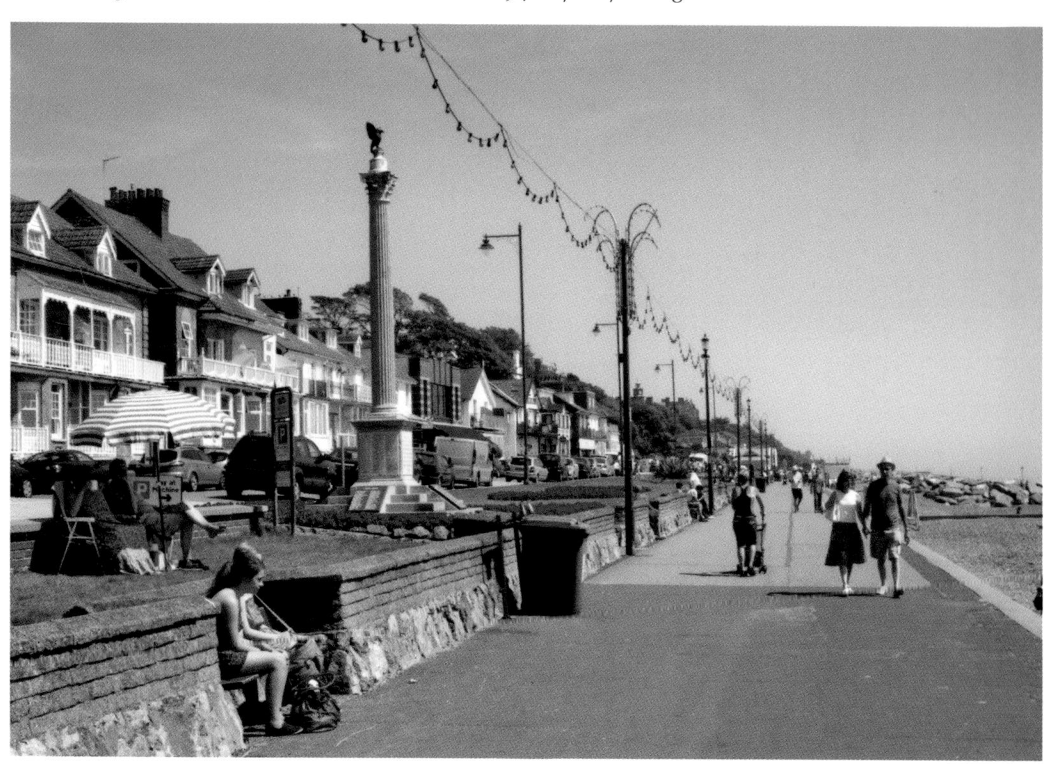

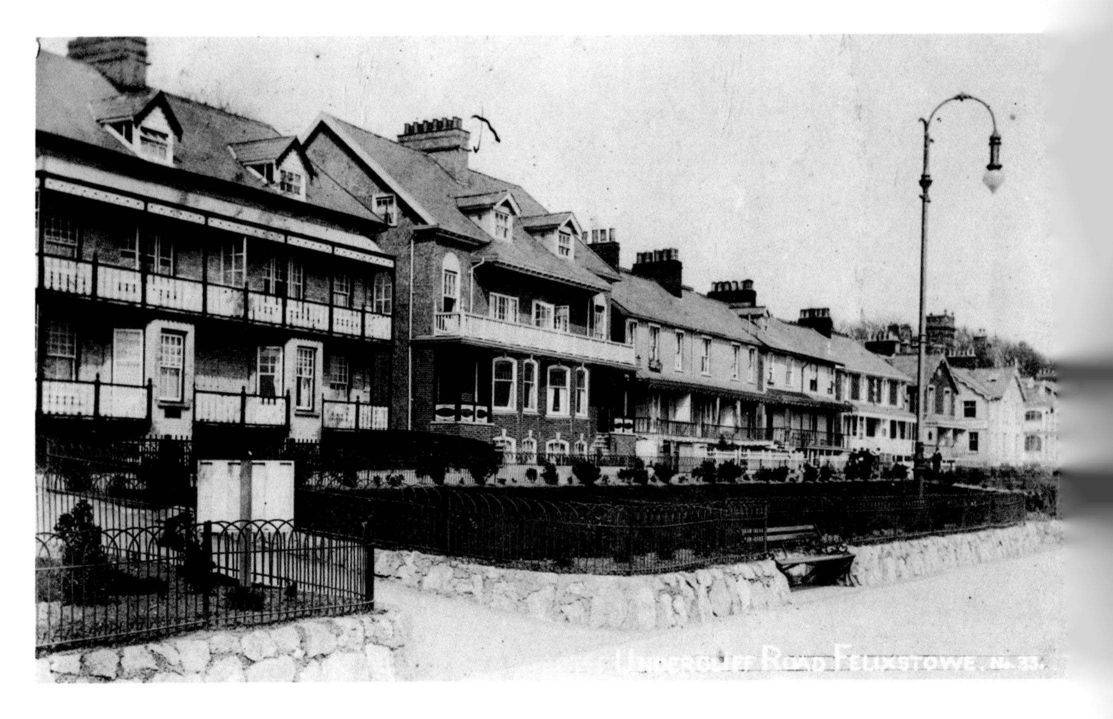

Undercliff Road *c.* 1908

'This is a good photo of our house,' says Emily in 1908 making a cross above the right hand side of the second property from the left. Over one hundred years on, the section of the sea front is instantly recognisable, although there have been many quite subtle changes to some of the properties. The first property was for many years the Empire Café.

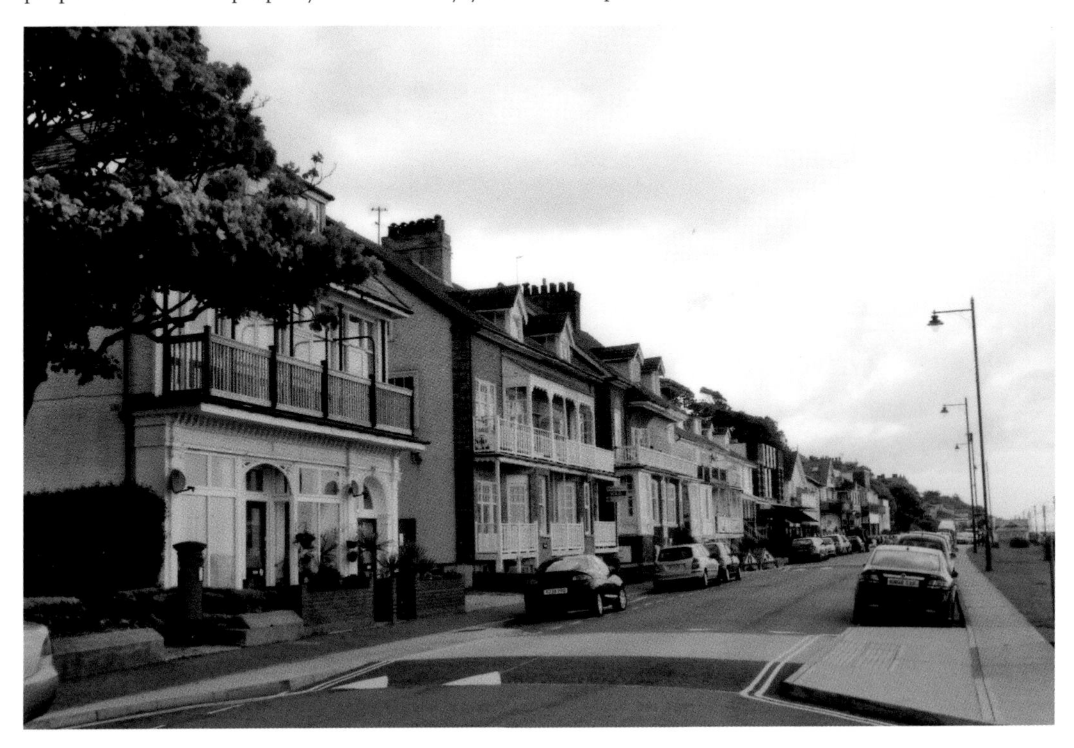

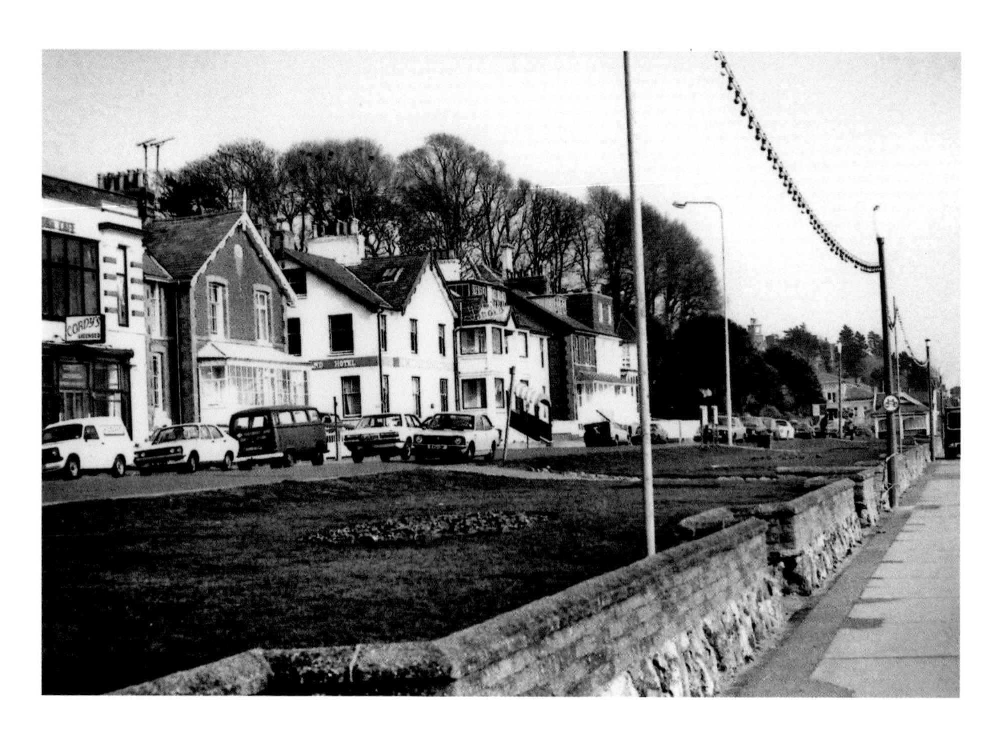

Undercliff Road ***c.*** **1980**
The famous Cordy's Alexandra Café is in the foreground. In 1950 it claimed the 'best position on the sea front', with a seating capacity of 500. William Cordy first opened a restaurant next to the Grand Hotel. In 1926 Leslie Cordy bought two houses on Undercliff Road West, demolished them and built the Alexandra Restaurant, opening it for the 1927 season. In 2000 the Yeo Group bought the business and a second refurbishment in 2010 created the popular Alex Café Bar with a brasserie on the first floor.

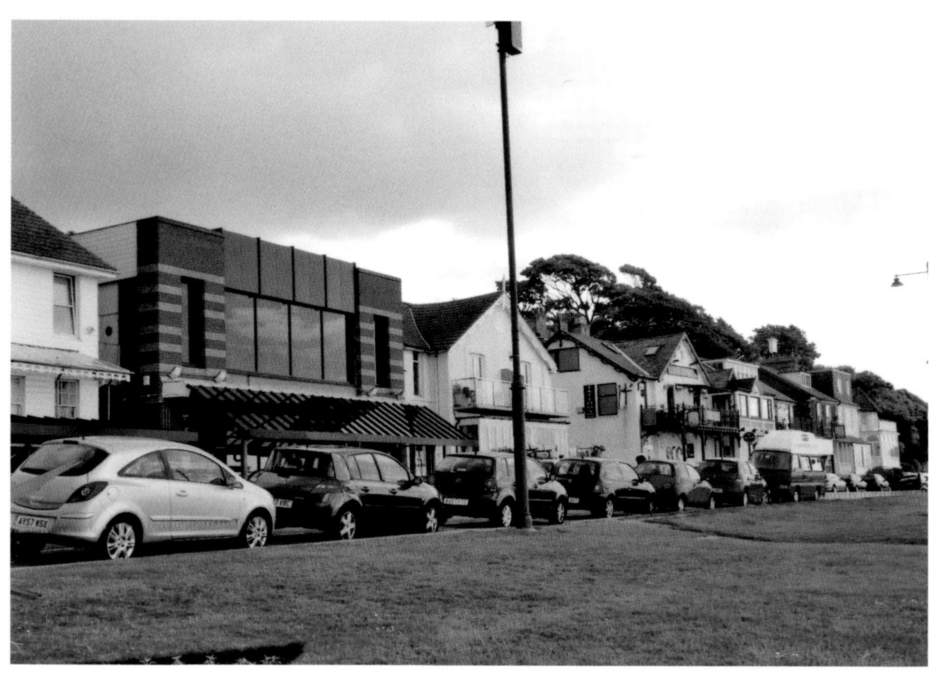

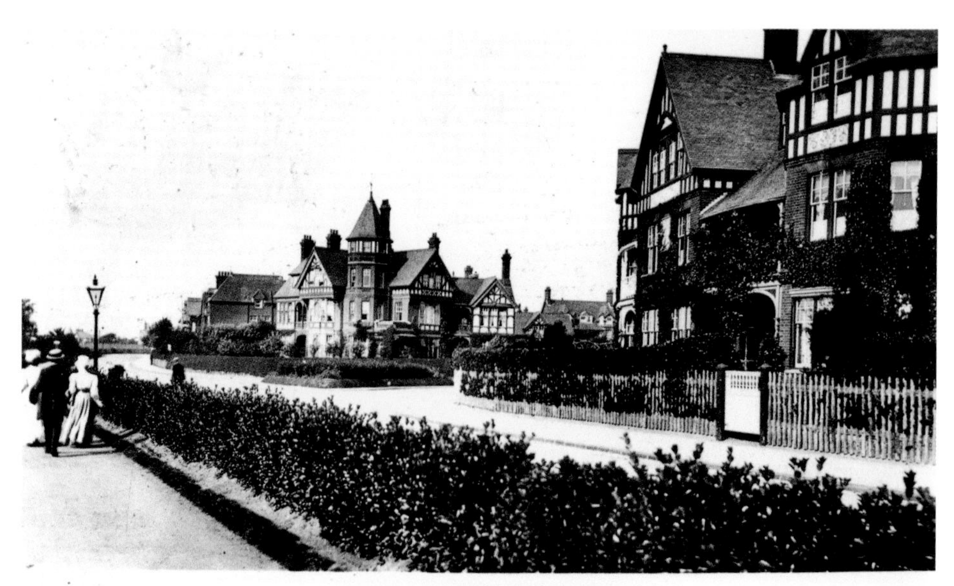
S 1295 WOLSEY TERRACE, FELIXSTOWE.

Wolsey Terrace *c.* 1908
The late nineteenth century development of the town saw the building of many fine properties on the cliffs with stunning views of the bay. The building in the distance at the top of Convalescent Hill is the late Victorian Kilgarth House, quite recently converted into apartments as Kilgarth Court. The message to Muriel reads: 'I hope you are keeping well and getting on alright at school. The two prominent houses are work I carried out here some years ago, thought you would like them, your loving Uncle.'

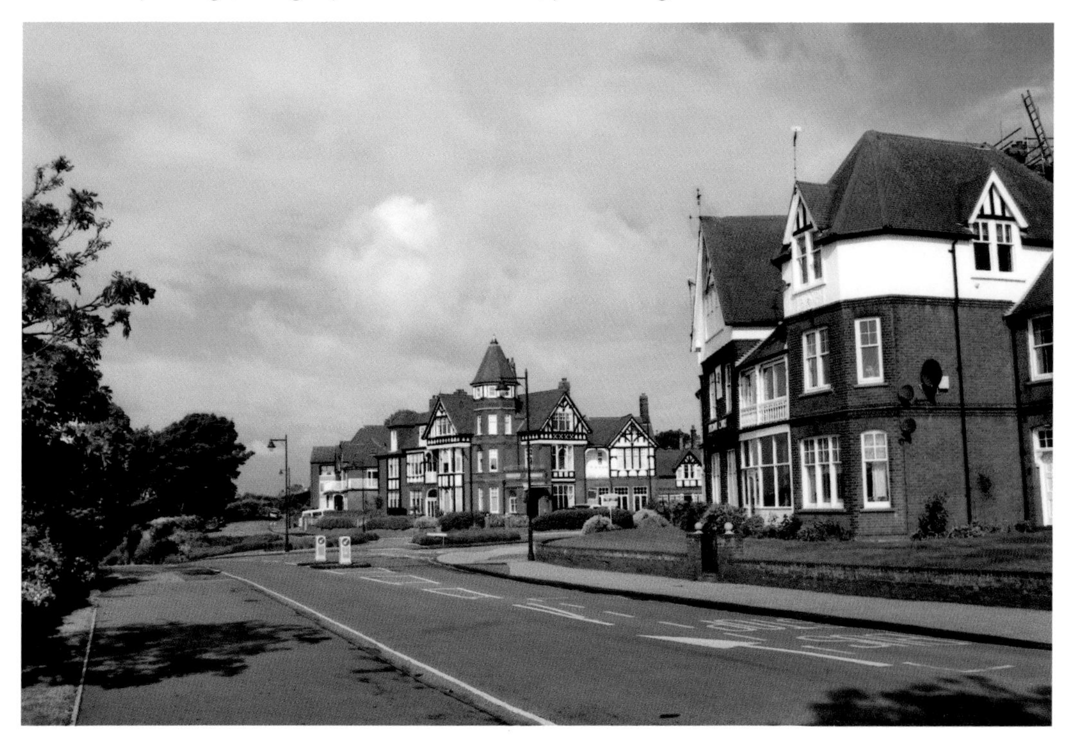

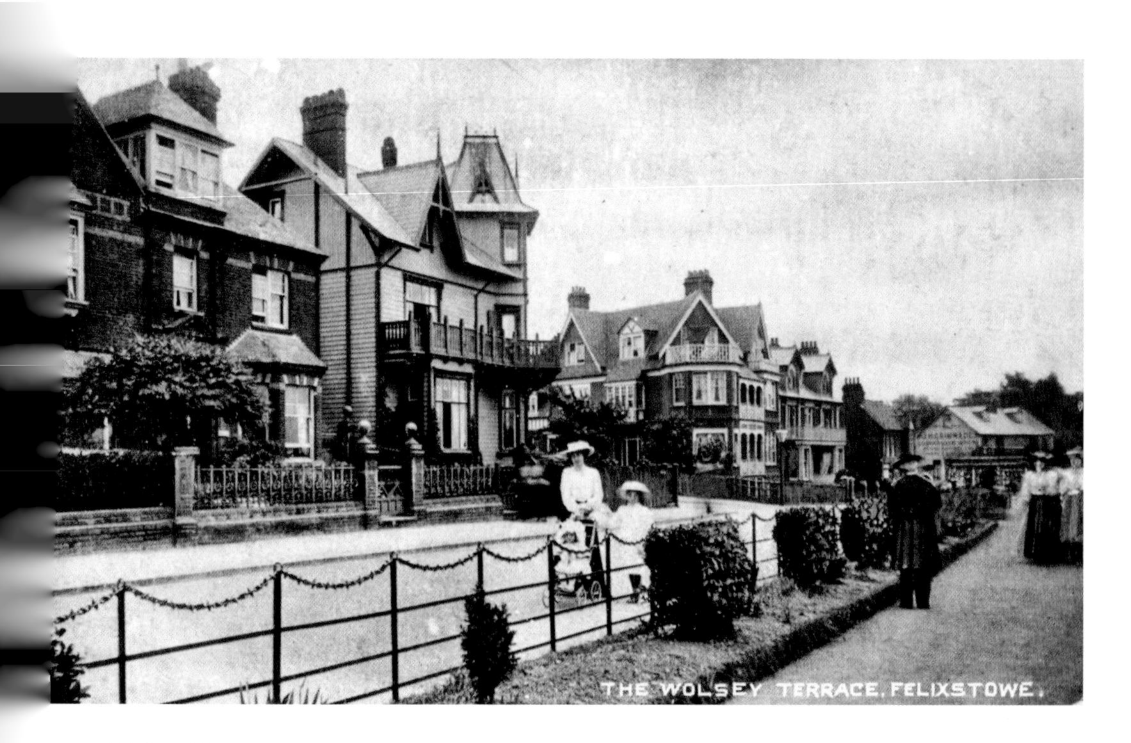

Wolsey Terrace *c.* 1909
The wooden clad building with its distinctive turret was the Eastward Ho College for Boys, established in 1883. After a period as the Glenroy Hotel it became St Peter's School and the building alongside it became the Eastward Ho! Hotel. Both buildings were demolished in 1971. Wolsey Court now stands on the site. The corner of the Waverley Hotel can be seen.

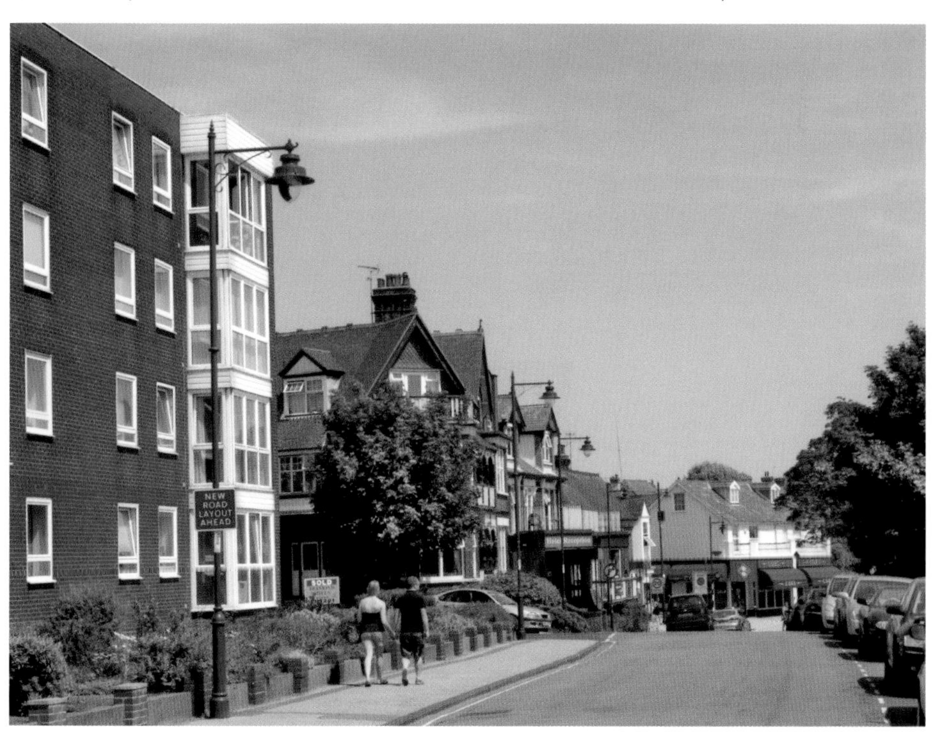

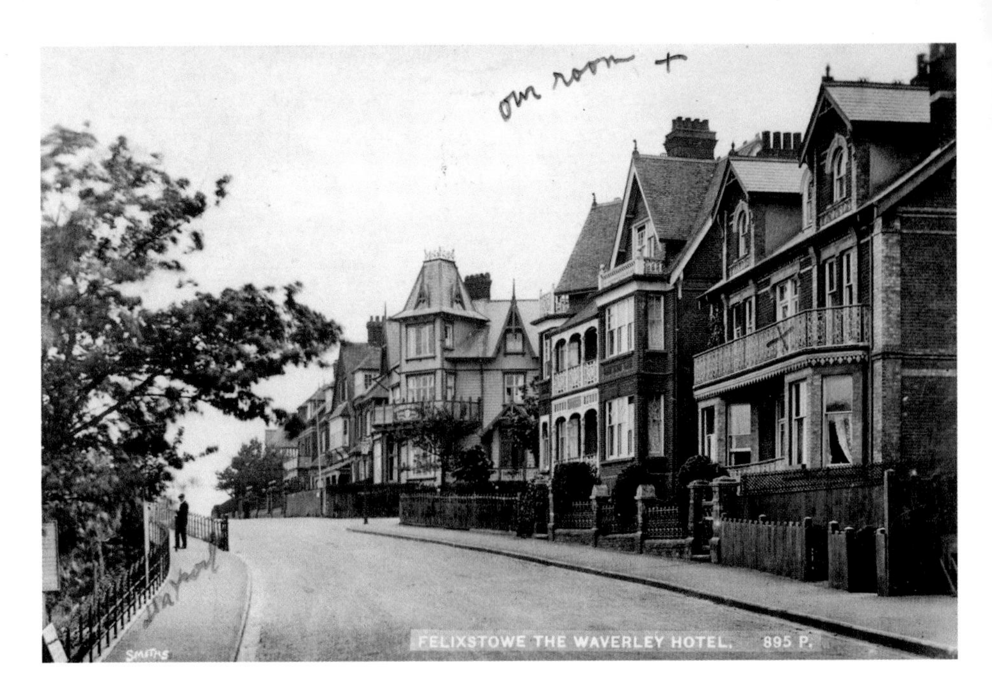

The Waverley Hotel *c.* 1918

The Waverley is one of the resort's longest established hotels still in business today. In the guide book for 1936 it is described as: 'Excellent position on Cliffs, facing South and Sea. Central for shops, Amusements, Golf and tennis. Own gardens with Croquet Lawn. Comfortable Lounges and Smoke Room. Large Recreation Room. 45 Bedrooms, H & C running water. Gas and Electric Fires.' There was also a Vita Glass Sun Lounge and Wireless. I couldn't find the croquet lawn, but there was space to park. The modern photograph shows the post office tucked in alongside the hotel.

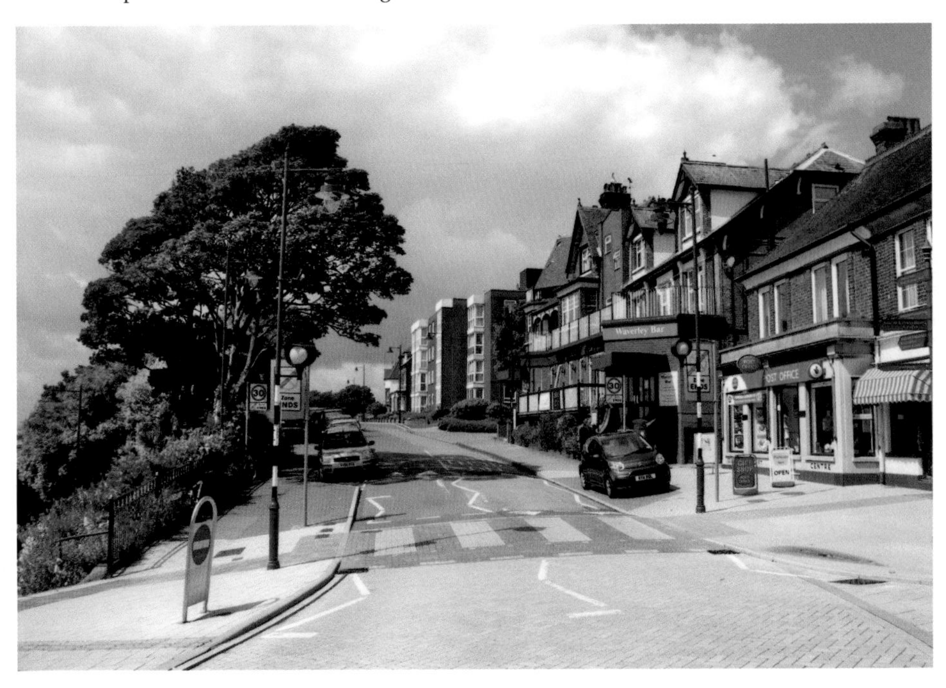

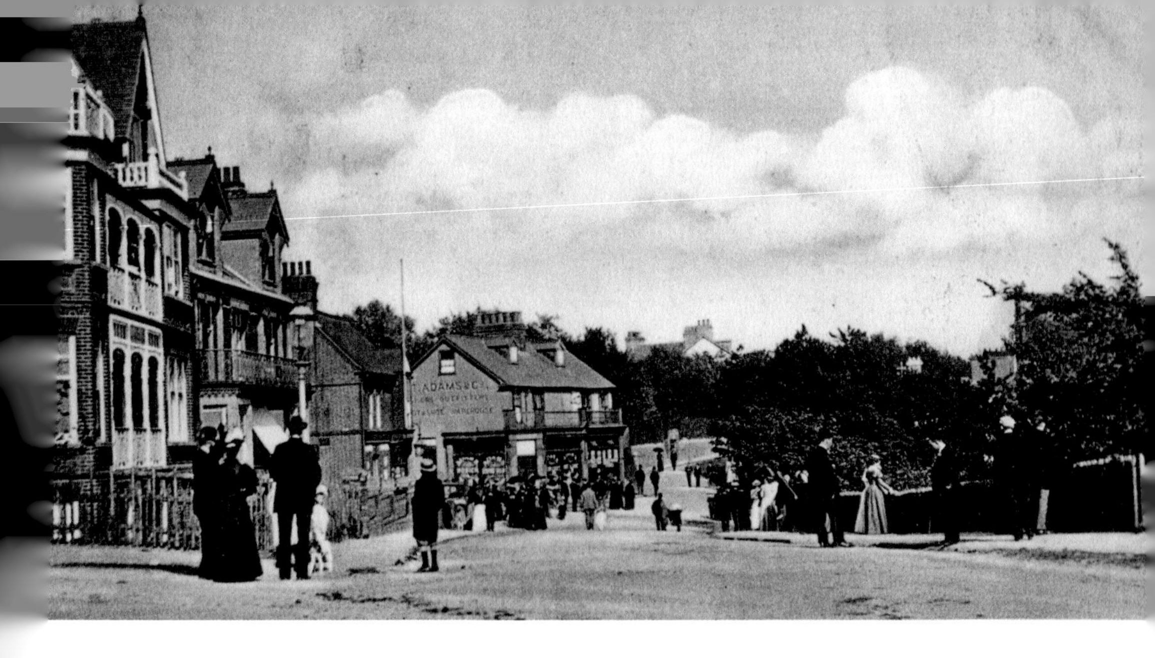

Top of Benthill ***c.*** **1907**

The Waverley and looking beyond to Adam & Co's outfitter's and shoe shop. The far side of the building was a separate restaurant, but today it is all Coes as my bird's eye view from the Waverley Hotel shows. South Beach Mansion can just be seen in the modern photograph through the trees on the right, beyond the road improvements at the top of Bent Hill.

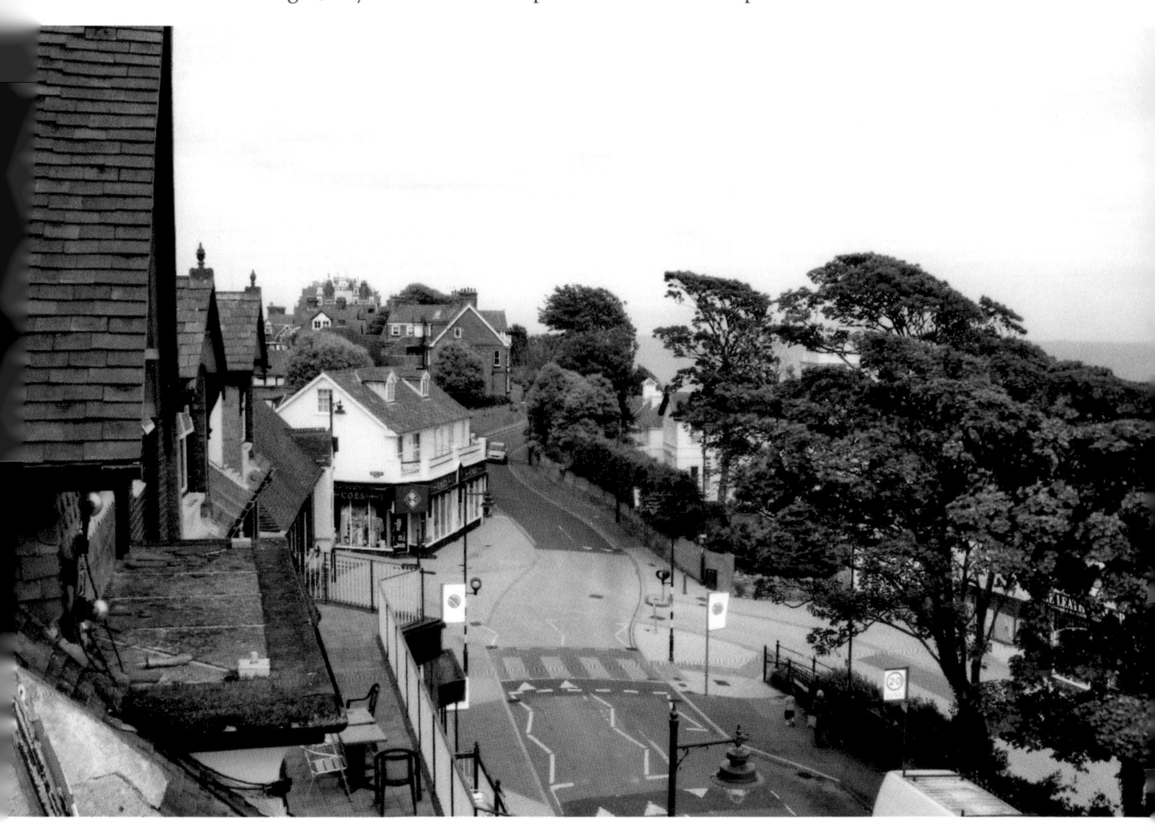

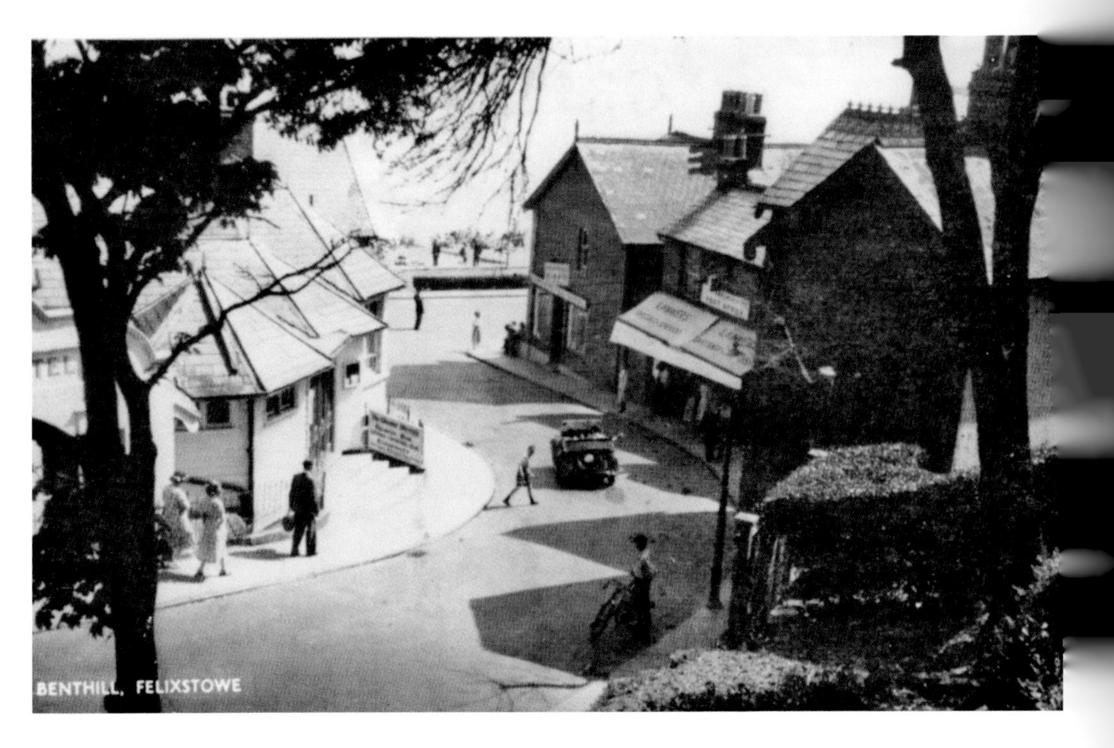

Bent Hill, 1950s

The side of the Grand Hotel is on the left. The cottage in the right foreground was demolished in 1956. The Grand's premises keep undergoing many changes and in 2010 the road itself was resurfaced with new footpaths. Bent Hill leads directly from the sea front into Hamilton Road and the main shopping area.

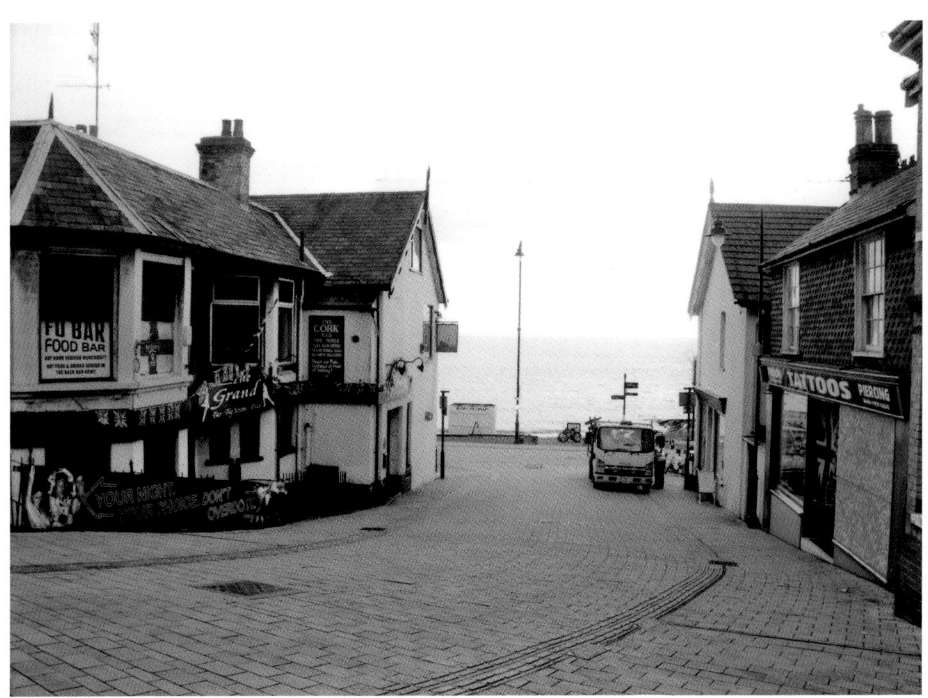

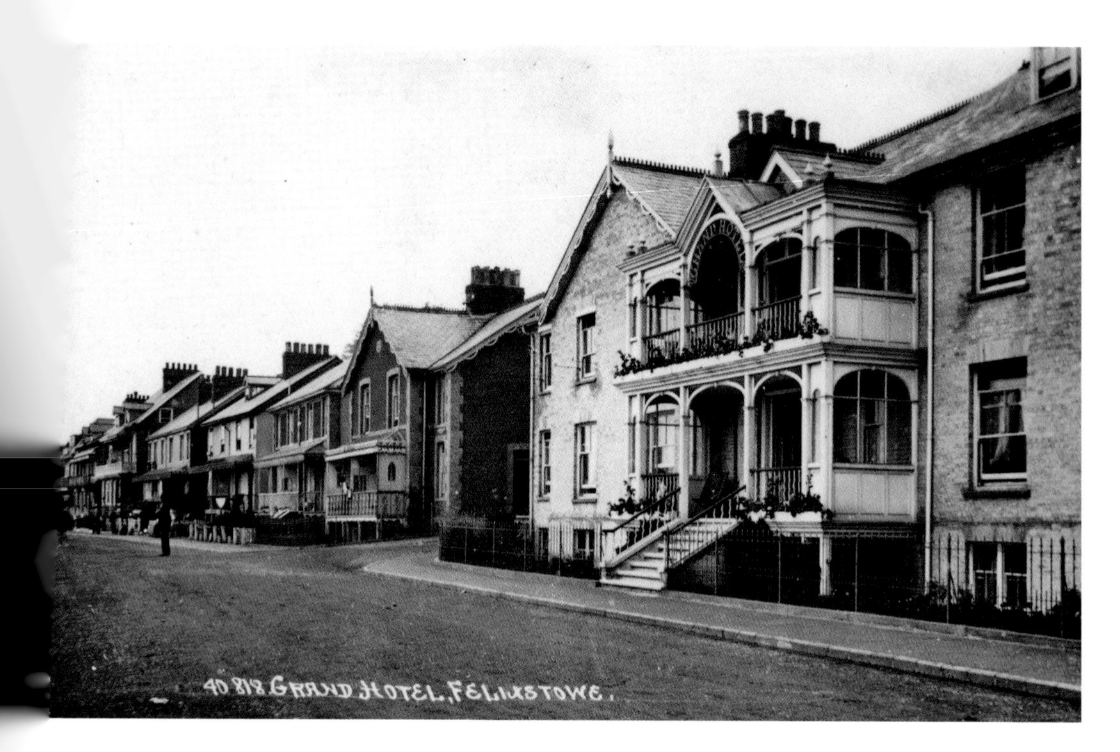

Grand Hotel *c.* 1910

The Grand Hotel dated from 1877 and was extended and renovated by T. W. Cotman in the early 1900s. After the Grand closed in the 1980s part of it became the Cork public house, named after the Cork lightship that could be seen from the sea front. Further along Undercliff are two houses that were demolished when the Alexandra Café was built in 1927.

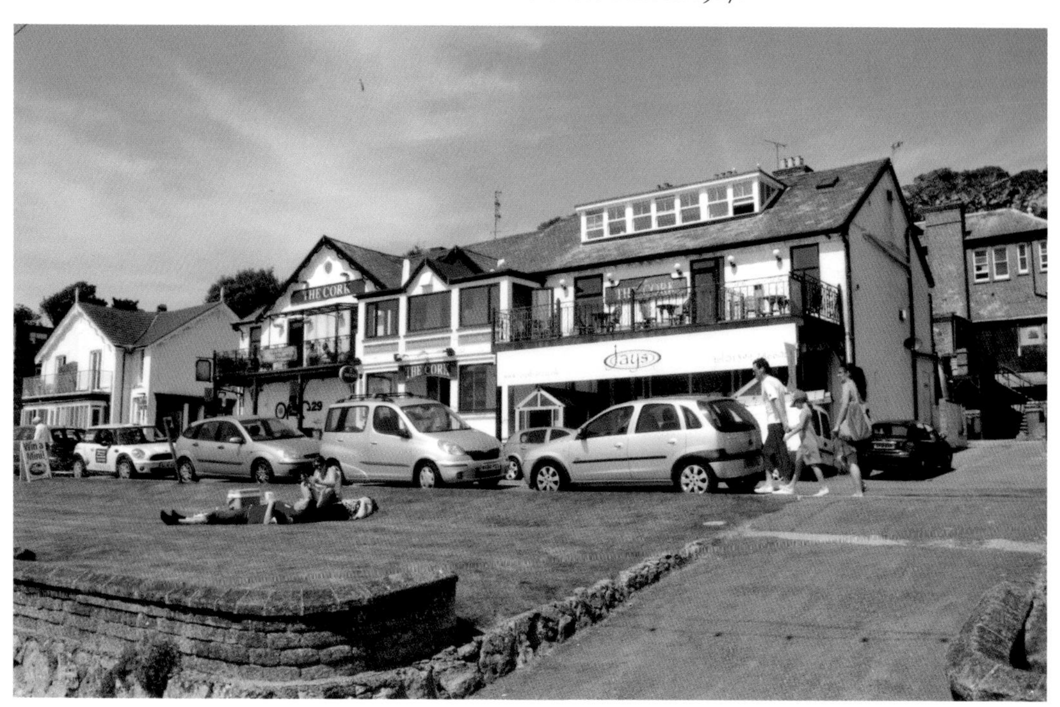

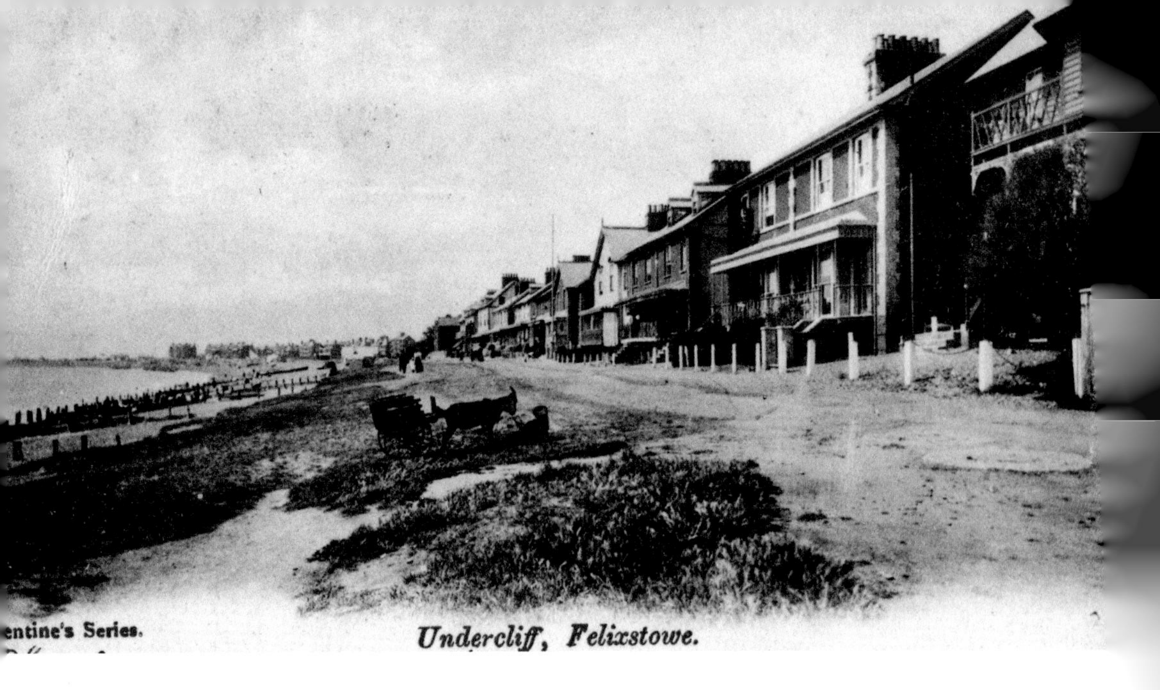

Undercliff *c.* 1902

A boy rests with his goat cart opposite Swiss Cottage, one of the wooden houses built by John Chevallier Cobbold at the foot of the cliffs. Pipes collected water from the cliffs to supply the houses. This photograph is taken before the pier was built, along with the promenade and its gardens. In 1902 the Urban District Council purchased the central cliff and began creating the gardens. It was the development of the gardens over the next nearly thirty years that was to make such a massive contribution to the resort's attraction.

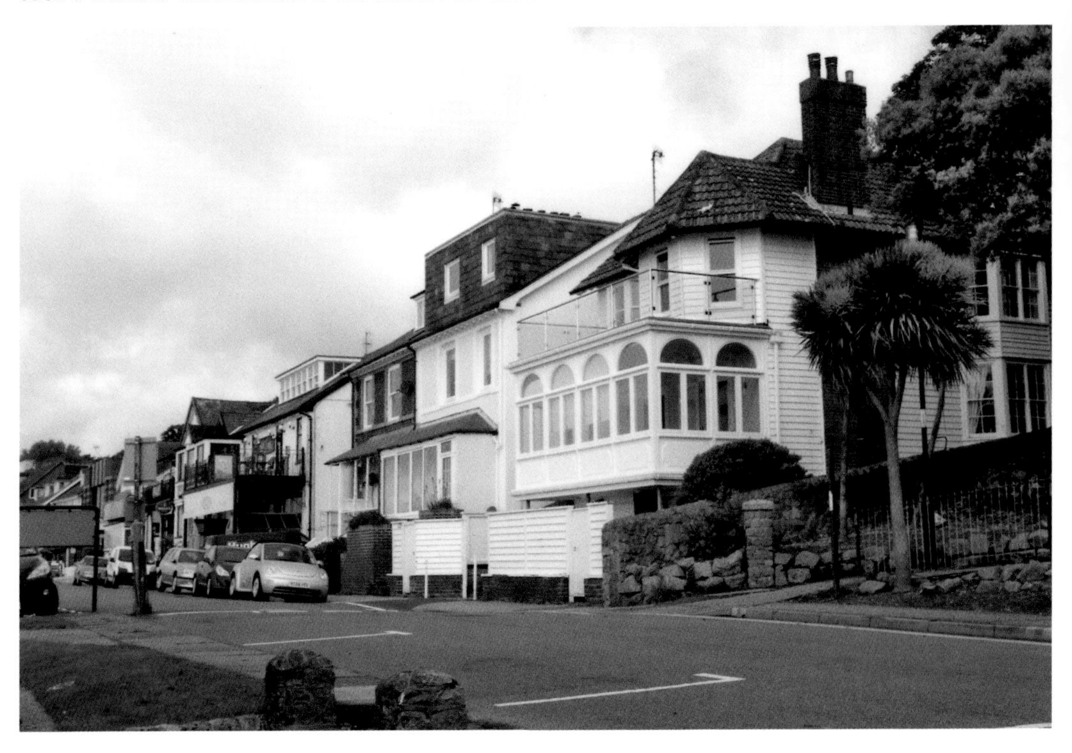

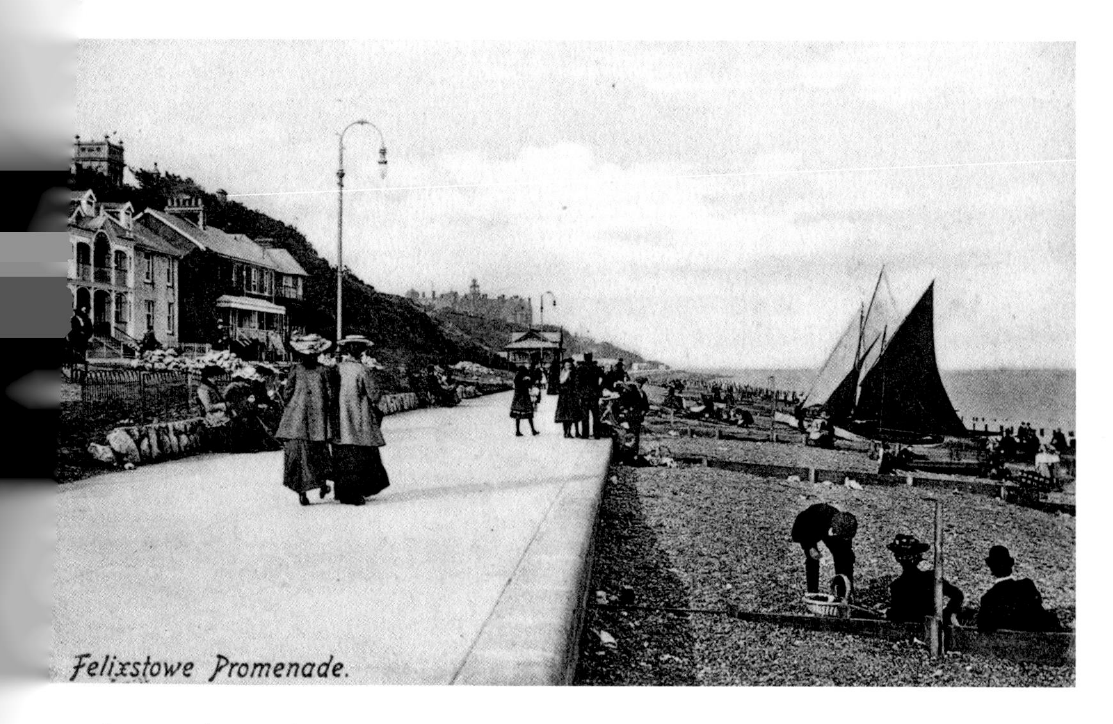

Promenade *c.* 1908

'I wish you were here to walk along this path with me. There isn't very much sand nearly all stones'. A romantic thought with some practical information, sent in July 1909 to a young lady in Lichfield. Felixstowe always saw itself as a genteel and rather exclusive resort. The distinctive tower of South Beach Mansion can be seen above the Grand Hotel. Built by Eley, the manufacturer of gun cartridges, this was where the Empress of Germany stayed. The 1898 Jubilee shelter can be seen in the distance. Today's view was taken looking the other way from the Victorian shelter.

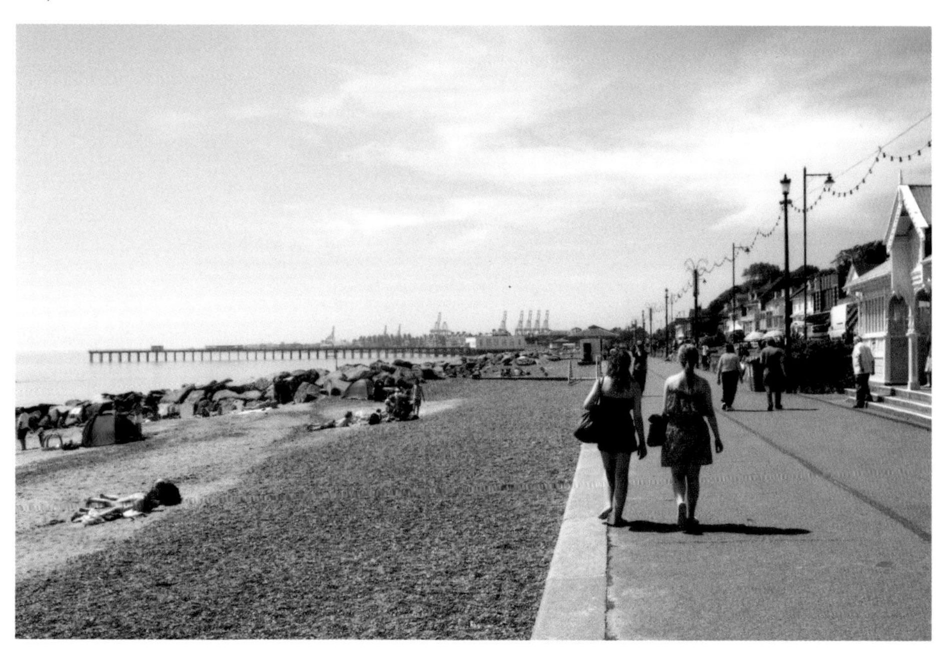

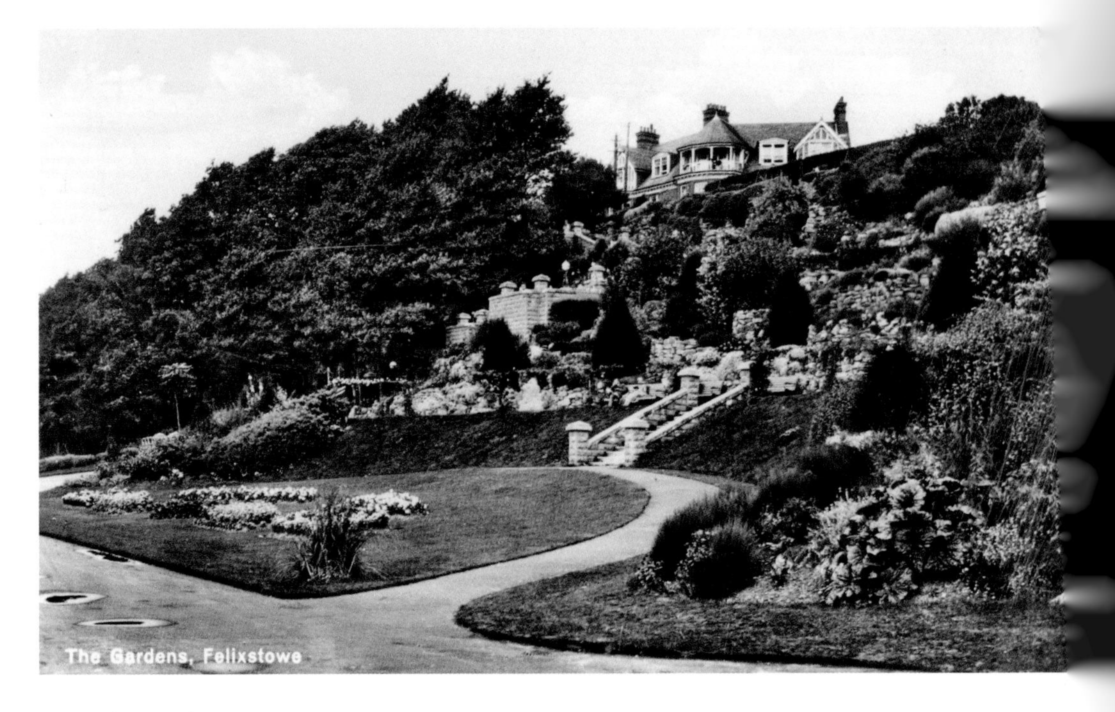

The Gardens *c.* 1934

The Ranelagh Steps Gardens run below South Beach Mansion, which can be seen to the left on today's photograph. There was a pram walk through these gardens conjuring up pictures of uniformed nannies walking their young charges. Wealthy families might come down for the season and bring their domestic staff with them. In July 2011 it was confirmed that with the support of a Lottery Heritage Grant some £2.76 million will be spent of refurbishment, improved access, especially for disabled people, lighting, furniture and seating along the seafront gardens.

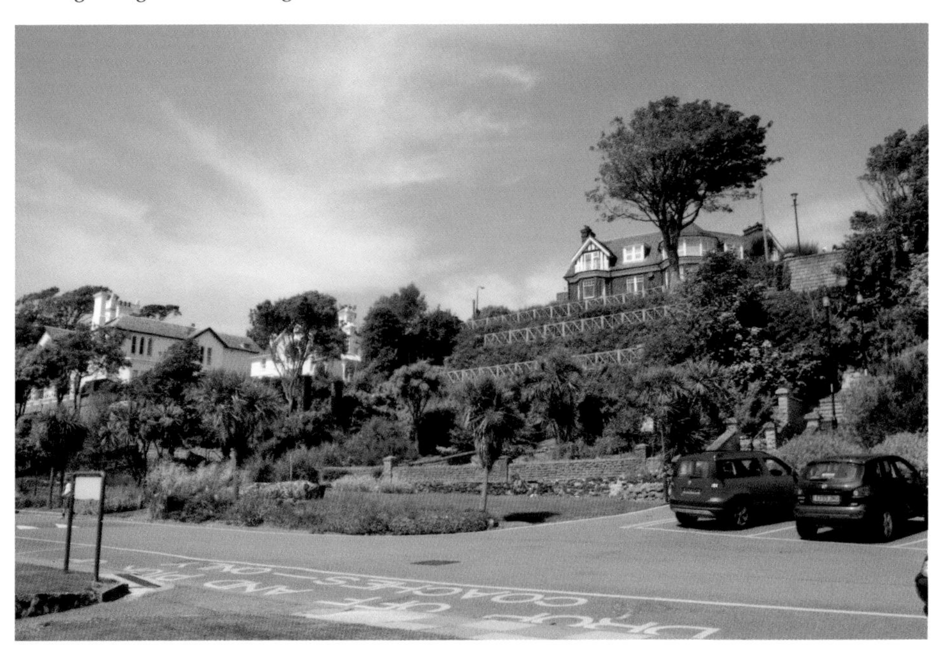

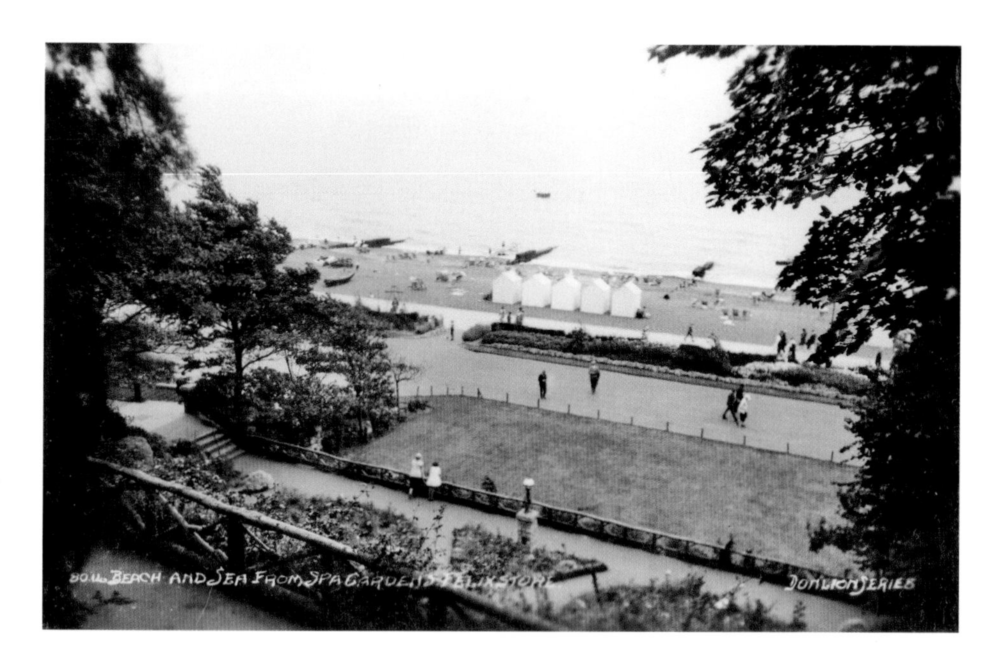

Beach & Sea from Spa Gardens ***c.*** **1925**

'The shrubs, the flowers, the winding pathways, the shady nooks, the glimpses of the sea through masses of foliage, combine to give the sea-front of Felixstowe a charm that grows upon acquaintance.' (*Ward Lock Guide*, 1921). Felixstowe was always proud of its hours of sunshine. The town's *Official Guide* for 1936 boasts: 'There is bathing at every state of the tide; there is sunshine of greater intensity and longer duration than anywhere else in England or Northern Europe; a health record unique; a water supply that never fails in the driest summer; a subsoil that absorbs all moisture; and a climate that is kindly in winter and positively ravishing in summer.'

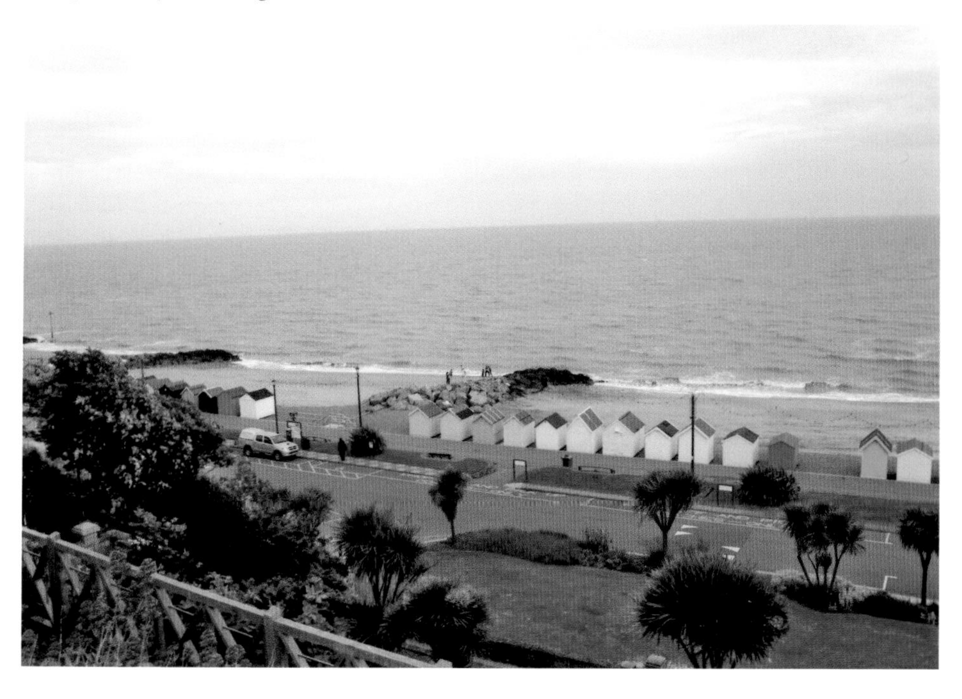

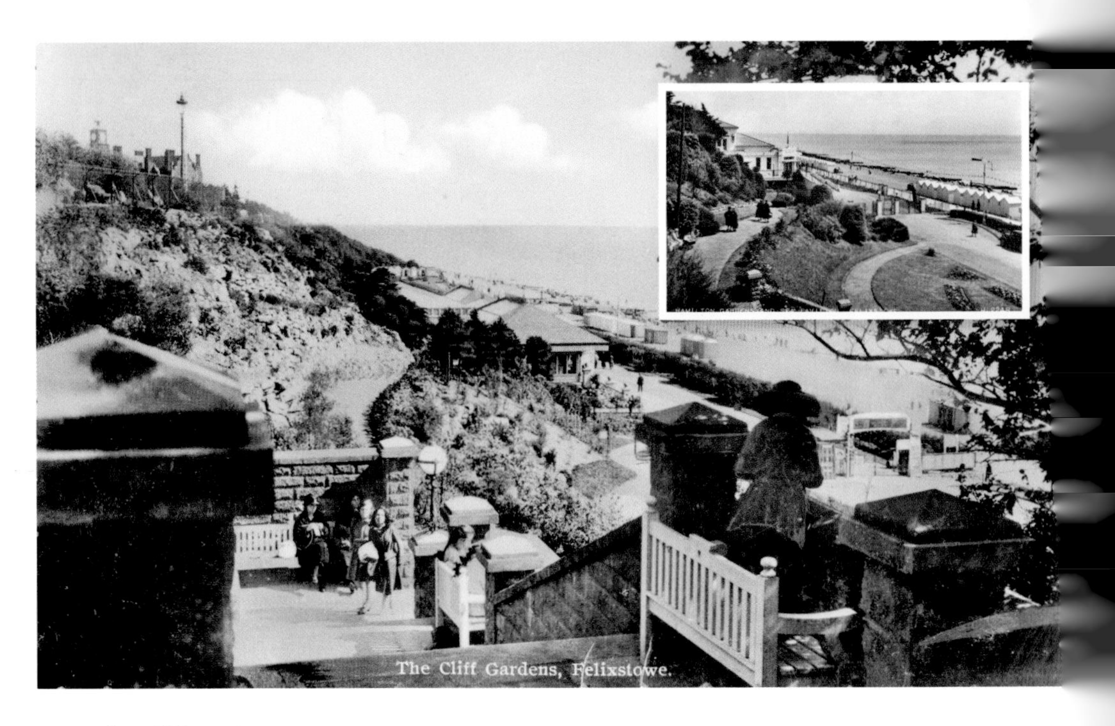

The Cliff Gardens *c.* 1929
In 1910 these steps replaced the original zigzag steps created 1903 to provide access from the cliff top to the new promenade. The new steps were designed by Harry Clegg, the District Council Surveyor, after he had completed the Spa Pavilion. By the mid 1950s (inset) the new Spa Pavilion had opened and everywhere appears neat and tidy. Today the gardens have Grade II listed status on the National Register of Parks and Gardens of Special Historic Interest.

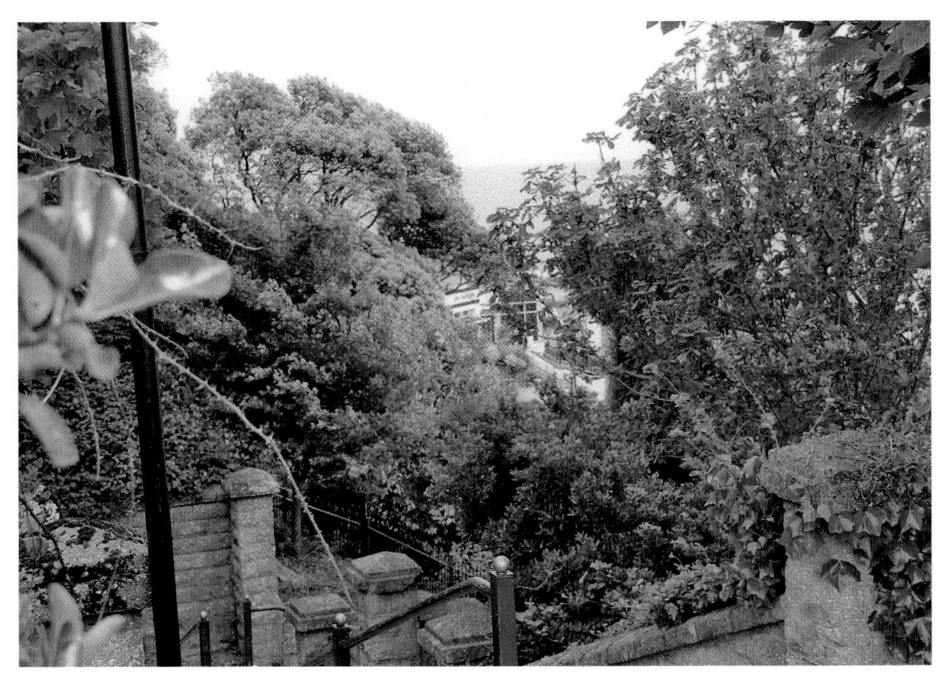

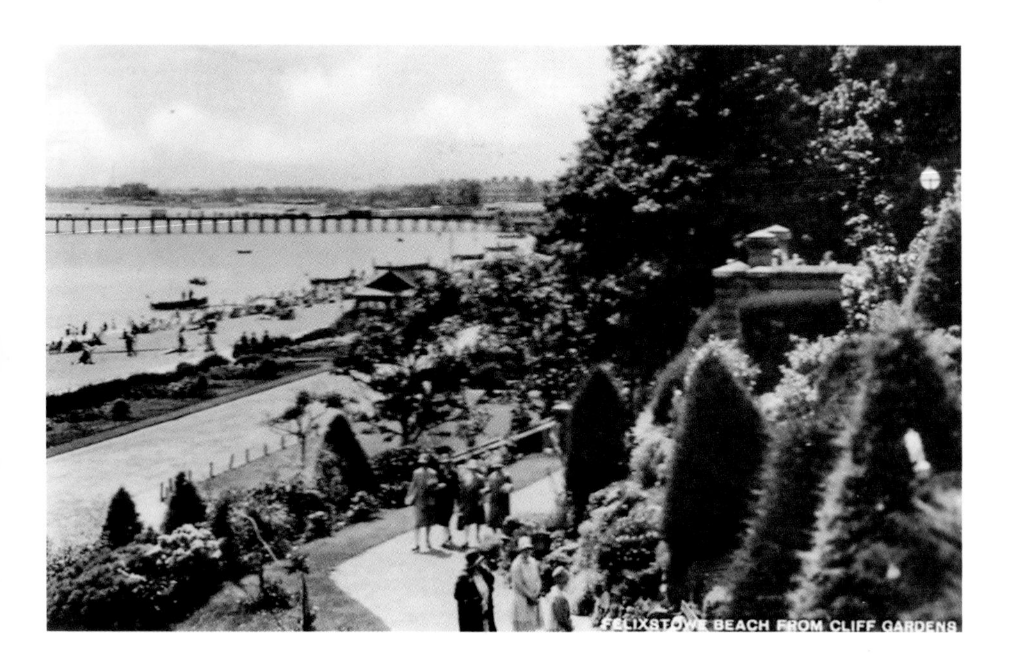

Beach From Cliff Gardens *c.* **1930**
The need for the restoration work is apparent. In places the foliage has become too massive and obscures the view. Some of the steps are in need of repair, so the news that a Heritage Lottery grant will be used to restore the gardens is very welcome. The whole section of gardens under South Beach Mansion (below) and the Spa need the spectacular views opening up again for public enjoyment. Work is due to begin in April 2013 and should take about a year.

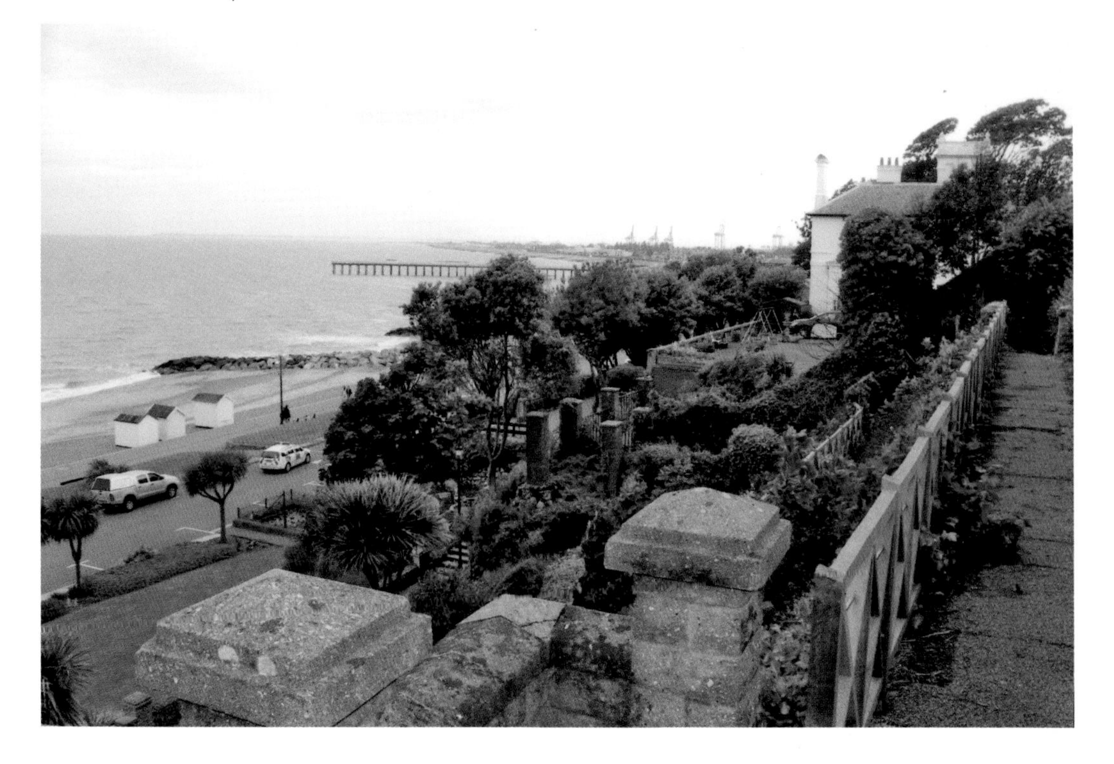

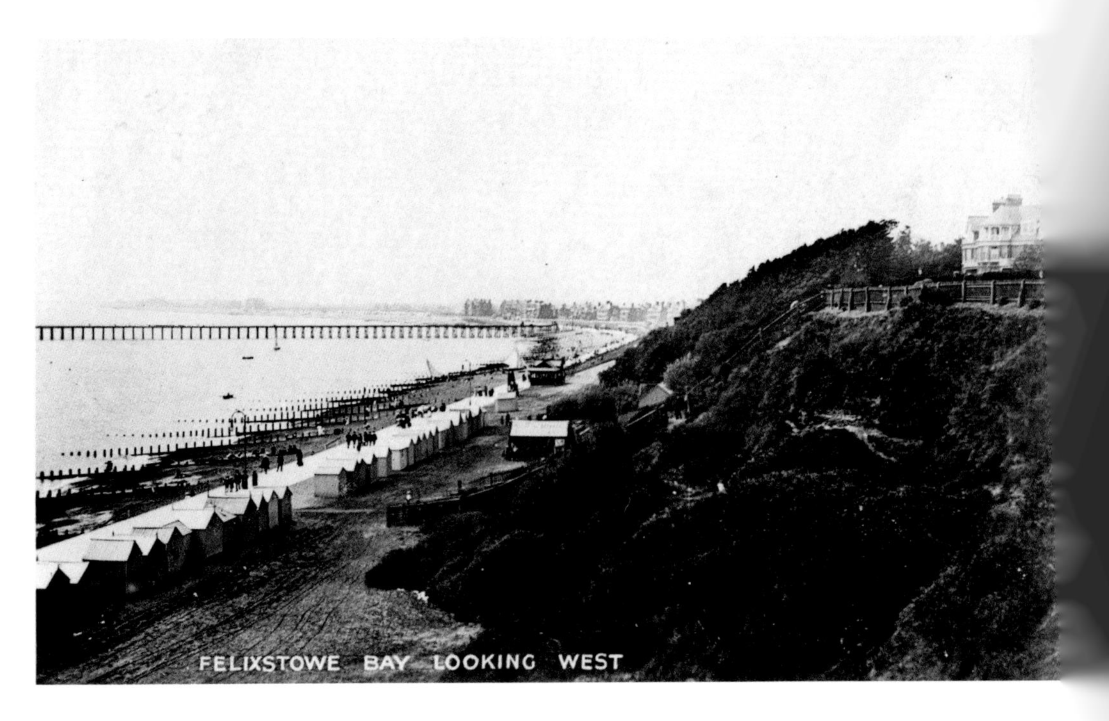

Felixstowe Bay Looking West ***c.*** **1905**
As well as the sea-water cure, Felixstowe had the added attraction of a natural spring situated below the cliff so it could promote itself as a spa. A pump was installed and the water was described as 'similar in taste to Apollinaris, and recommended in its aerated state, as a gentle aperients, anti-dyspetic, and anti-gout water. The Felixstowe waters belong to the same muriated saline class as those at Baden-Baden and Wiesbaden.' In 1907 a bandstand was erected near the spring. Shelters and the pump house are both awaiting restoration.

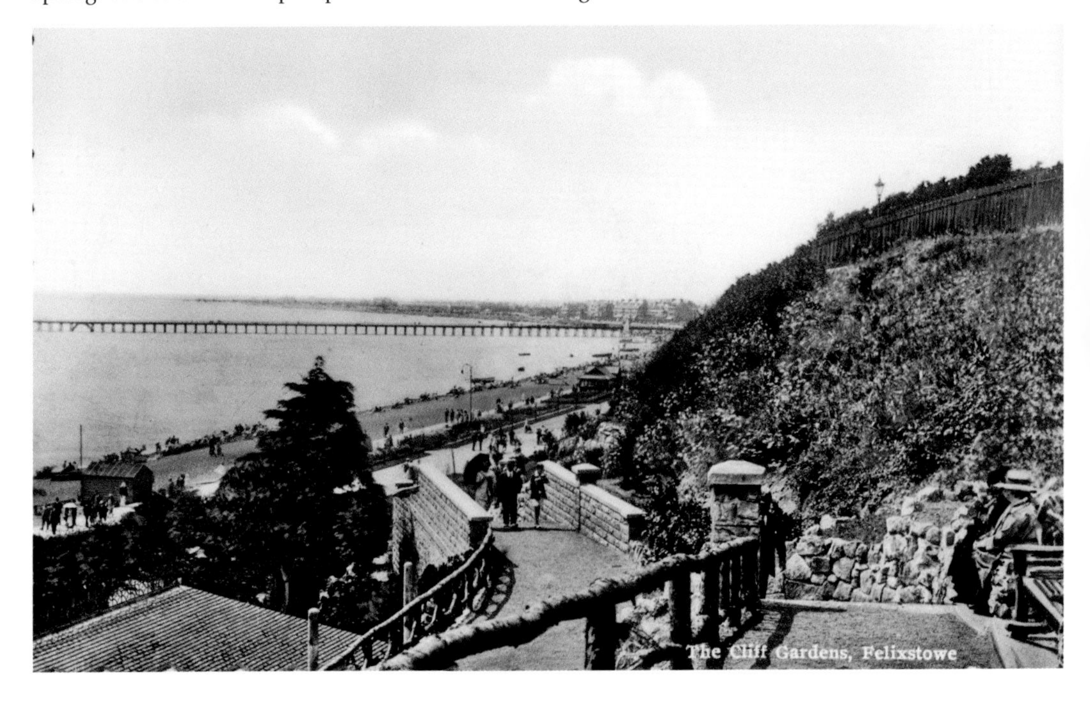

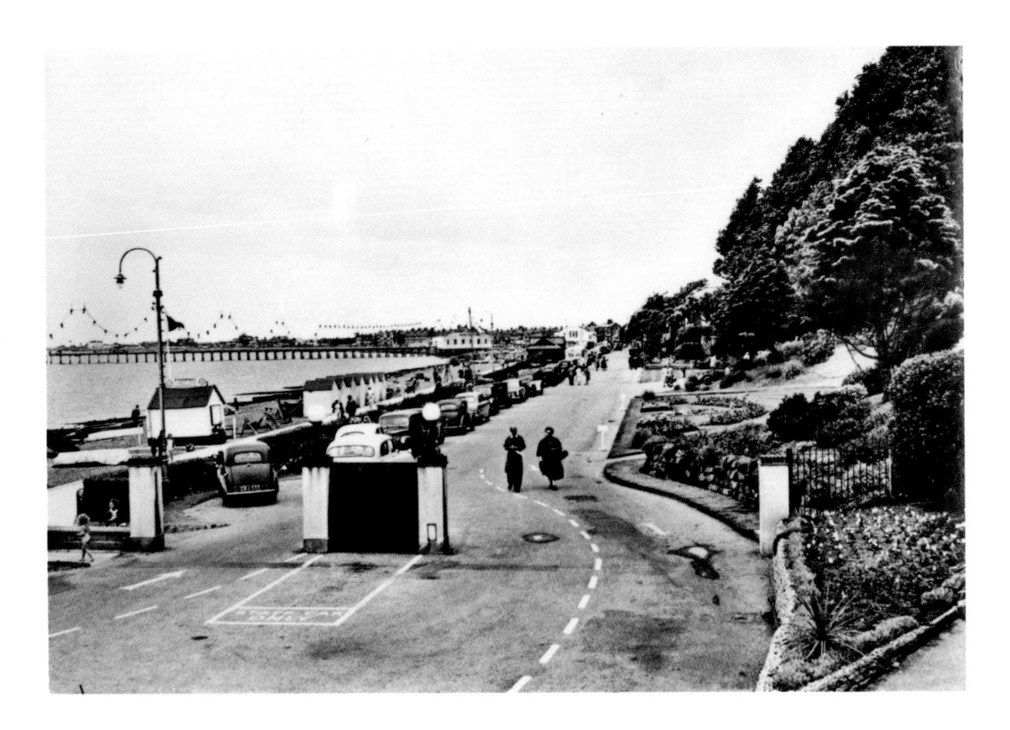

Spa Gardens ***c.*** **1955**

The Gardens are such a delightful feature of the sea front that their restoration should give a huge lift to the town for residents and visitors. *Ward Lock & Co's 1921 Guide* states how: 'Some years ago the Medical Officer of Health wrote "If steps were taken to utilize to the full the Undercliff of Felixstowe, the central cliff portion of which is one of the sunniest and at the same time most sheltered portions of the whole coast, it could not fail to have a most important bearing on the future growth and prosperity of the town".'

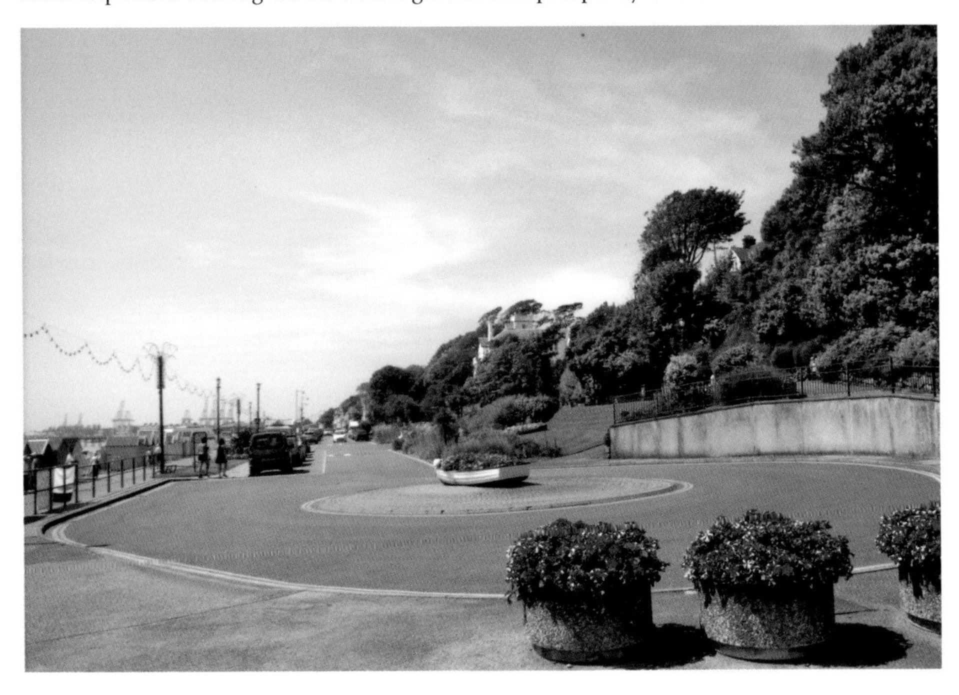

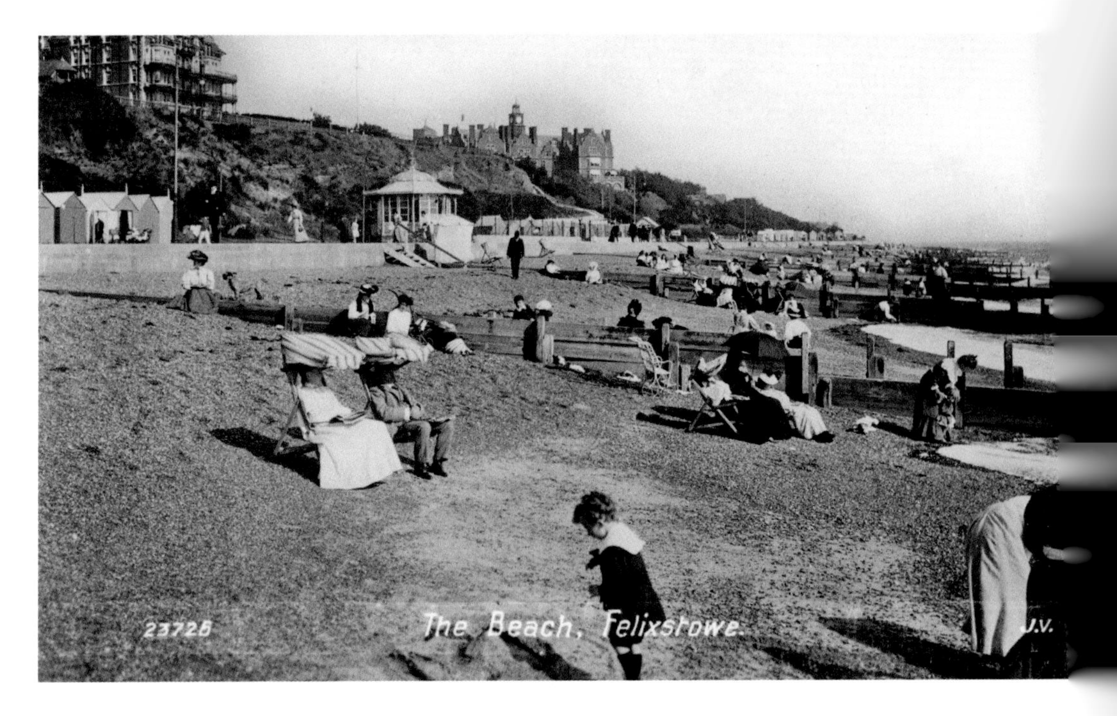

The Beach 1908

The Cliff Hotel built in 1908 can be seen and a splendid new bandstand at the foot of the cliffs. In 1909 this bandstand was incorporated into the new Spa Pavilion. The first Spa Pavilion was designed by Harry Clegg and built by local builder Harry J. Linzell. There was seating for more than 600 people and it was based on the Floral Hall at Bridlington and indeed known for a time as the Floral Hall. It became a popular entertainment venue. There were resident orchestras and always a concert party season.

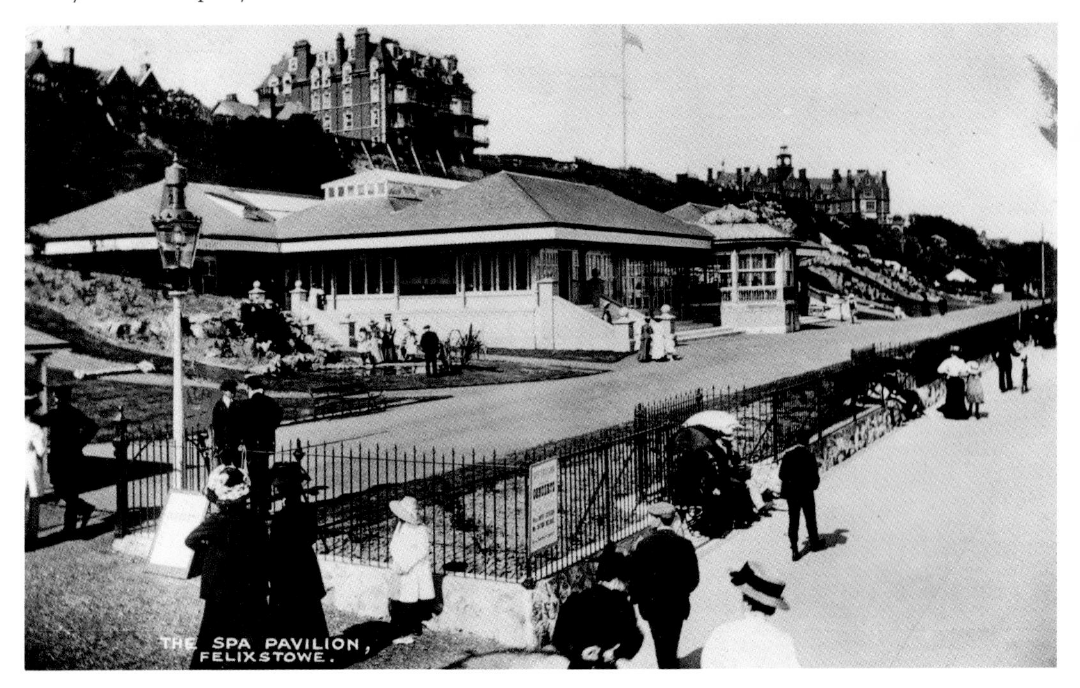

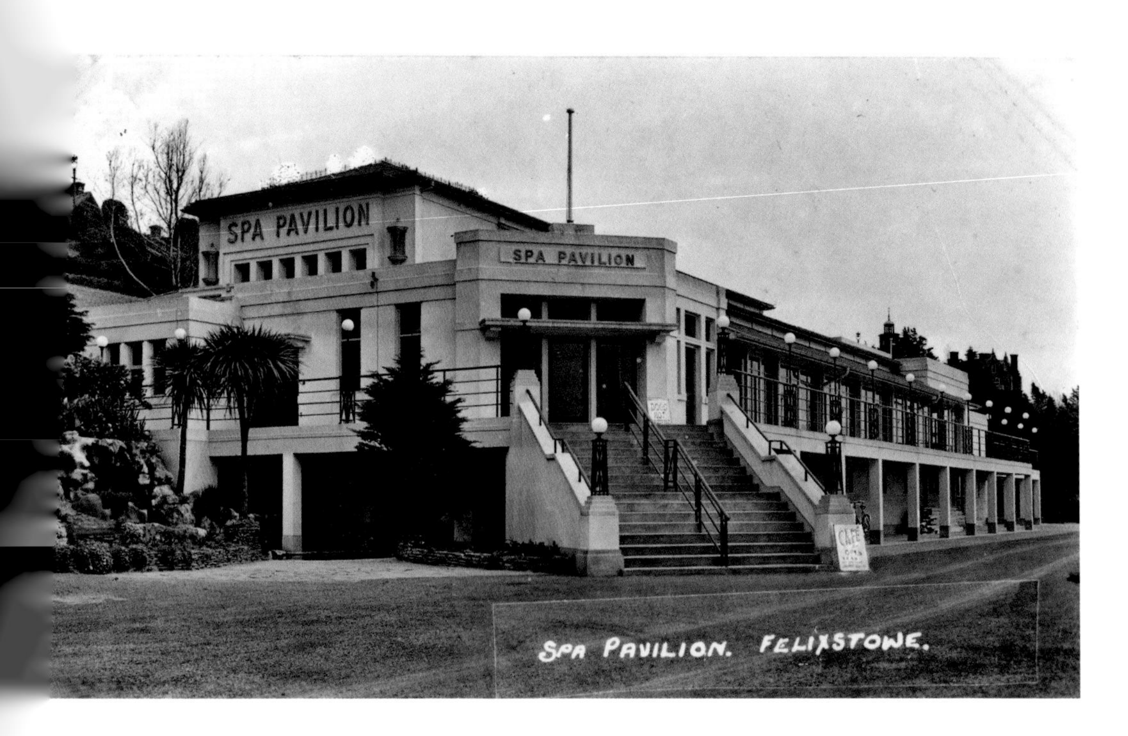

Spa Pavilion *c.* 1950
In 1938 it was demolished and replaced by the Spa Pavilion designed as a theatre. Damaged by bombing in 1941, it reopened in 1950. It was the home for many successful summer shows such as, 'Starlight Rendezvous' in 1965. It was extended in 1973 and for 1974 Barry Kent and Joe Church starred in 'Starnite 74'. It attracted big names – I saw Max Bygraves there and the unforgettable Tommy Cooper, but after many successful years as a centre for seaside entertainment, its future is now uncertain and with a nearly 900 seat auditorium, it is a challenge to fill.

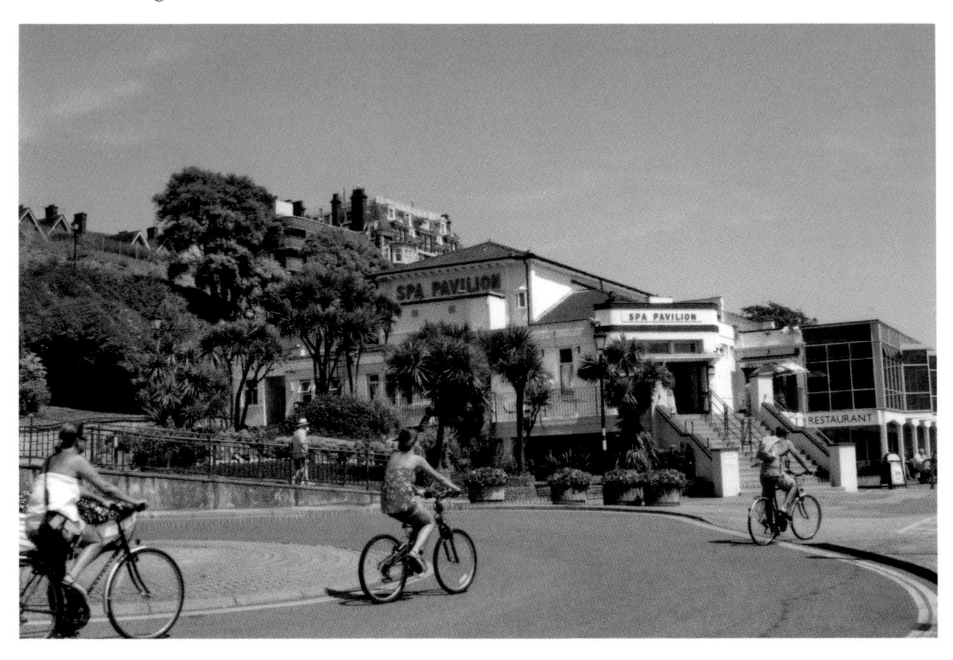

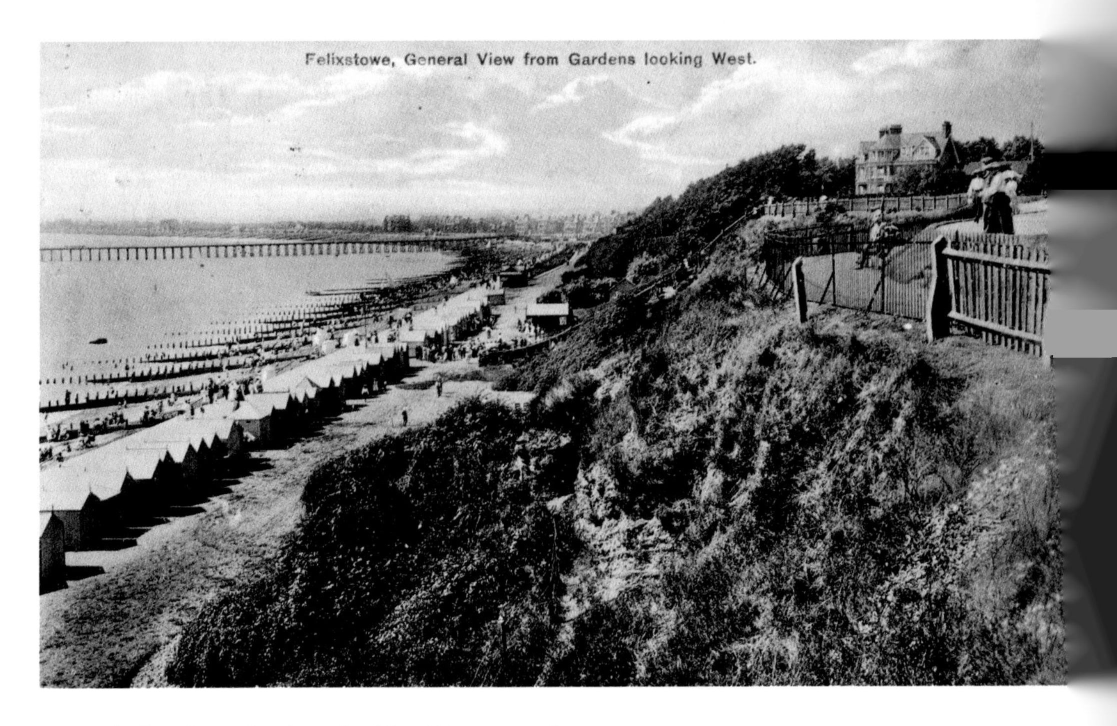

General View from Gardens, looking West *c.* 1906

The new pier can be seen, but there is no Floral Hall and the gardens have yet to be laid out on the cliff side. There is a long line of bathing huts and a queue of people presumably visiting the Spa to buy the healthy water. Some tents can be seen on the sands. As West Carnie wrote in 1898: 'You must have a tent on the beach. It is a delightful fashion, for you can with the aid of a tent live almost entirely on the sands, breathing the pure air as it comes straight from the sea.'

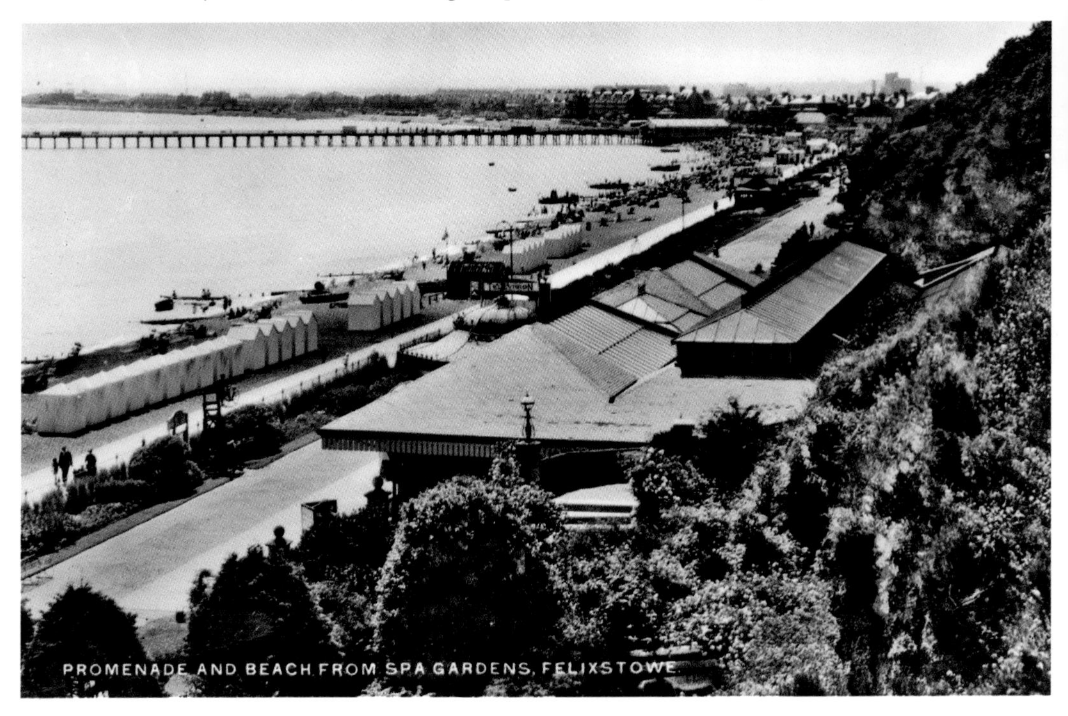

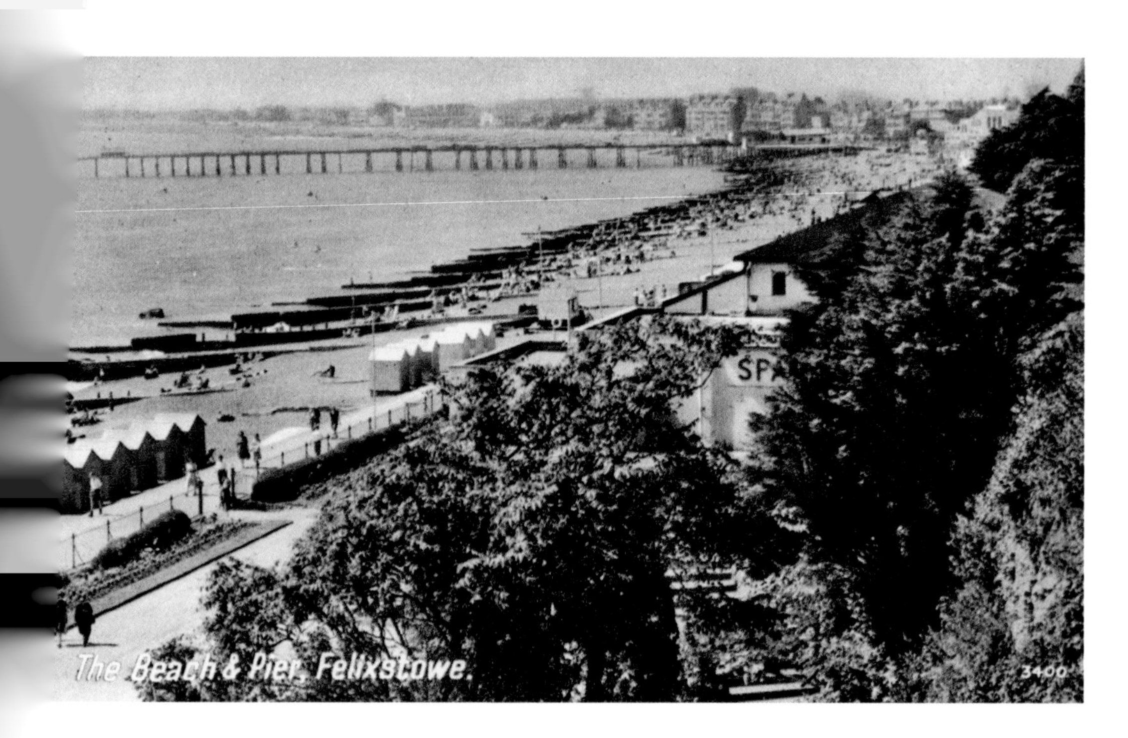

The Beach and Pier, 1950s

The previous photograph from around 1932 shows the roof of the first pavilion and the promenade which was constructed in 1903 from Manor End to Cobbold's Point giving the holidaymakers and residents a 3-mile stretch for 'promenading'. The view from the Hamilton Gardens has always been one of the delights of the resort, but over the years the trees and bushes have increasingly obscured the scene and some of the steps have been closed. Hopefully these problems are about to be addressed.

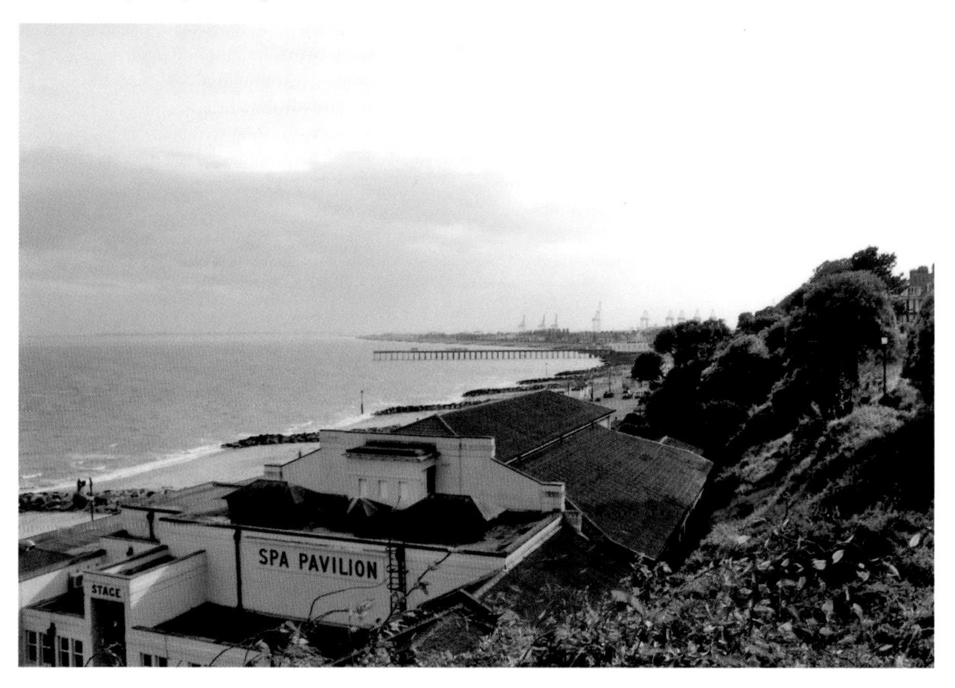

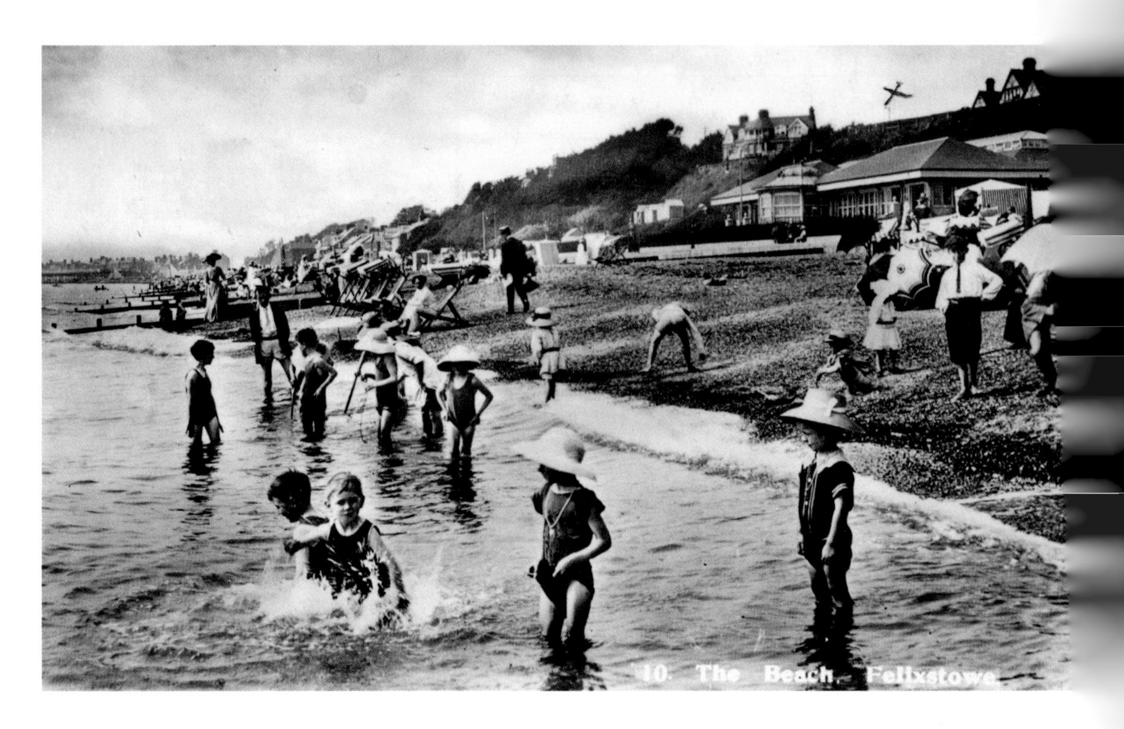

The Beach *c.* 1914

'Dear Brother, We have heard our company are going to have free passes given out for four days leave. We are going to move the other side of London. You may expect me any time after then...' – a young soldier perhaps billeted at Felixstowe during the First World War? Like most seaside resorts Felixstowe had a bumper August bank holiday in 1914, but within months everything changed when the country went to war.

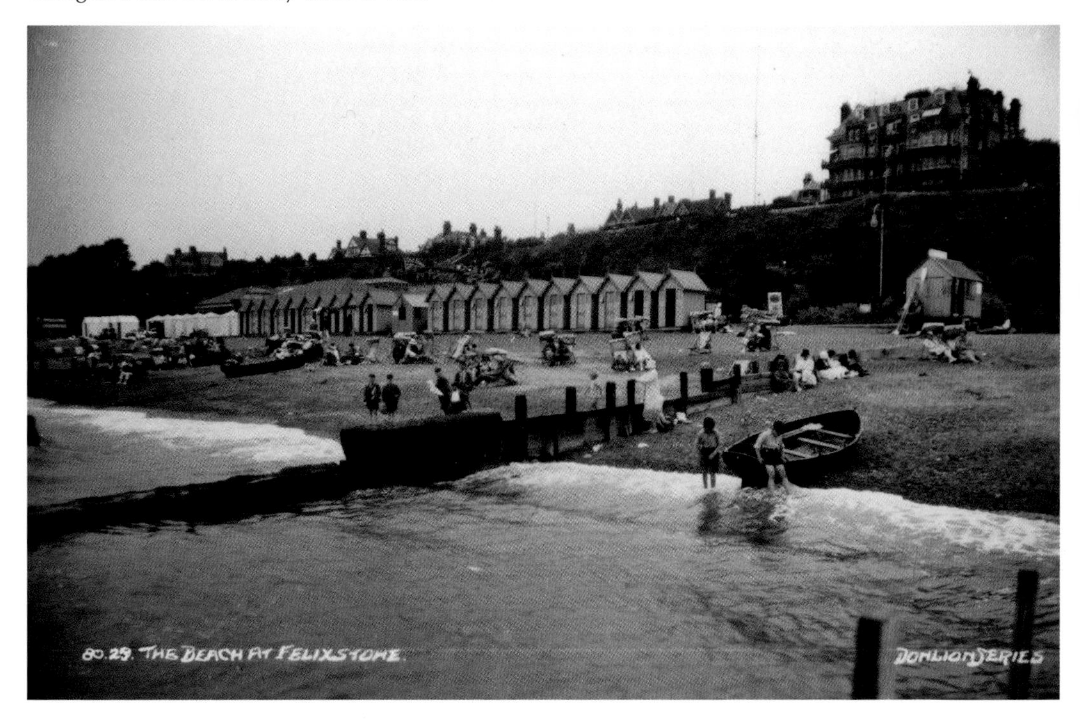

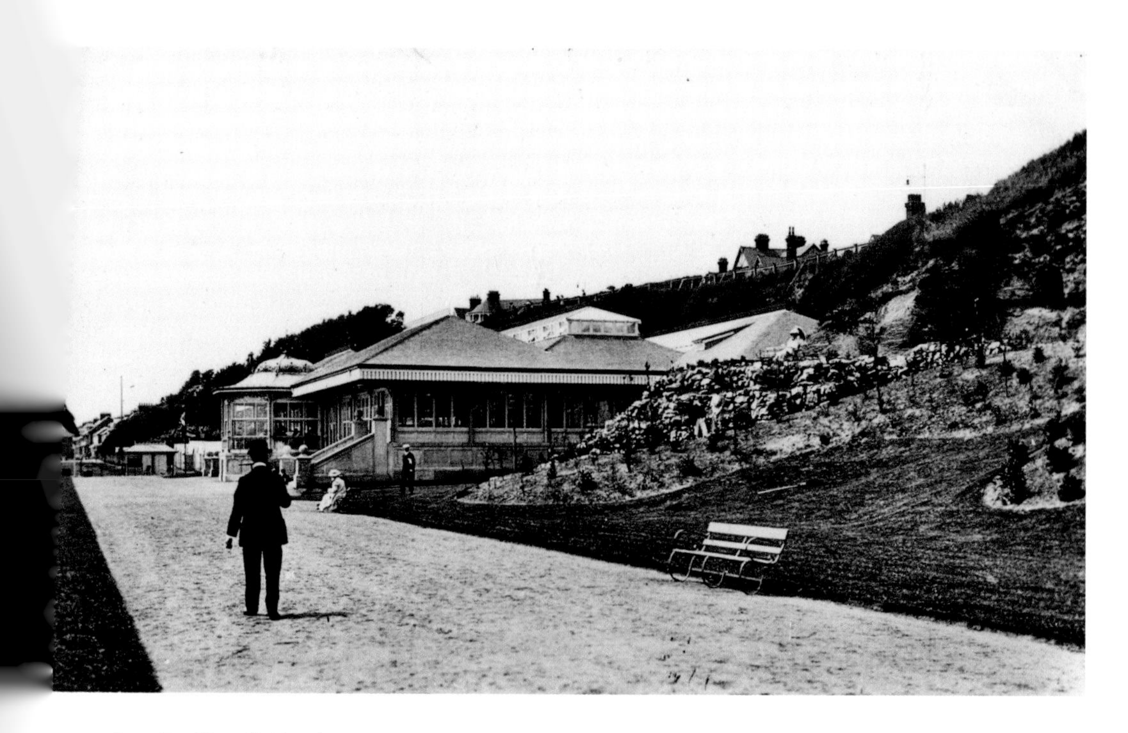

Spa Pavilion & Gardens *c.* 1912

A different angle on the new Floral Hall showing the bandstand and the windows overlooking the sea front. It will probably take 'a different angle' to save the Spa too. One hundred years on, this is such a fundamental part of Felixstowe's seaside history, that it must be saved. There is huge local goodwill, but today's difficult times demand more imagination, a viable business case and a more buoyant British holiday industry.

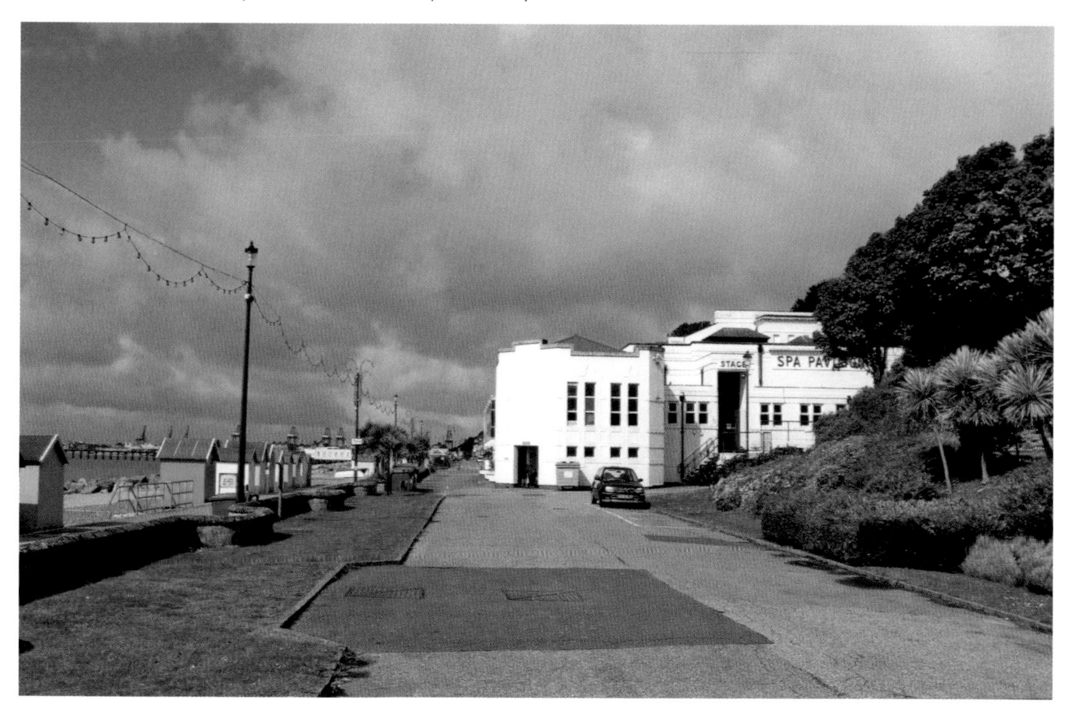

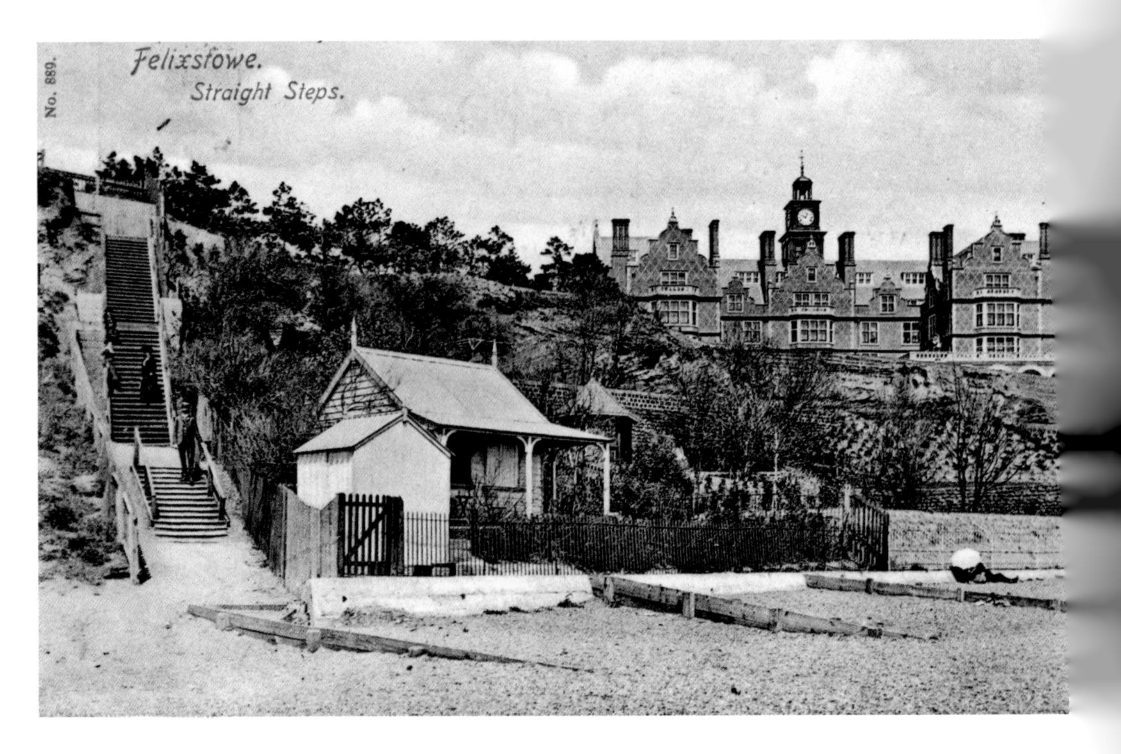

Straight Steps *c.* **1904**
The new Felix Hotel and its cliff gardens can be clearly seen. The tennis courts and croquet lawn ran alongside the Bath Road, the other side of Cobbold Road and to the rear of the Bartlet where the Felixstowe Lawn Tennis Club courts have been since 1884. The cliffs in the foreground have yet to be landscaped. In 1907 the Serpentine Steps (below) were completed. These replaced the Straight Steps. They appear to be constructed from Pulhamite, which was a speciality of the local firm of Pulham builders. They made the artificial stone from sand, shale and cement.

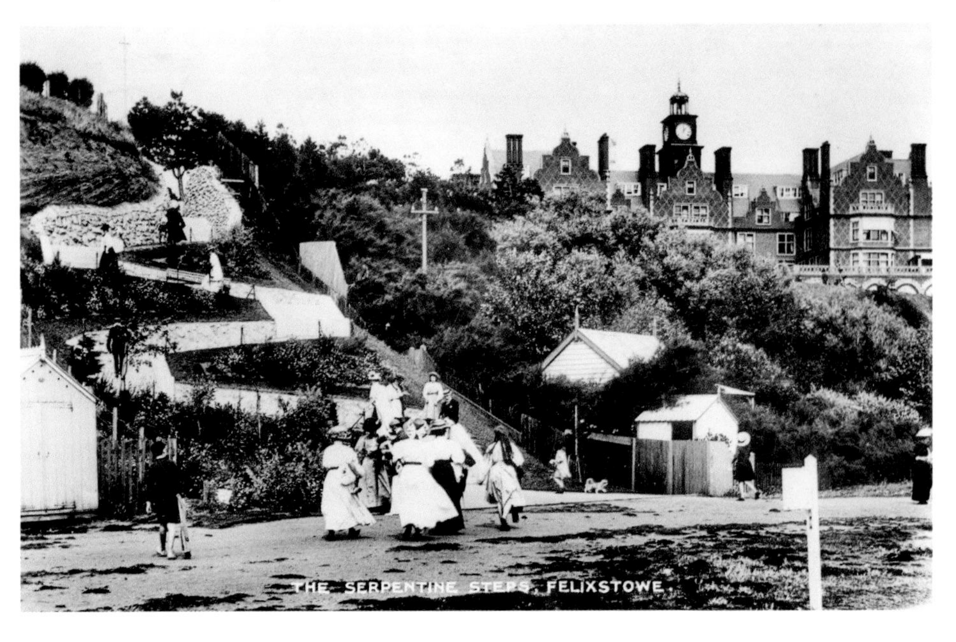

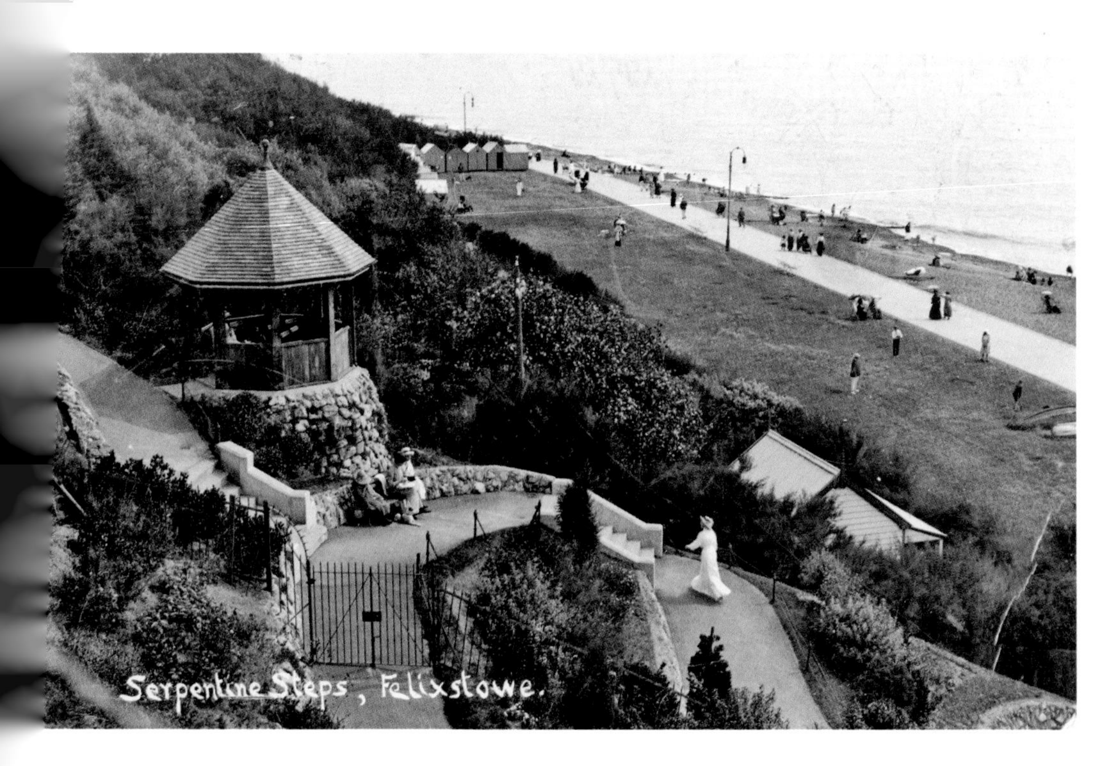

Serpentine Steps *c.* 1913

The round shelter appears to have been added to the steps soon after they were built. This is one of the features that will be refurbished. It is easy to see from today's photograph how the Serpentine Steps have been lost in the growth of trees and foliage. Clegg's original design has a coherence that needs to be reasserted. A new heritage trail will be part of garden's restoration.

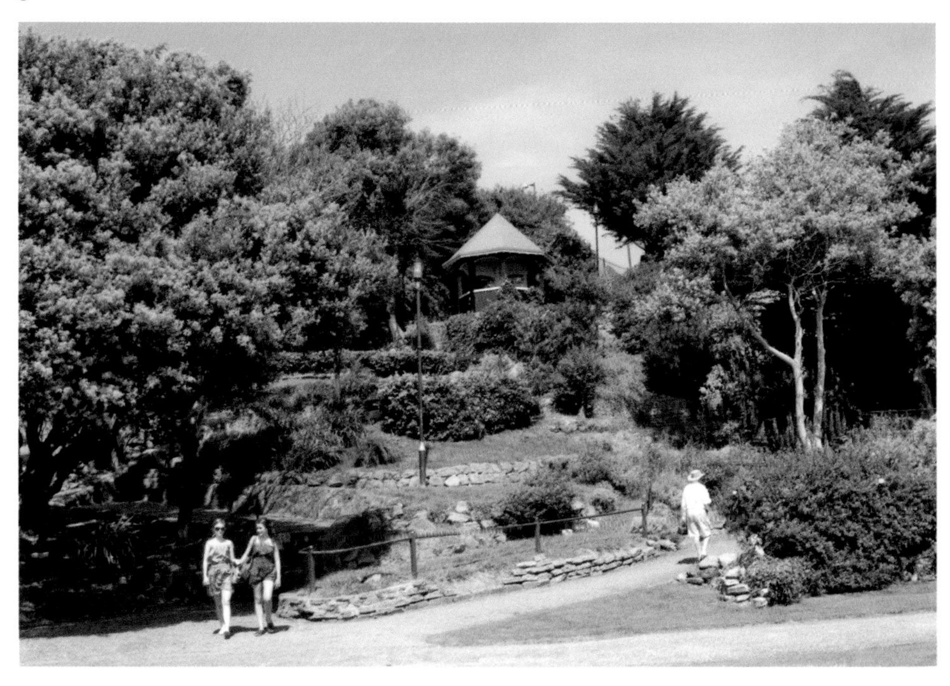

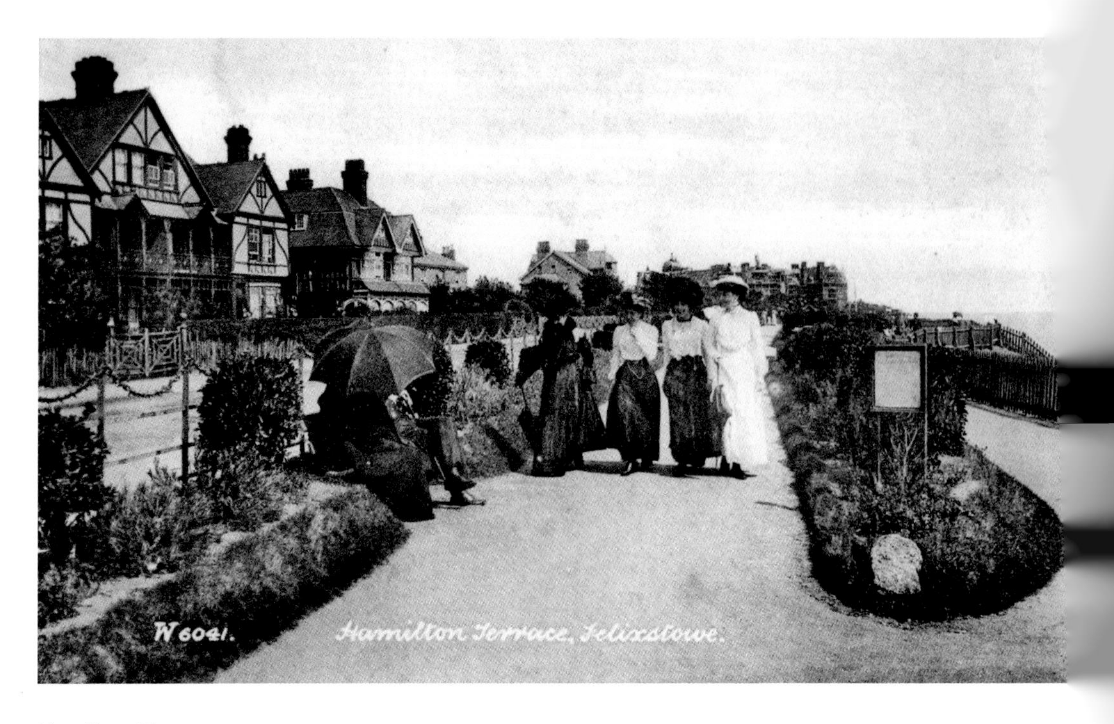

Hamilton Terrace *c.* 1905

This could be a little earlier than 4 August 1905 when Lillie sent it back to London to Winnie for her collection, telling her that she was 'having a jolly time bathing', as the Felix Hotel still seems to be under construction in the distance. Seagull Cottage is on the left and South Cottage where the German princes stayed is beyond that. By 1908 Quilter's Cliff Hotel, with its magnificent balconies, has been built.

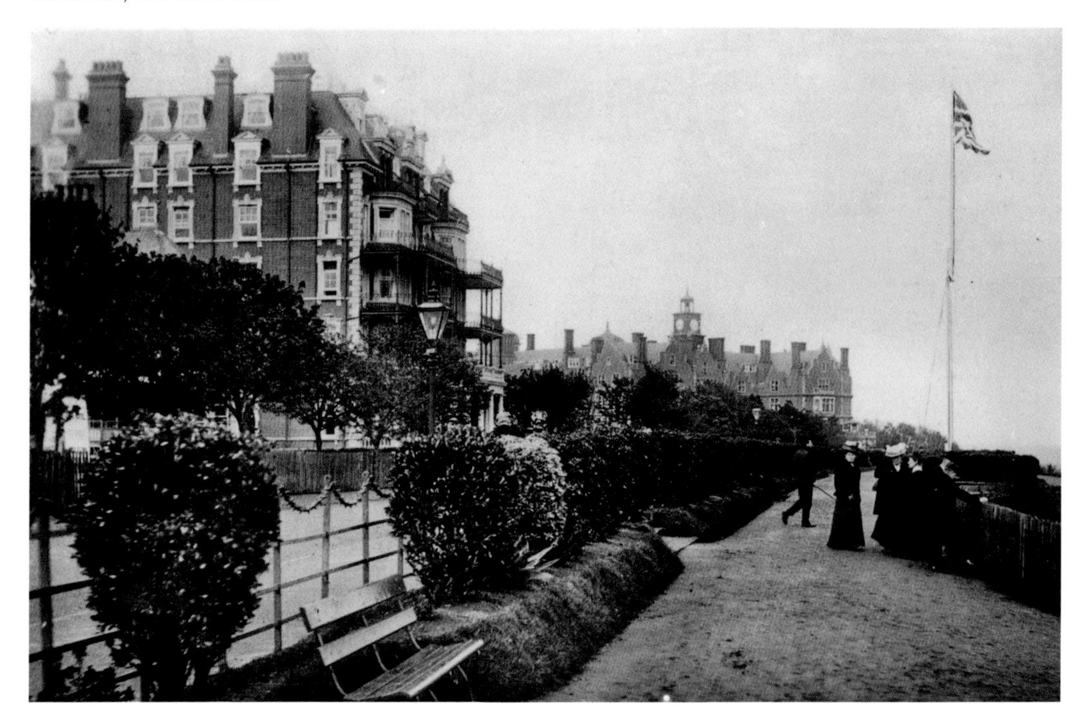

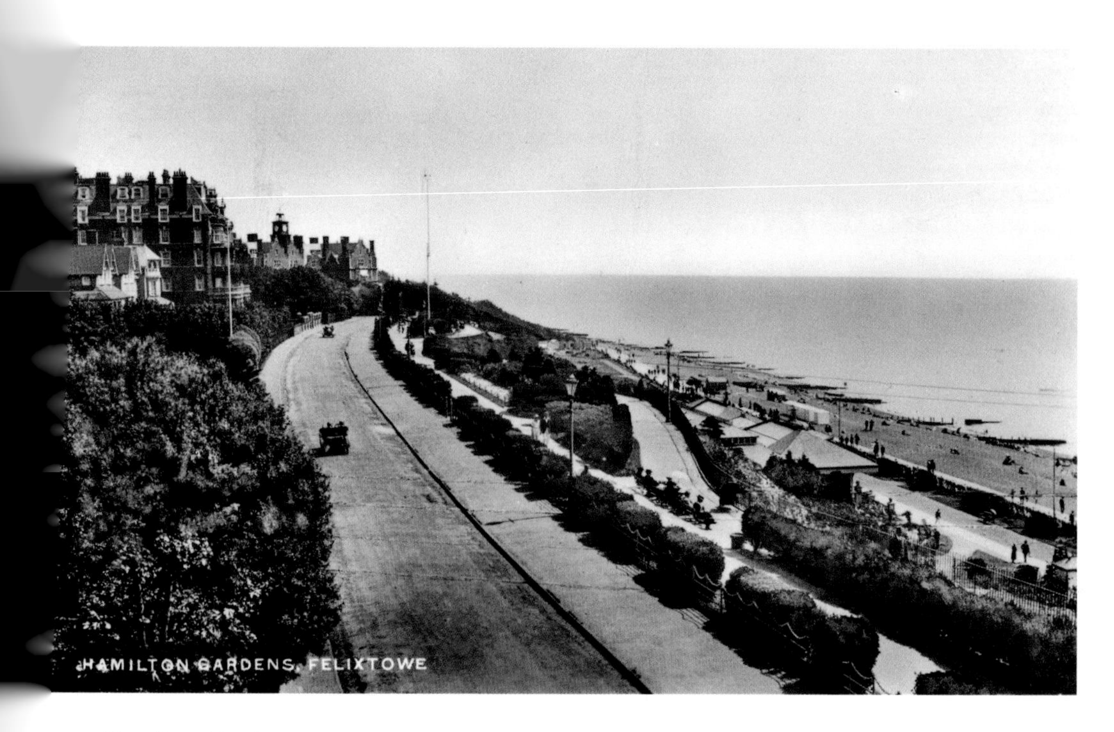

Hamilton Gardens ***c.*** **1932**

It is possible to see the smaller South Cliff House this side of the Cliff Hotel. South Cliff House was demolished in 1973 and 1981 saw the completion of Rosemount on its site. I'm sure the building is very functional with every modern convenience. The view shows how the gardens and paths down the cliff had become such an attractive feature in the twenty years or so since they were laid out.

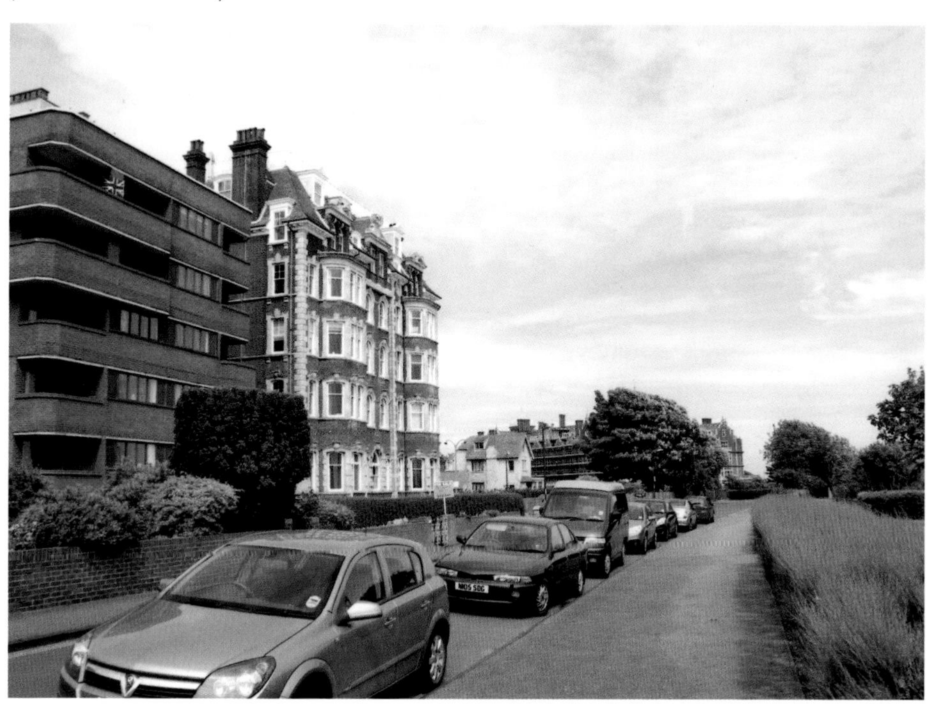

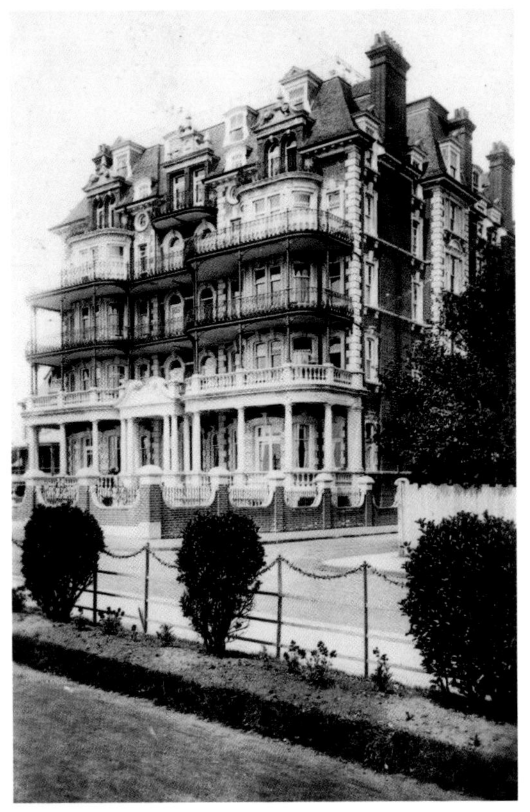

Cliff Hotel *c.* **1908**

The splendid Cliff Hotel designed by Henry William Buxton for John Crowle as a 'first class boarding house'. It was a temperance hotel, but after Crowle's death and a legal battle, it obtained a drinks licence and was run by George Quilter and his sister, Mary, as a first class hotel. During the First World War it was a military hospital. In 1956 the Cliff Hotel was bought by Fison's, who had already acquired the Felix Hotel. They removed the balconies and refurbished it. Today it is the Headquarters of Brinor International Shipping & Forwarding Ltd.

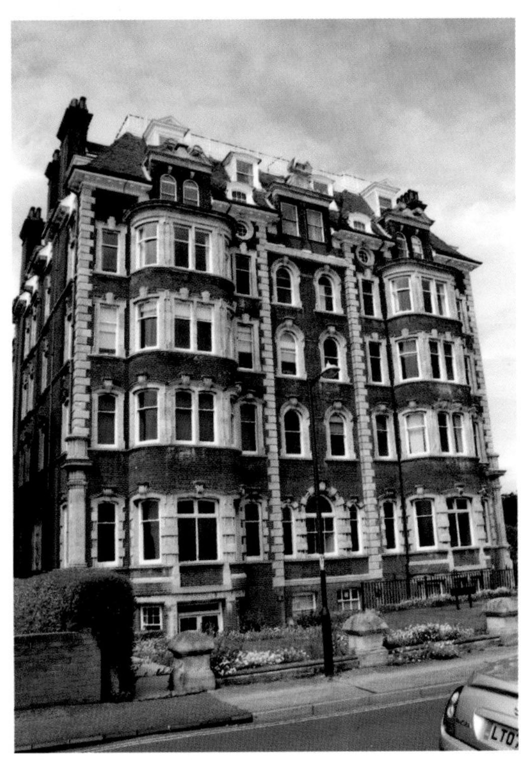

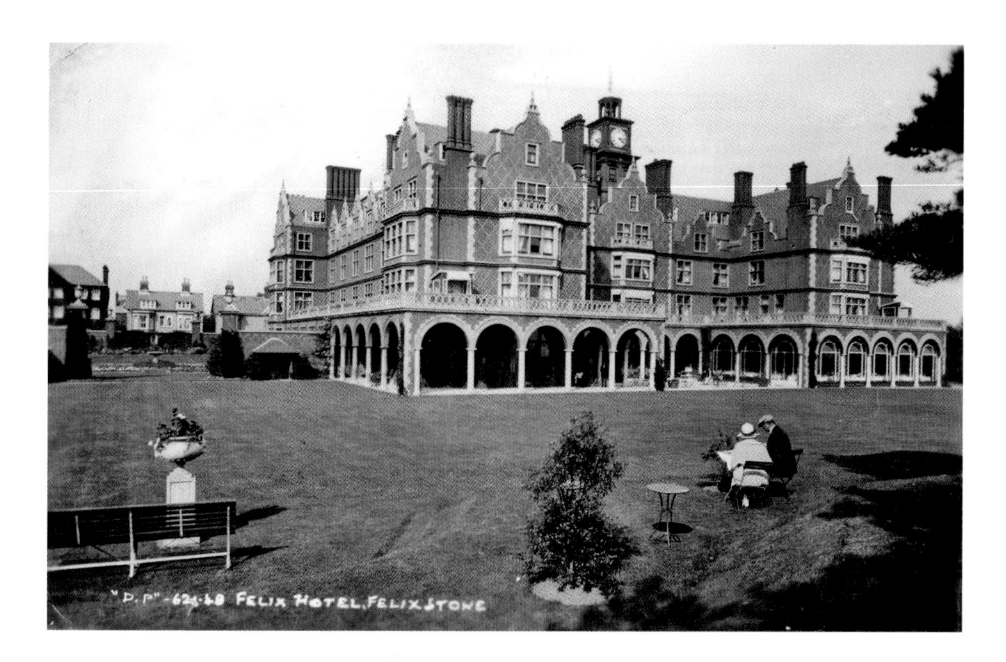

Felix Hotel *c.* **1923**

Originally the Balmoral, there was an early change of name for this magnificent hotel often described as 'the finest hotel on the East Coast'. Thomas William Cotman designed it for Douglas Tollemache, the Ipswich Brewer, and it opened in May 1903. Its gardens ran down the cliff to the sea front. In 1919 it was bought by the Great Eastern Railway Company. In 1936 it was advertised with '250 rooms with Hot and Cold Running Water. Radiators in most rooms. Ball Room. Hot and Cold Sea Water Baths, 8 Hard tennis courts, 20 grass tennis courts, 2 full sized croquet lawns, 18 hole putting course.'

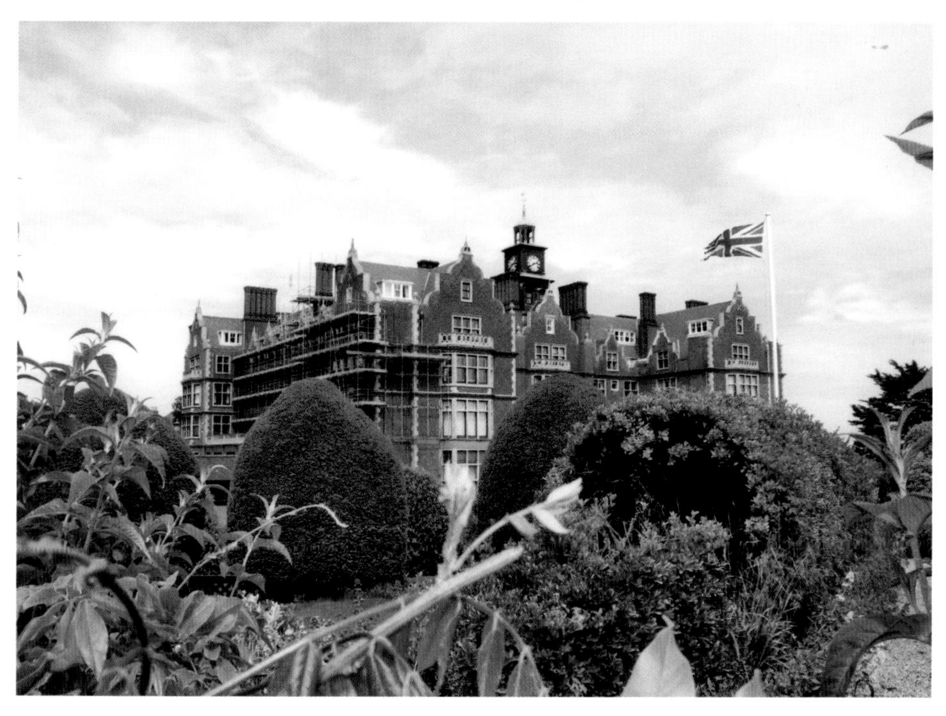

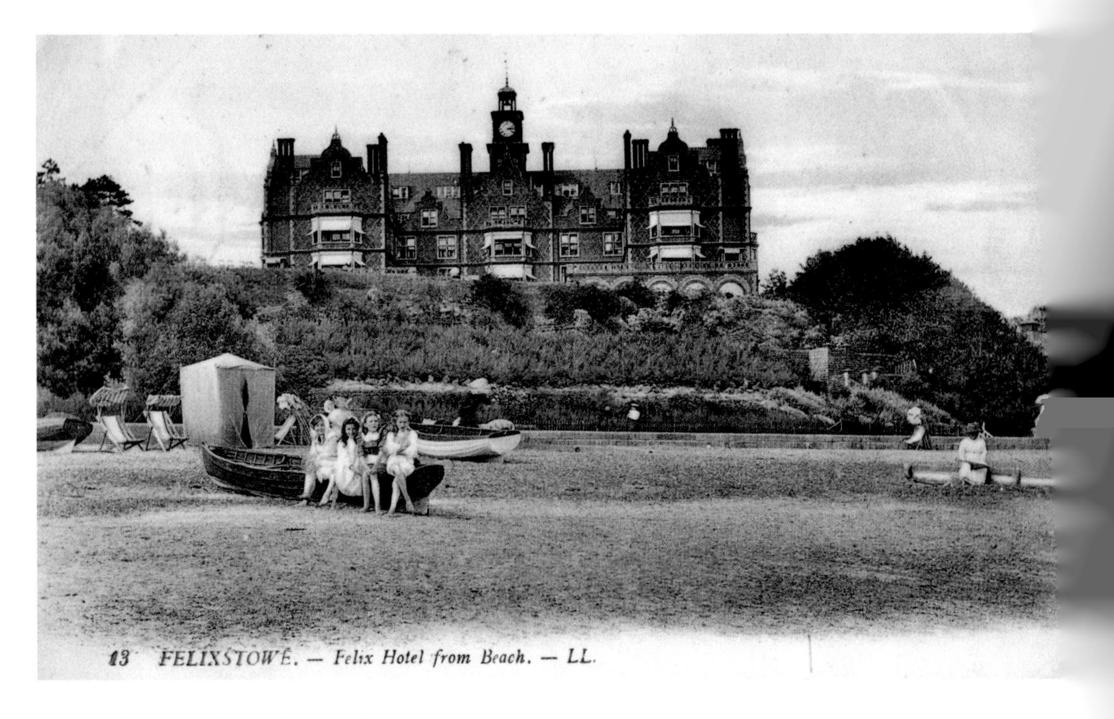

Felix Hotel from the Beach *c.* 1913

In 1952 the building was bought by the Fison's group. It was converted for office use and renamed Harvest House and the company presented the Cliff Gardens to the town. In 1973 incredibly Fison's were granted planning permission to demolish and replace it with modern offices, despite a public outcry, but it was listed Grade 2 that summer and the Secretary of State revoked the decision. Norsk Hydro took over the offices in 1982 but in 1985 the building was converted into luxury retirement flats for the over 55s, thus keeping one of the resort's most iconic buildings.

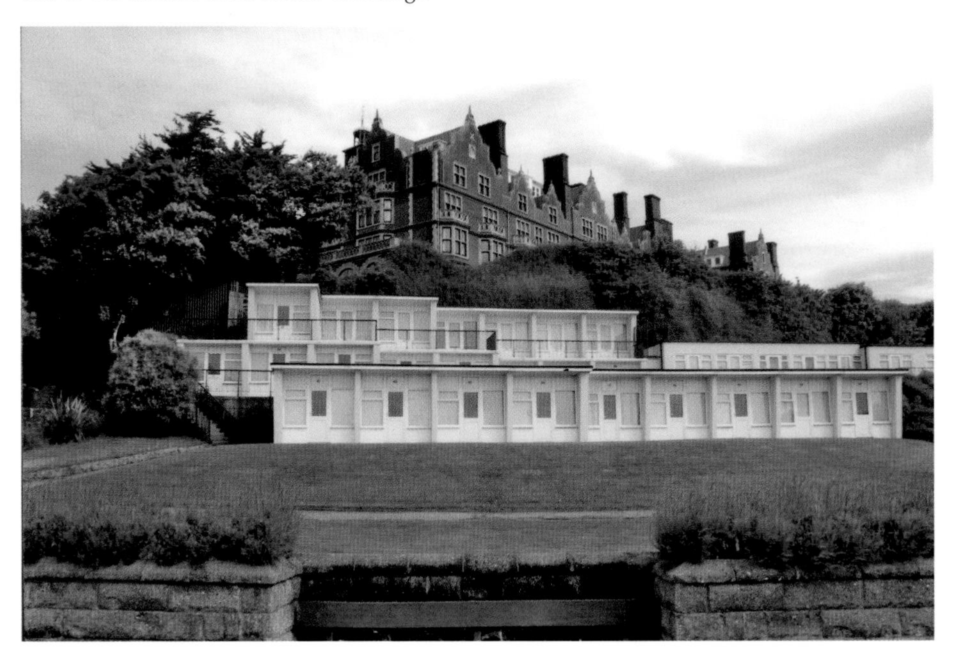

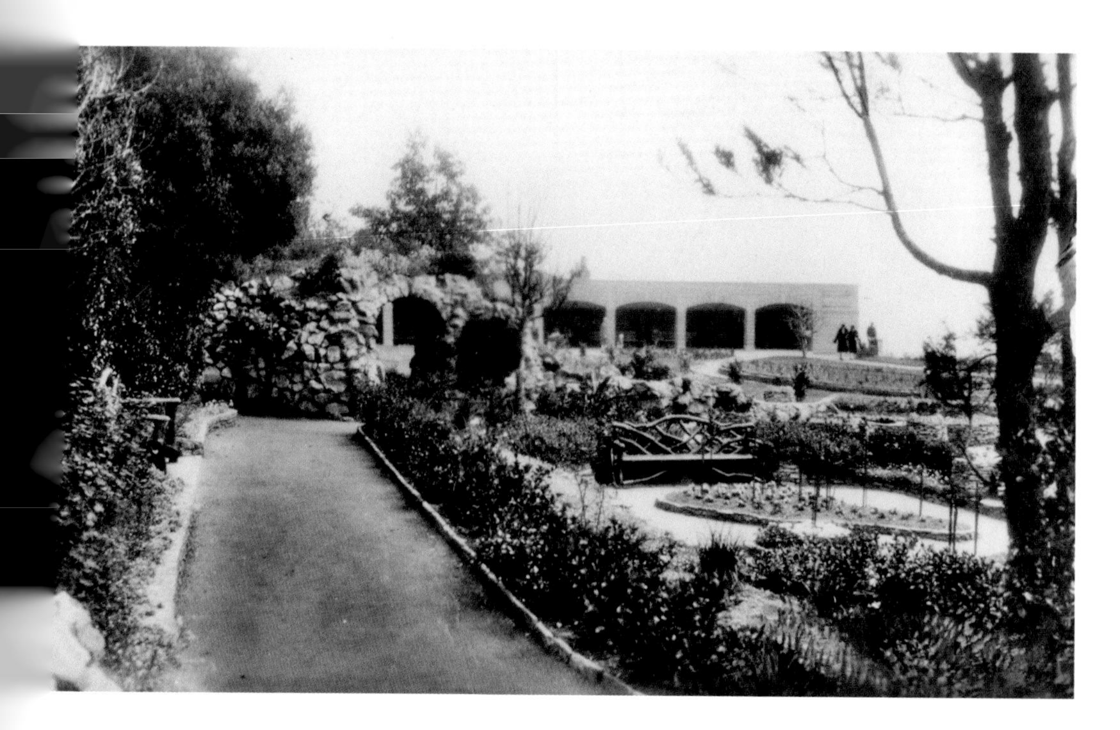

New Cliff Gardens ***c.*** **1930**
These formal gardens with the Long Shelter were laid out by the Urban District Council and officially opened by the Lord Mayor of London in 1928. Nestling under Cliff House with its café, they contain a sunken garden and an attractive water feature and archway before ending at the Long Shelter. The Long Shelter was demolished in recent years but most of the original features survive.

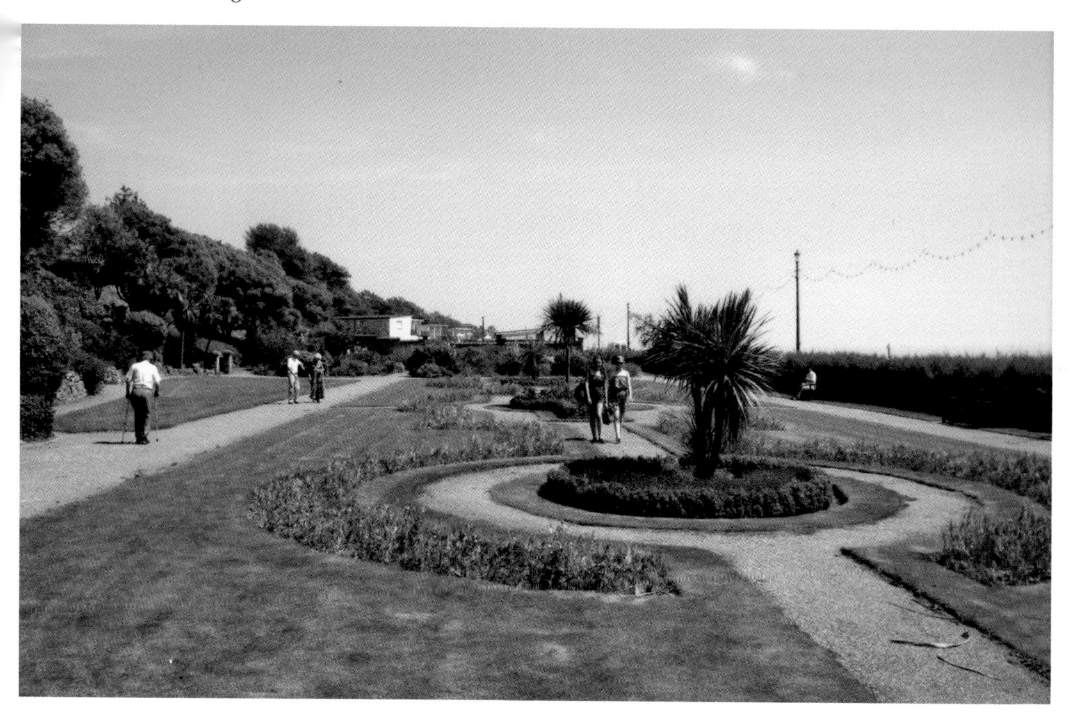

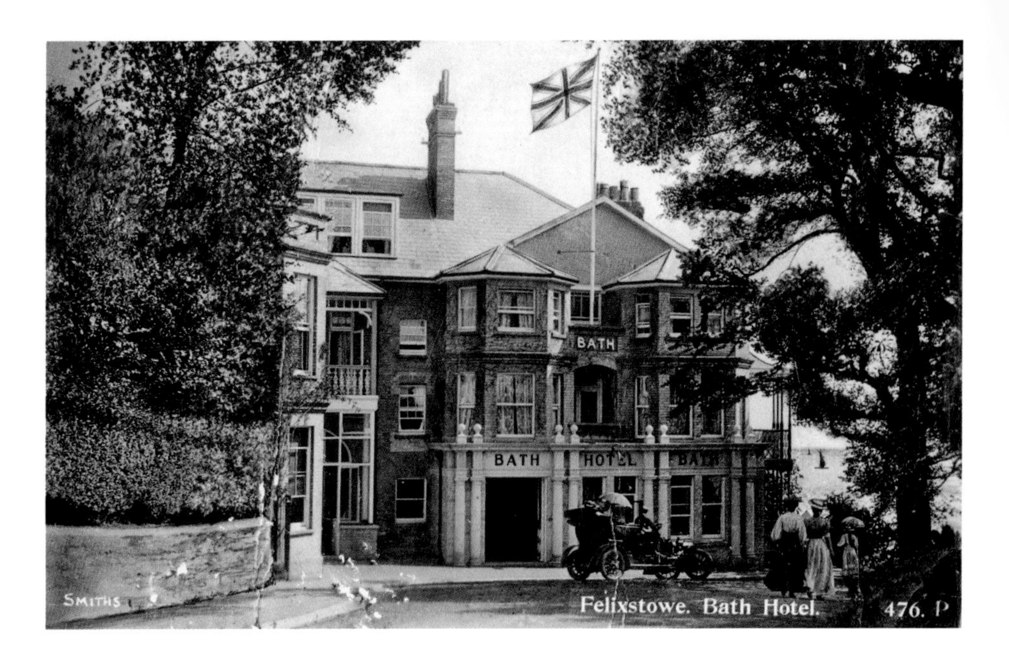

Bath Hotel ***c.*** **1908**

One of the most significant hotels in the resort and one of the earliest built by John Chevallier Cobbold, the Brewer, in 1839 as the Hamilton Arms, after Lord Hamilton who owned a large estate nearby and from whom he purchased the land. Over the years the hotel was greatly extended and the name changed to the Bath, presumably because of the popularity of sea water baths and bathing. On the 28 April 1914 before the hotel opened for the summer season it was destroyed in a fire caused by Hilda Burkett and Florence Tunks, militant suffragettes. It was never rebuilt.

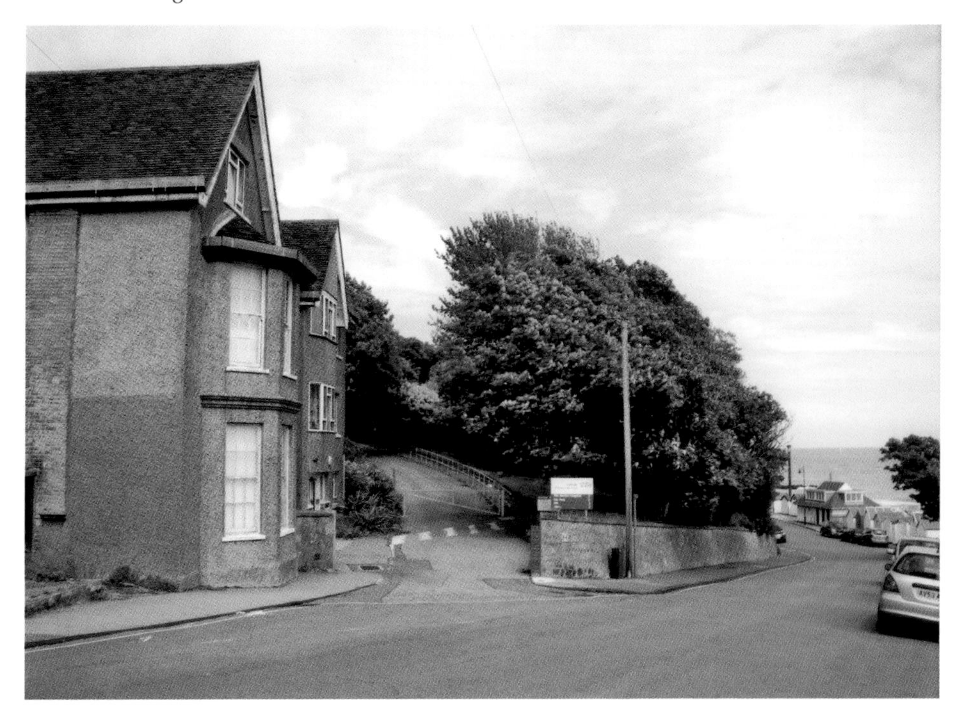

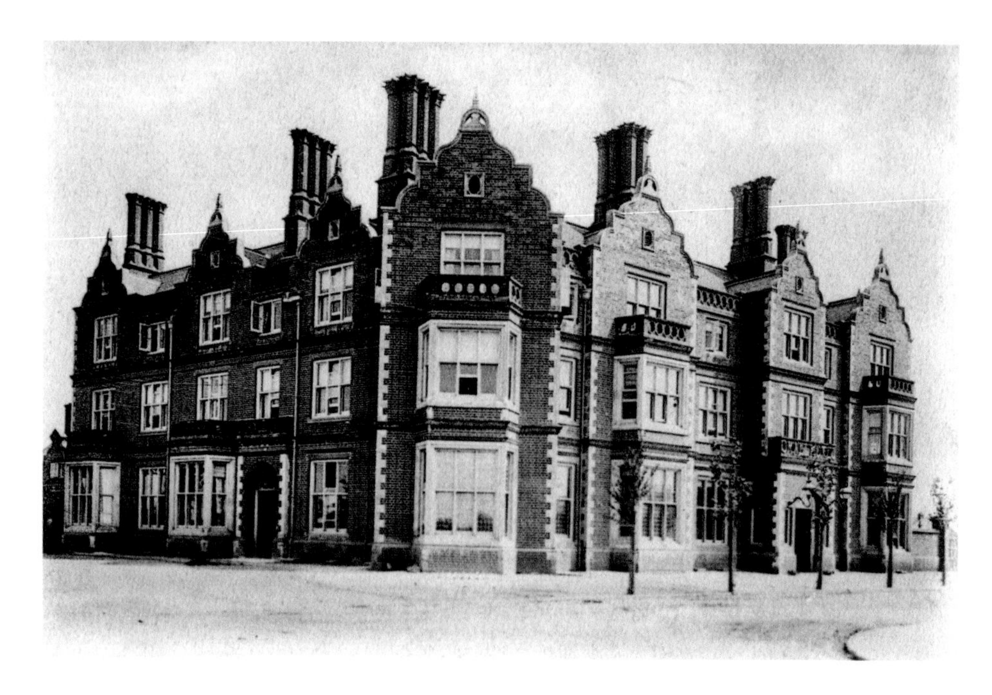

Orwell Hotel *c.* 1908

Douglas Tollemache, who built the Felix Hotel, had already opened the Orwell in 1898 opposite the new town station, so it was perfectly placed for the growing numbers of rail visitors. In the 1930s the Orwell was advertised as the 'Garden Hotel... Close to Sea Front... Nearest Hotel to Golf Links'. Its private grounds and gardens included an eighteen-hole putting course. It was refurbished in 2003 with fifty-eight *en suite* rooms and retains all its traditional charm. For a while in recent years it was known as the Elizabeth, but, despite the name boards still in place, it is the Orwell again.

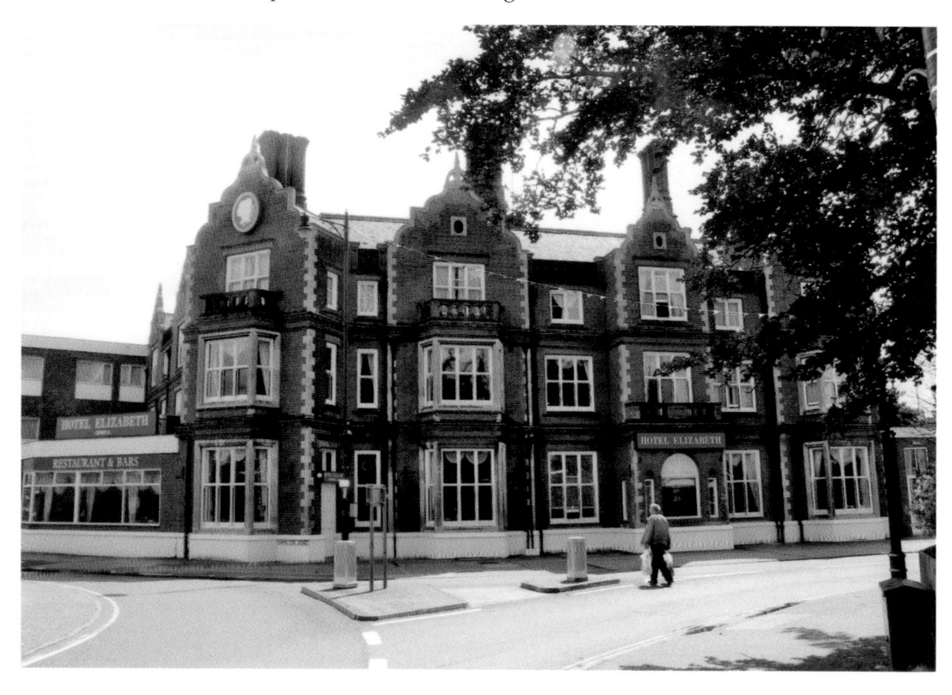

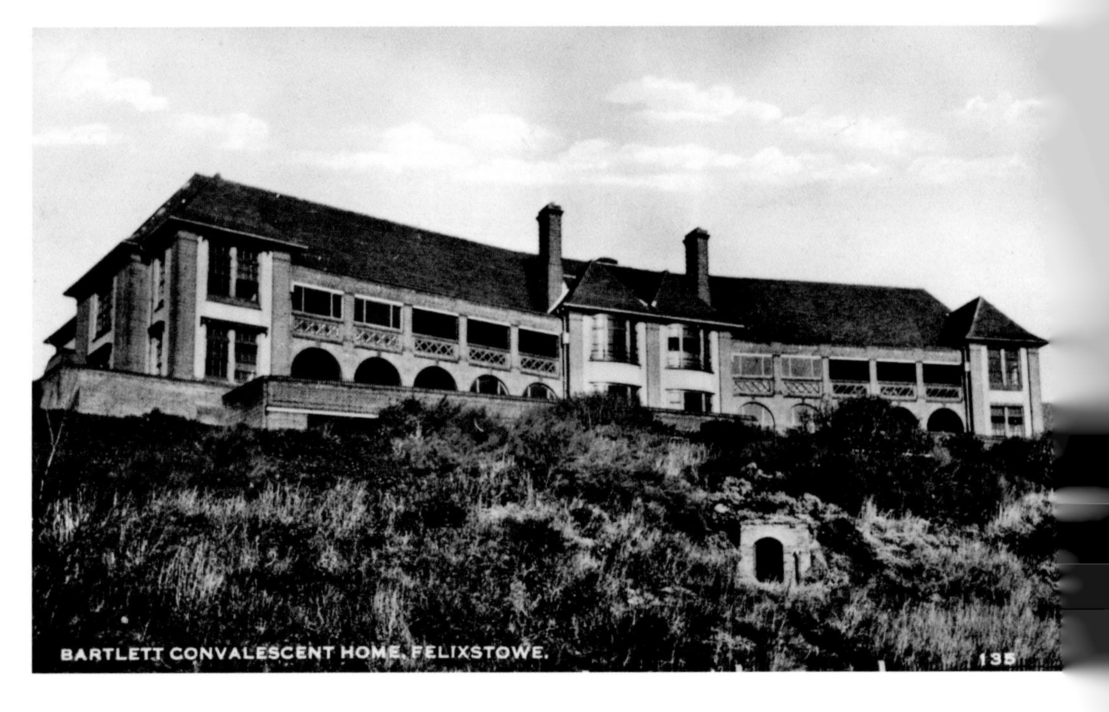

Bartlet Convalescent Home *c.* 1936
Dr John Henry Bartlet, former governor and surgeon at the East Suffolk and Ipswich Hospital bequeathed the money for a new convalescent home in his will. It was opened in 1926 and the building incorporated Martello Tower R in its foundations. The surviving part of the Bath Hotel became part of the nurses' accommodation for the new home. The Bartlet closed at the end of January 2008 and despite a campaign to save it as a convalescent home currently awaits conversion into luxury apartments.

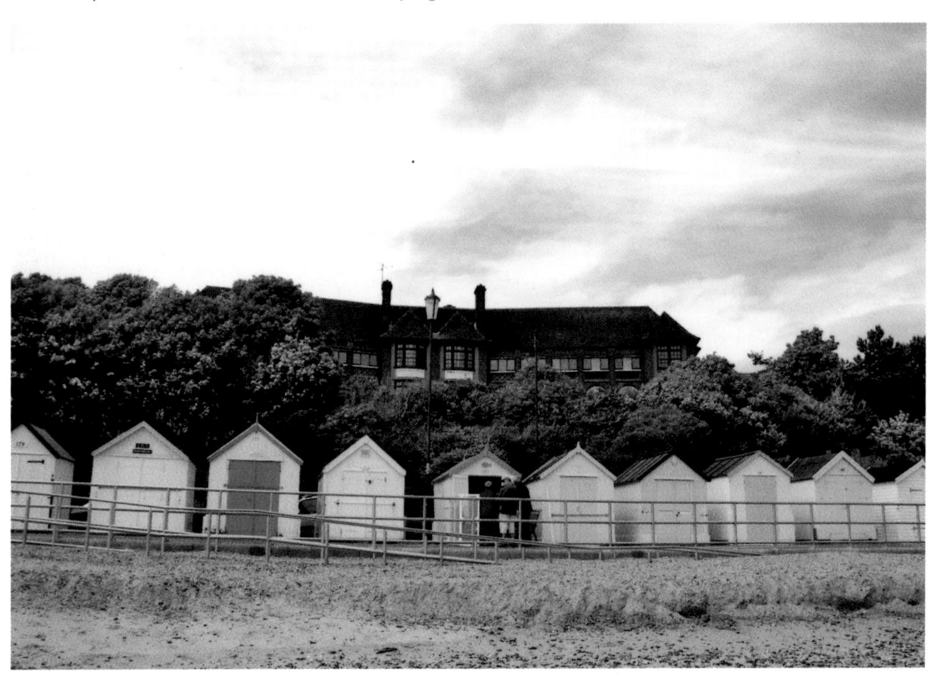

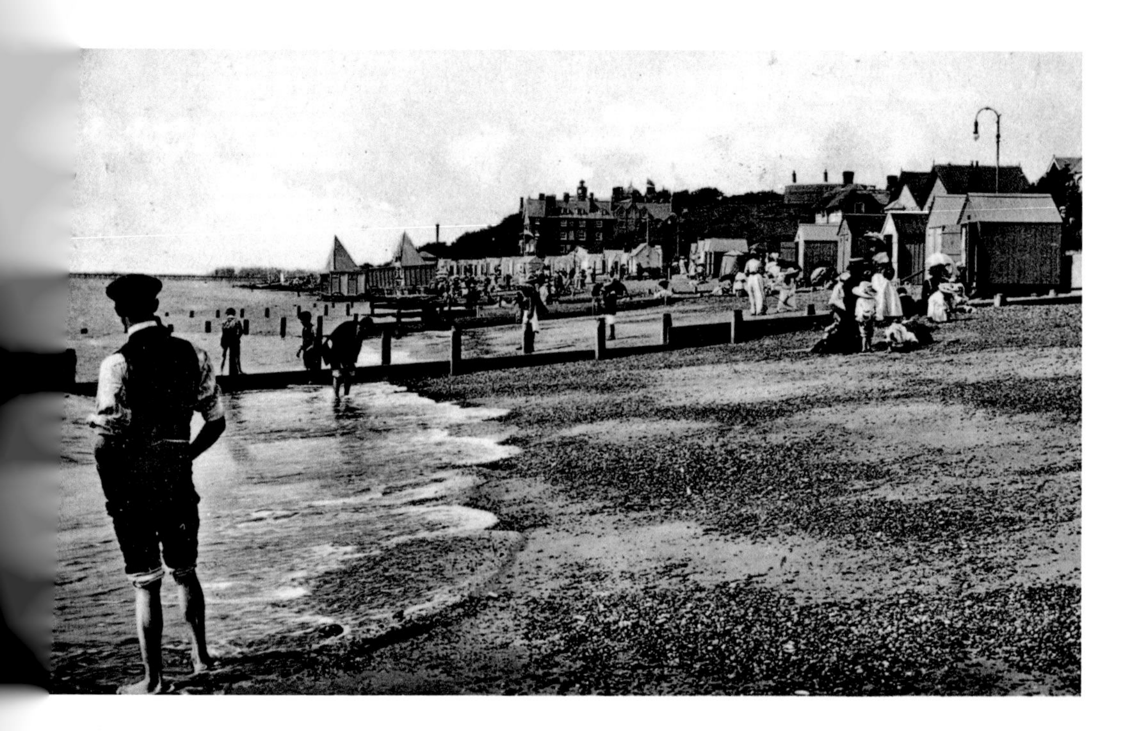

East Beach *c.* 1909

One of the joys of being at the seaside, is to roll up the trousers and go for a paddle. For many Edwardian holidaymakers and day trippers they probably didn't do much more than this, but what a change from the normal routine! The Felix Hotel can be clearly seen, as can the Martello Tower that was incorporated into the Bartlet site. Because the tide does not go out for miles and the beach shelves quite gradually, Felixstowe has always been popular for sea bathing.

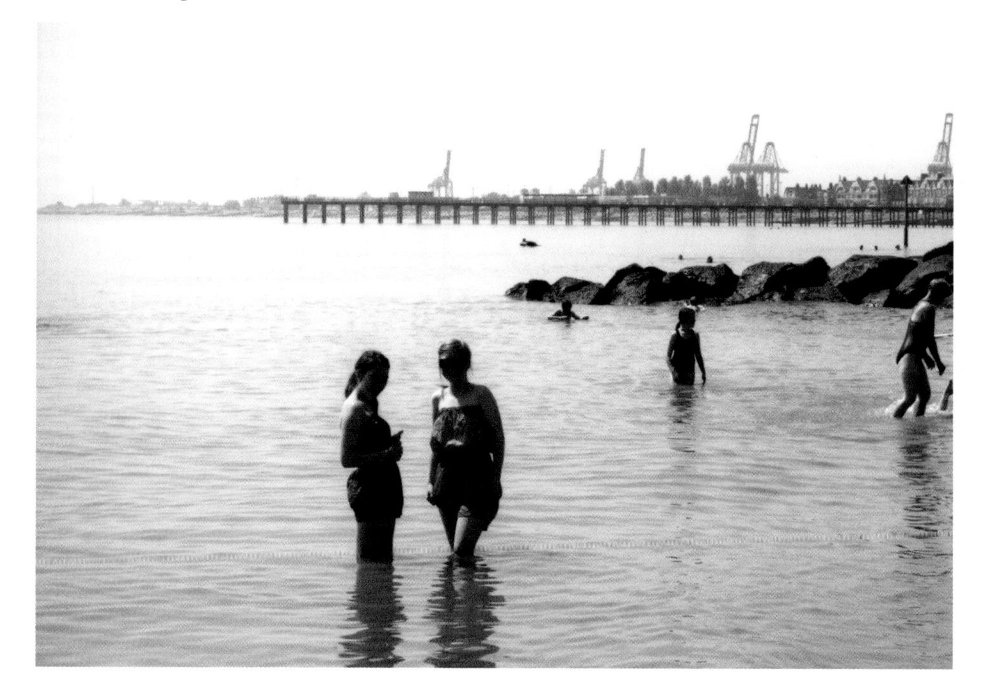

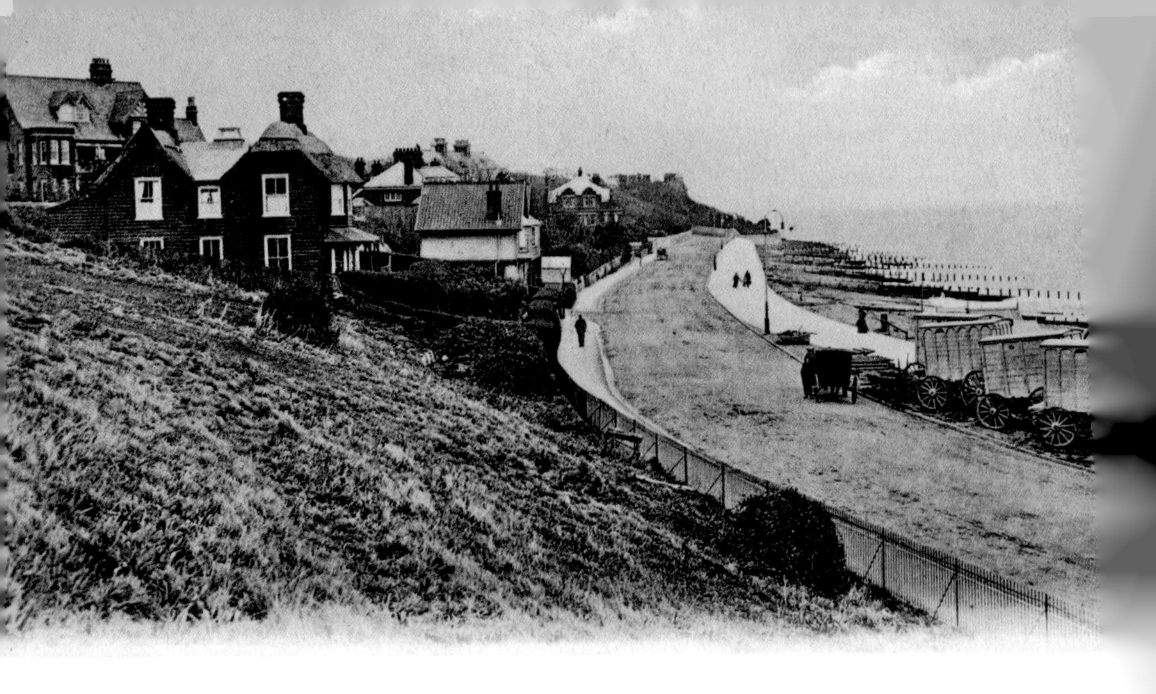

Cobbold's Point *c.* 1904

'We meander up and down here daily', so wrote Bessie in August 1904 to Leytonstone in Essex. In 1912 Lottie wrote home to Stoke Newington: 'I am having a good time. We had a regatta here on Wednesday, it was rather interesting to watch it especially the water polo. It is rather like football, only played in the water with hands. Both photographs appear to have been taken from the mound near the Martello Tower where the Bartlet was built. Cobbold Point is named after John Chevallier Cobbold (1797–1882) brewer, railway pioneer and Member of Parliament for Ipswich from (1847–1868).

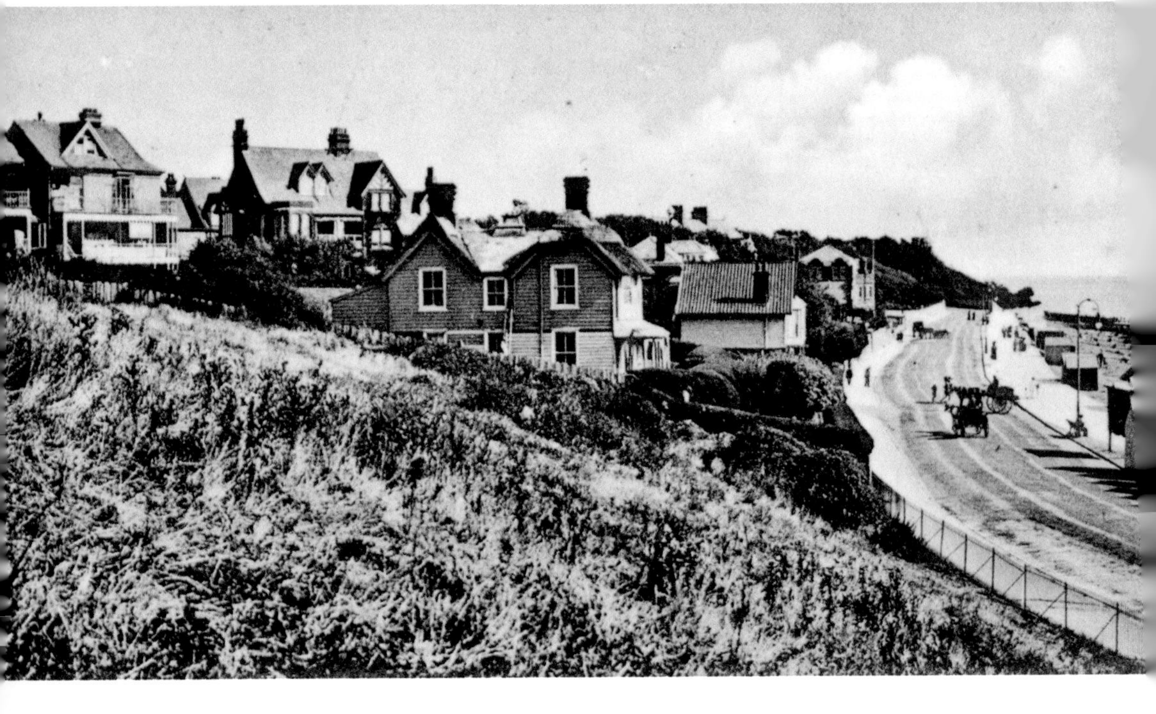

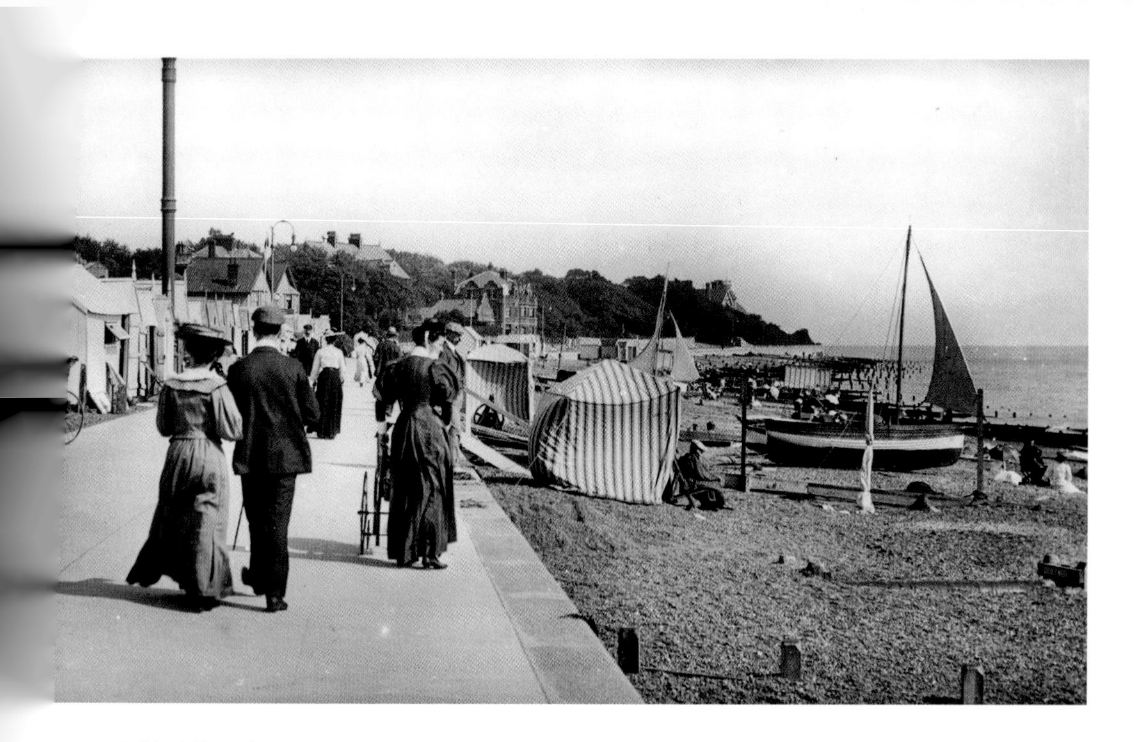

Cobbold's Point *c.* 1912

The Fludyer Arms Hotel in the middle distance began as a wooden building around the time of the Bath Hotel. William Smith, the licensee, operated bathing machines and hot and cold salt water baths. The present building being renovated by the Yeo Group as a fourteen-room pub/restaurant dates from 1903. Samuel Fludyer owned Felixstowe Lodge and then sold it to John Chevallier Cobbold. After building the Bath Hotel in 1839 Cobbold developed other sea front properties. As much as anyone he was responsible for the development of Felixstowe as a select seaside resort.

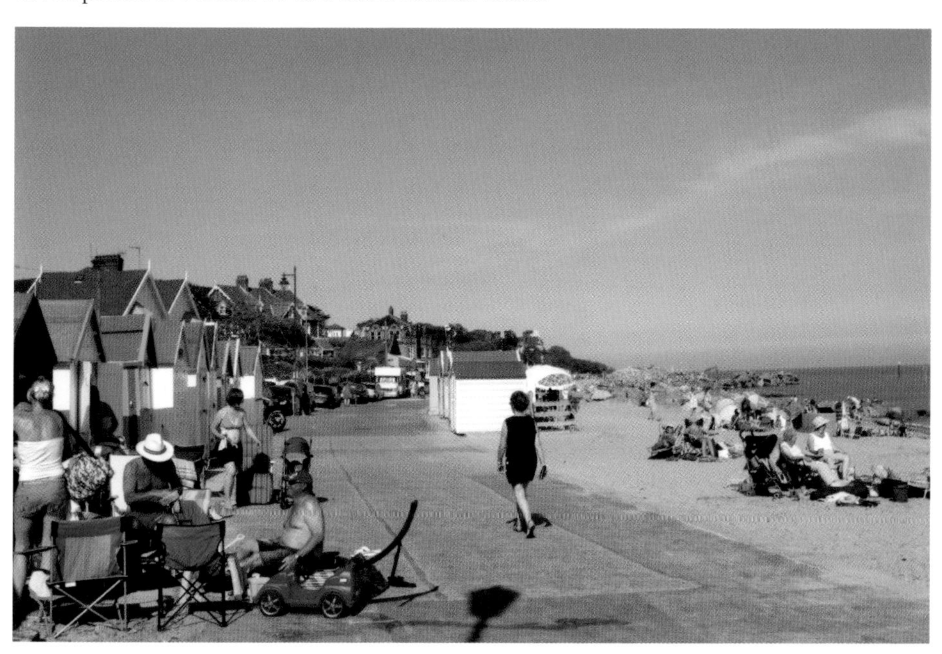

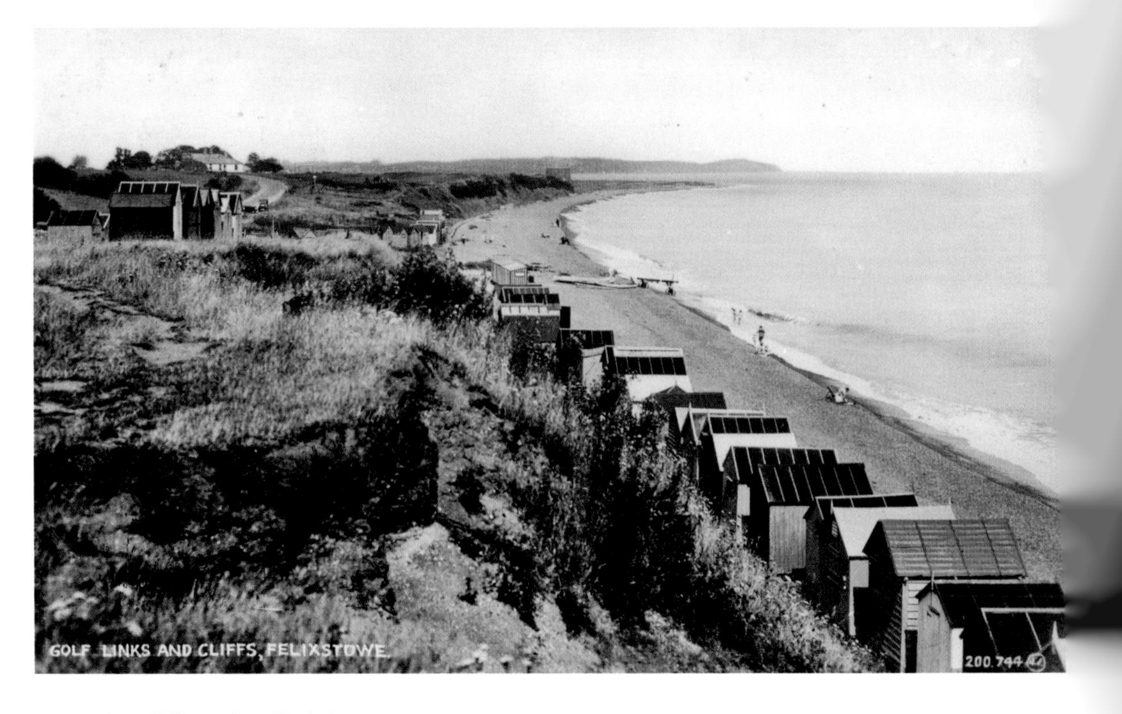

The Cliffs and Golf Links *c.* 1928

The sea defence works currently being engineered will include a new promenade around Cobbold's Point to Jacob's Ladder. There is a delightful sweep of the cliffs and lovely sands as the coast curves round towards the mouth of the River Deben and Felixstowe Ferry. The golf club was founded in 1880, one of the earliest in England and considered later to be one of the finest in Europe. The Right Honourable Arthur Balfour, Prime Minister from 1902–1905 and Foreign Secretary from 1916–19 was captain of the club in 1887.

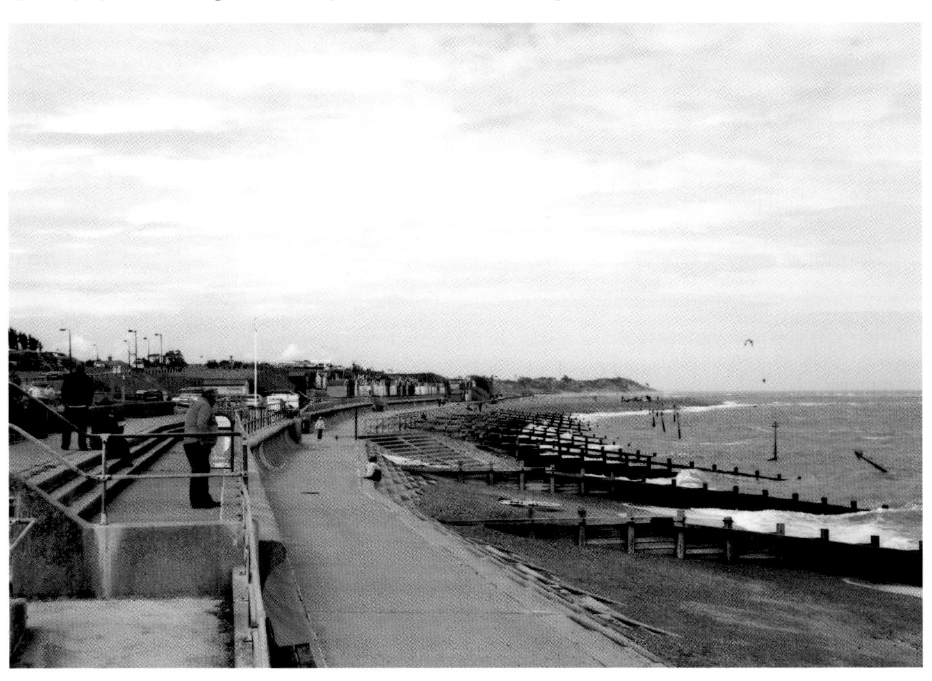

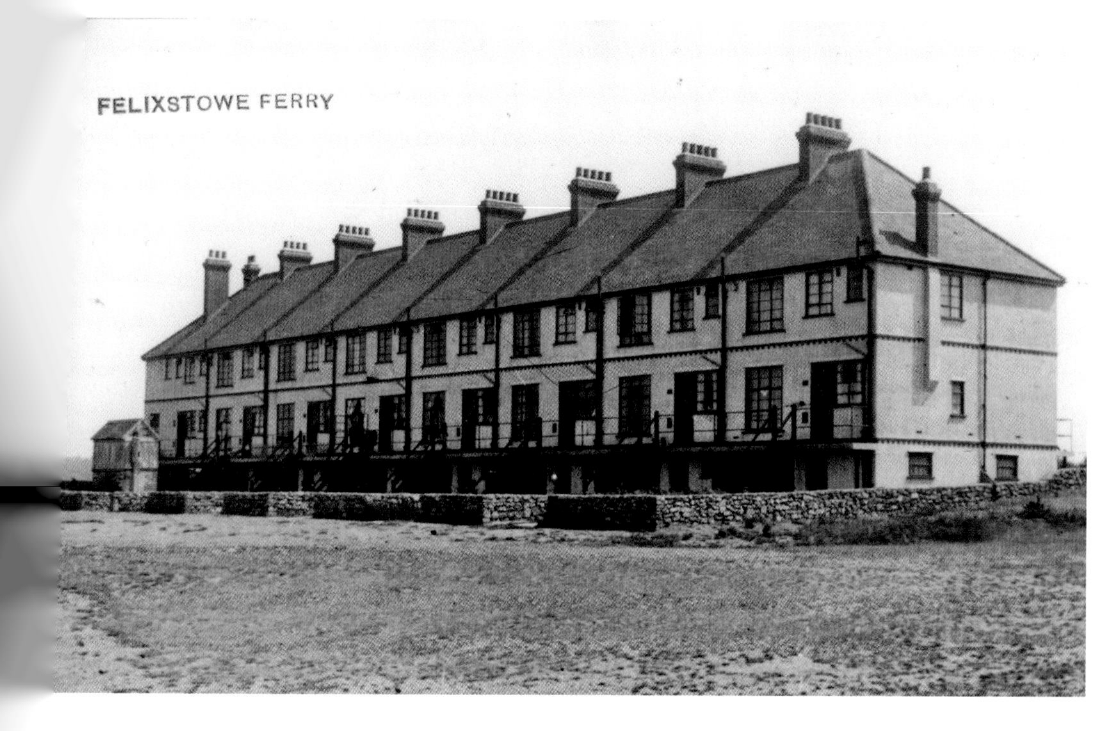

Felixstowe Ferry *c.* 1938
Harbour Villas, a rather stark row of eight houses, were built on the site of an old house, known as 'The Manor House' in 1937. Martello Tower U is close by.

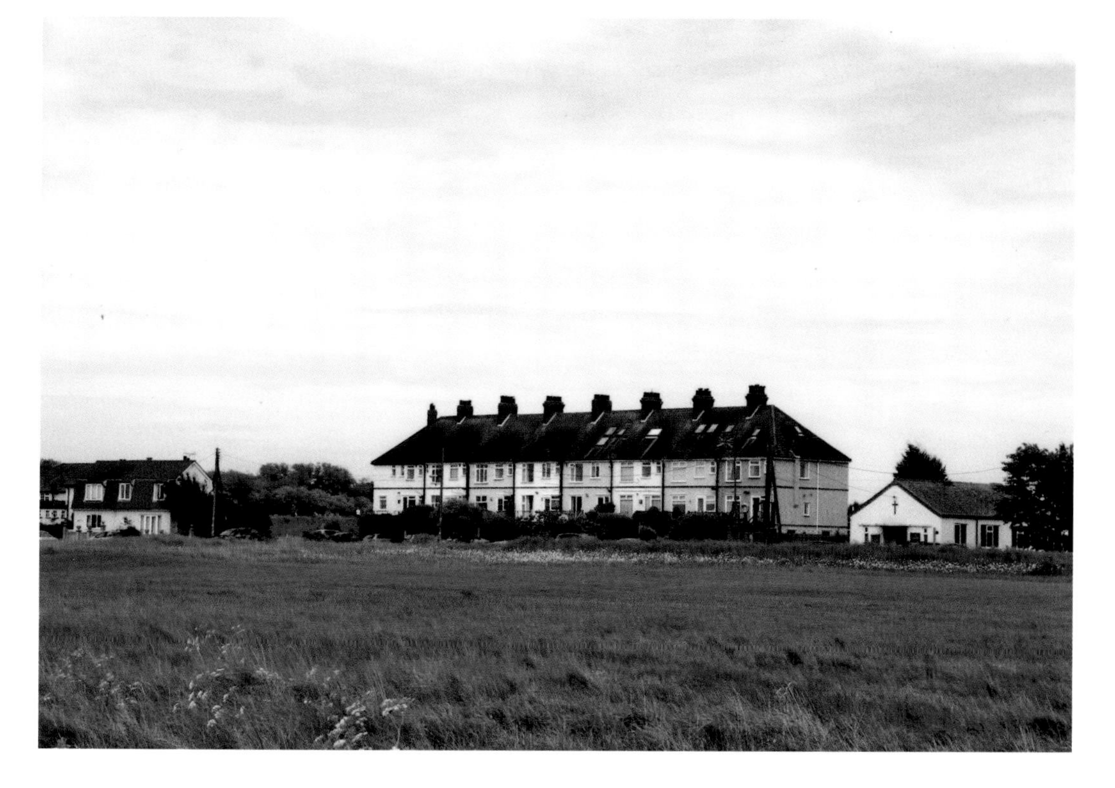

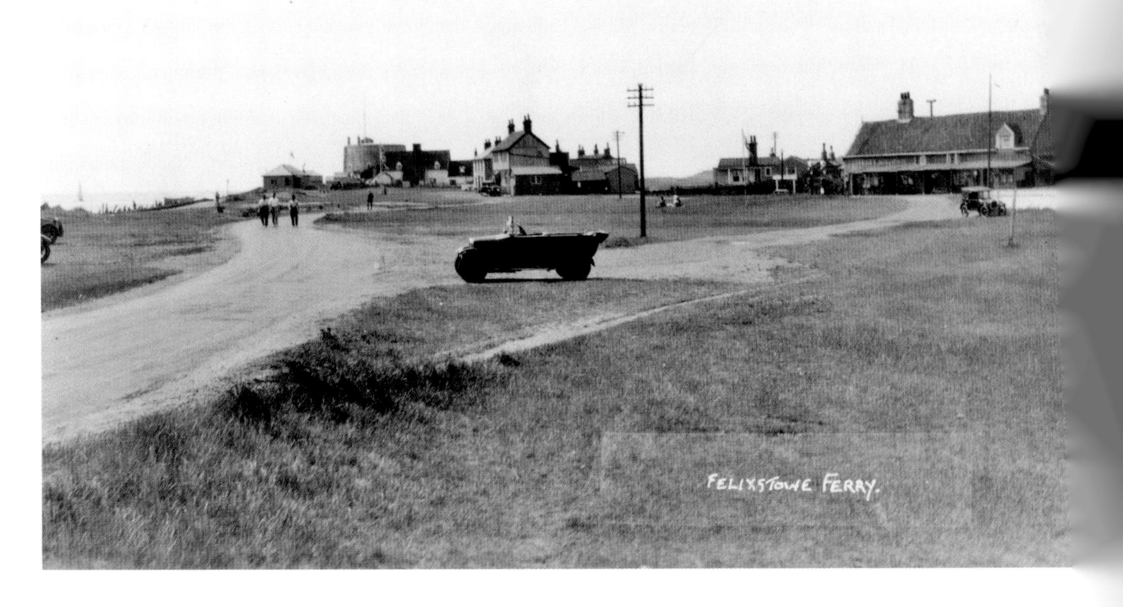

Felixstowe Ferry, 1920s

A wide view before the clay sea wall was built in 1970. The building to the left of the Martello Tower, which was the ladies' clubhouse for the golf course, was lost to the sea. The Old Manor House can be clearly seen, then the Victoria Inn and coming round to, on the right, the Ferry Boat Inn. The Ferry soon became a favourite destination for weekend motorists. Felixstowe sailing club is based here.

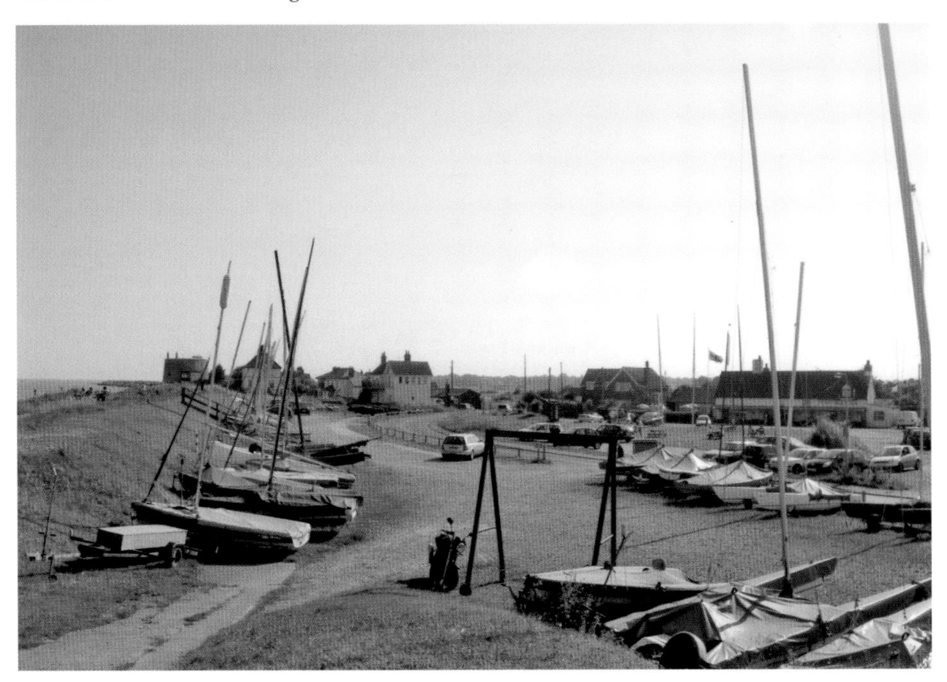

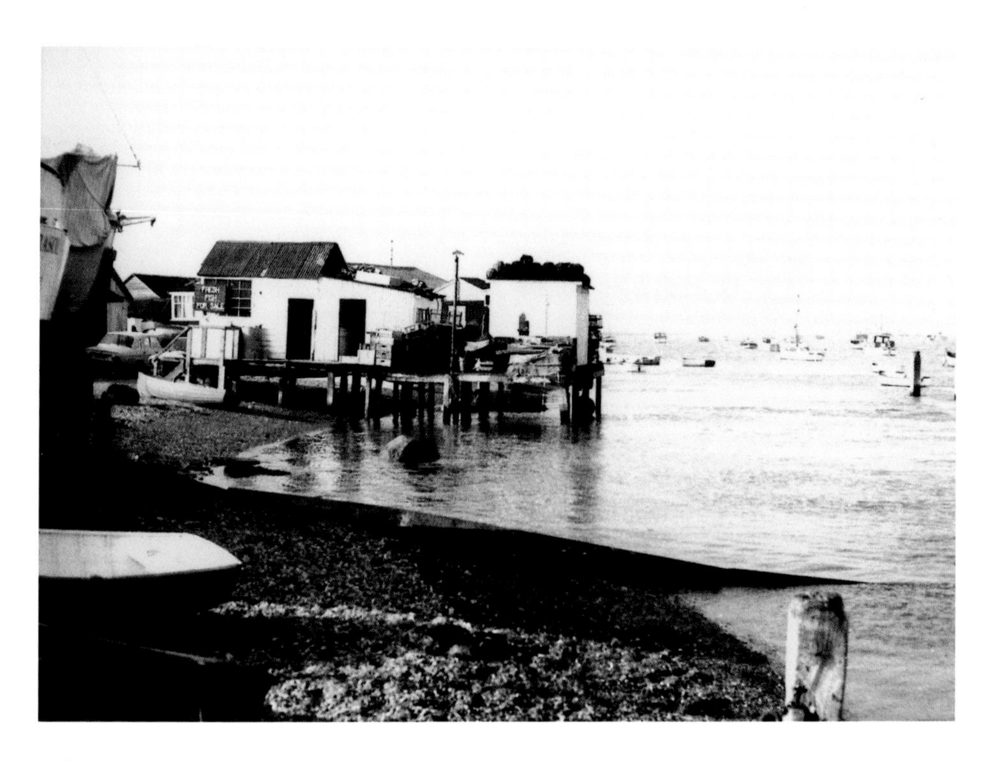

Felixstowe Ferry, 1980

'Fresh Fish for Sale' then and now, except the day's catch had been sold. This is a busy and popular spot. As well as the old fishing huts and the ferry, there is café/restaurant as well as the Ferry Boat Inn and the Victoria. The small car park is often full, as there is so much to see with the colourful yachts and other craft moving in and out of the River Deben.

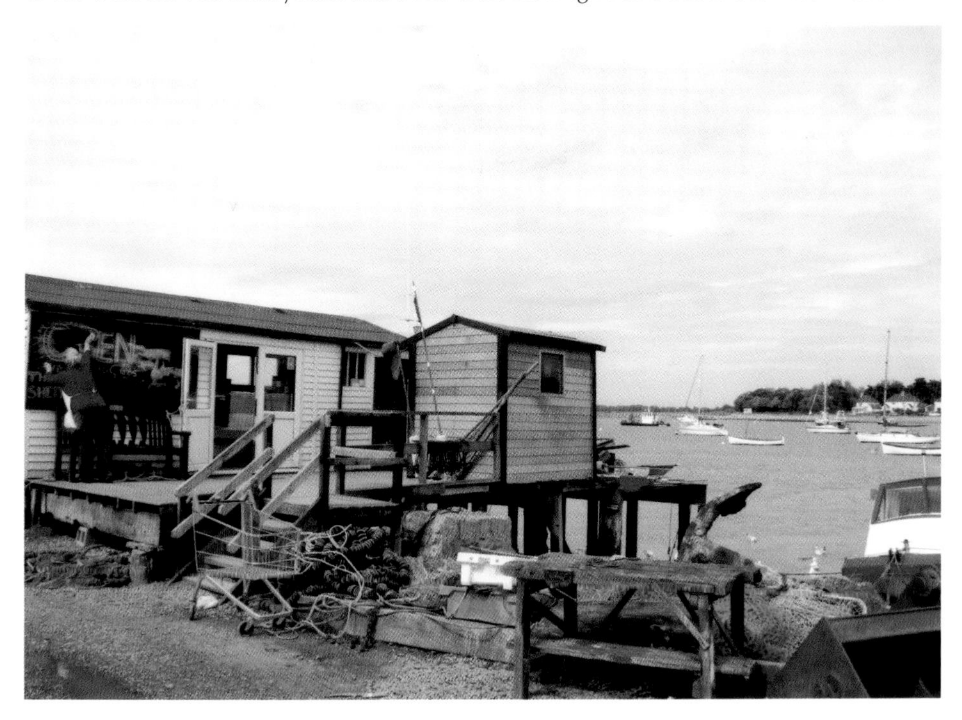

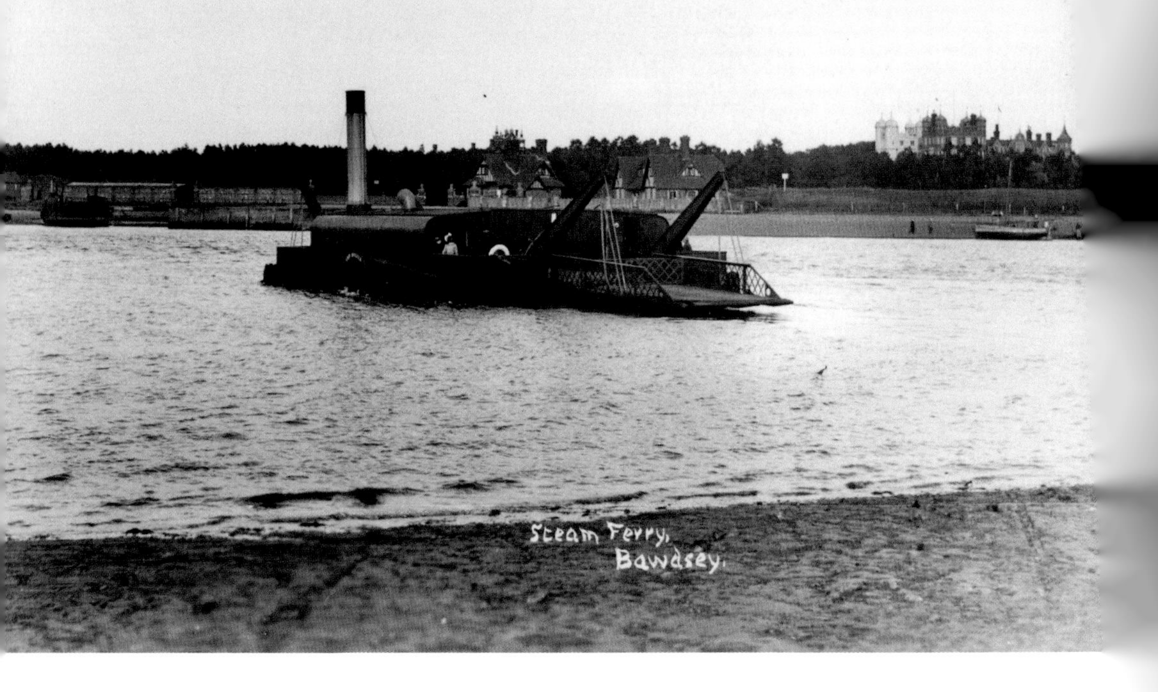

Steam Ferry, Bawdsey *c.* 1910

William Cuthbert Quilter, one of the founders of the National Telephone Company and an extremely wealthy man, dreamt of creating his own coastal town at Bawdsey across the Deben from Felixstowe Ferry. In 1881 he bought Bawdsey Estate of some 9,000 acres, constructed sea defences and in 1886 began work on his manor. In 1894 he opened a steam ferry service with two chain ferries, the *Lady Beatrice* (above) for the summer and the *Lady Quilter* (below) for the winter.

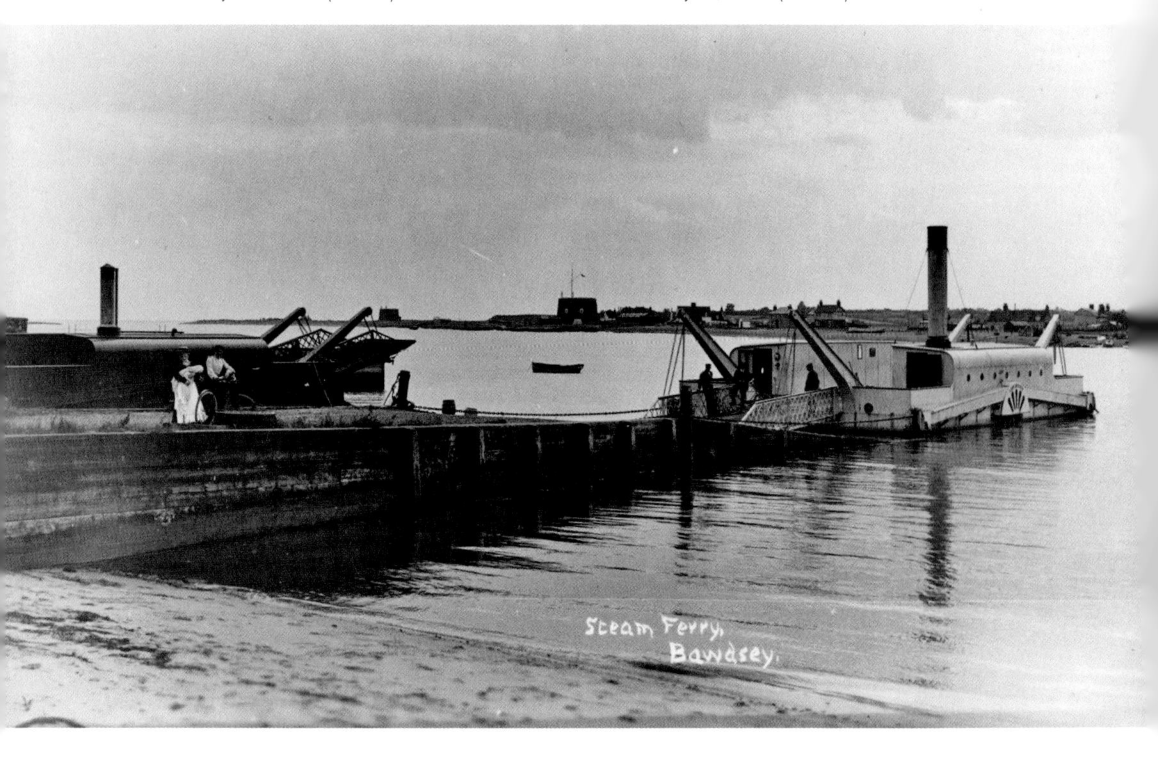

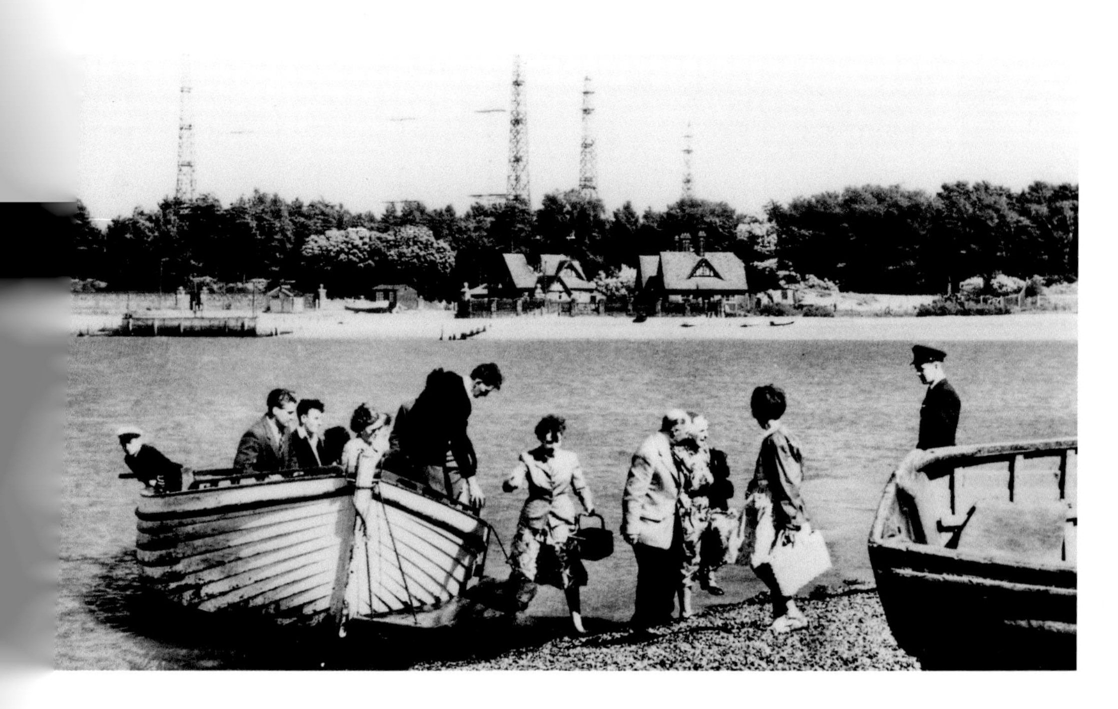

Deben Ferry ***c.*** **1955**

After Quilter's death in 1911 the family continued to run the ferries until 1931, until a launch replaced them. The steel transmitter towers are from the RAF days at Bawdsey and there are wooden towers, which appear faint on this photograph. Today there is a steady stream of passengers waiting on the landing stage, many of them with bicycles cycling the coastal path. The ferry runs daily from the 1 April until the end of September and during the rest of the year weekends only.

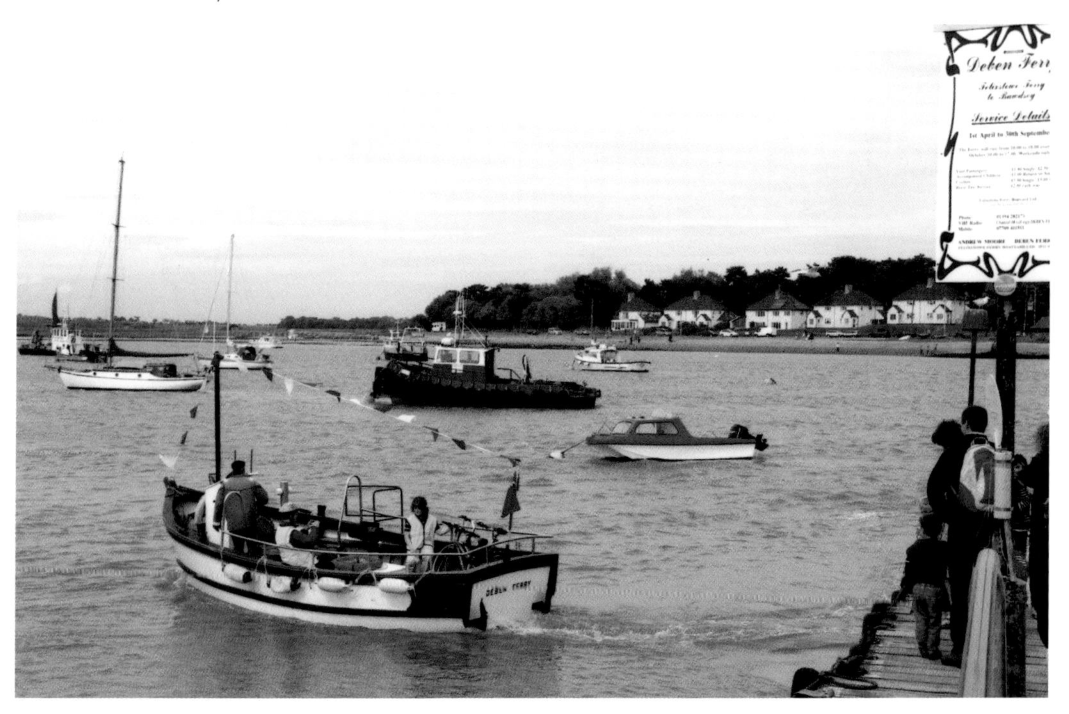

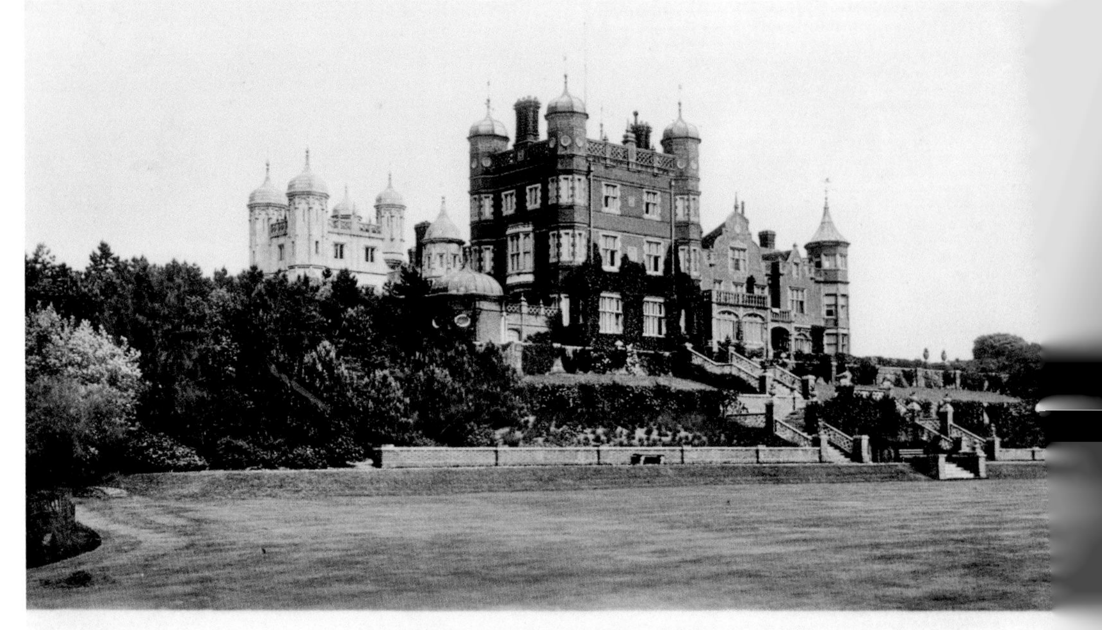

Bawdsey Manor *c.* **1908**

It was said that Quilter vowed to add a tower for every million he added to his fortune partly made from his stockbroking firm of Quilter, Balfour & Co. He was a MP for Sudbury (1885–1906) and created a Baronet in 1897. The white tower to the left was his last extension to the manor completed in 1905. Lady Quilter developed the formal gardens and a Victorian kitchen garden. The rockery seen below is an artificial cliff of Pulhamite and is 110 metres long.

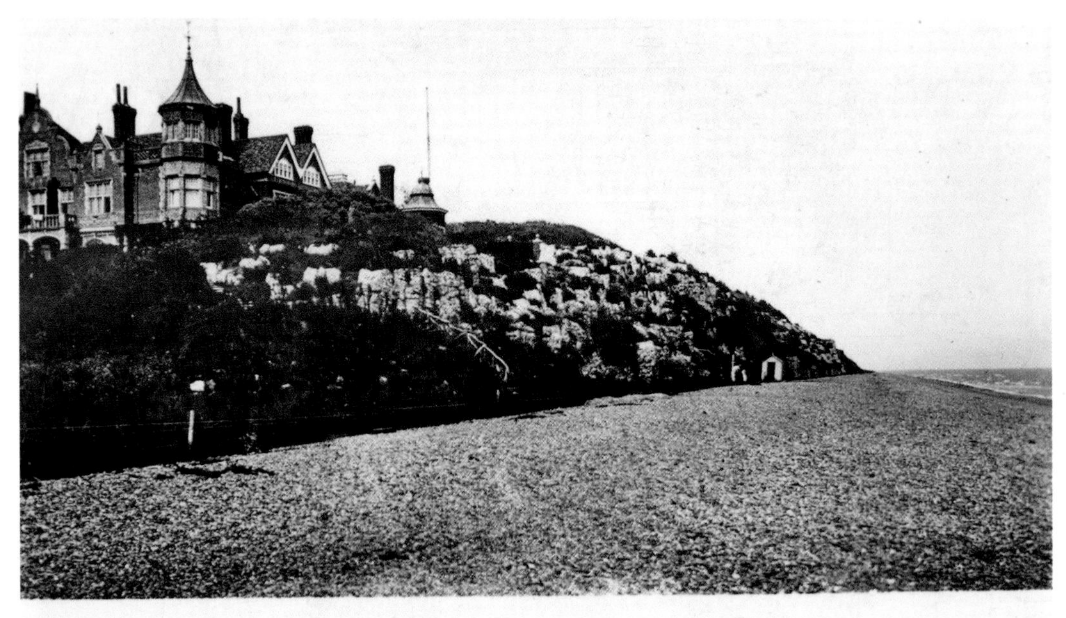

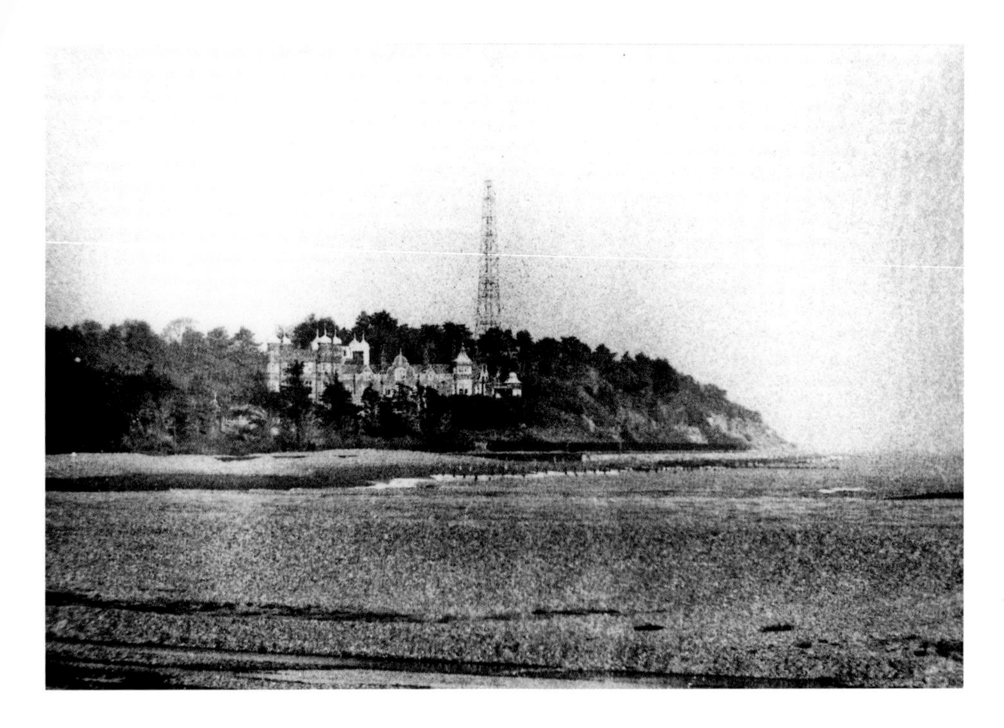

Bawdsey Manor, 1980

In 1936 the RAF bought Bawdsey. It had been selected as a site for a new research station for the development of radio direction finding. Robert Watson Watt was the first Superintendent and in May 1937 the first Chain Home Radar Station was developed on the site. During the Second World War, Bawdsey was in the forefront of the defence of the country and photographs show wooden receiver towers and steel transmitter towers, of which one can be seen here. The RAF left in 1994 and Bawdsey Manor was bought by the Toettcher family and is now a conference and wedding venue.

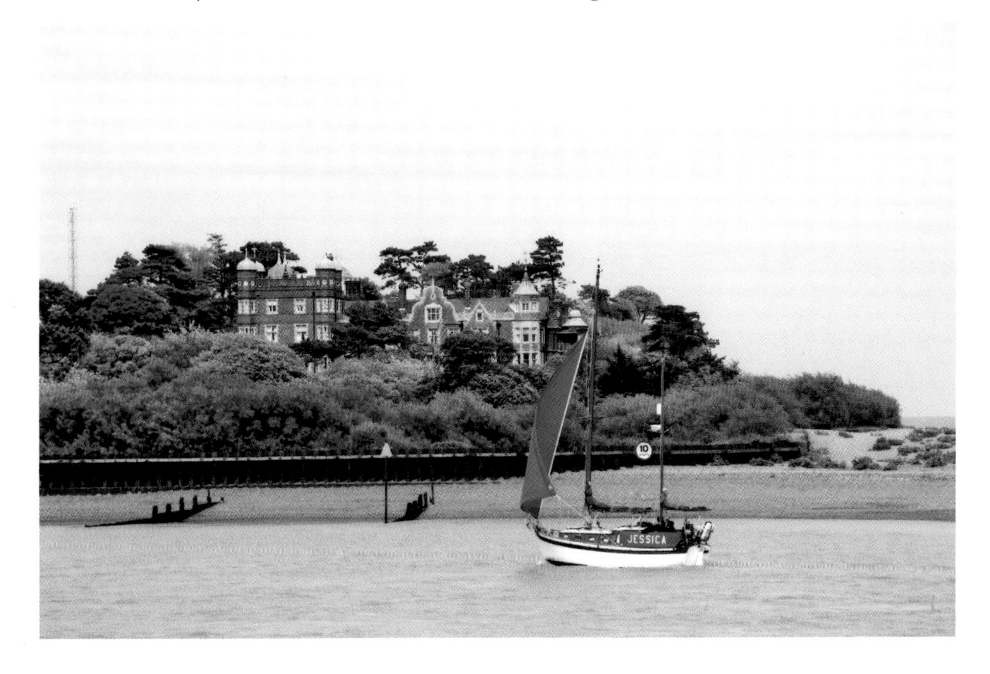

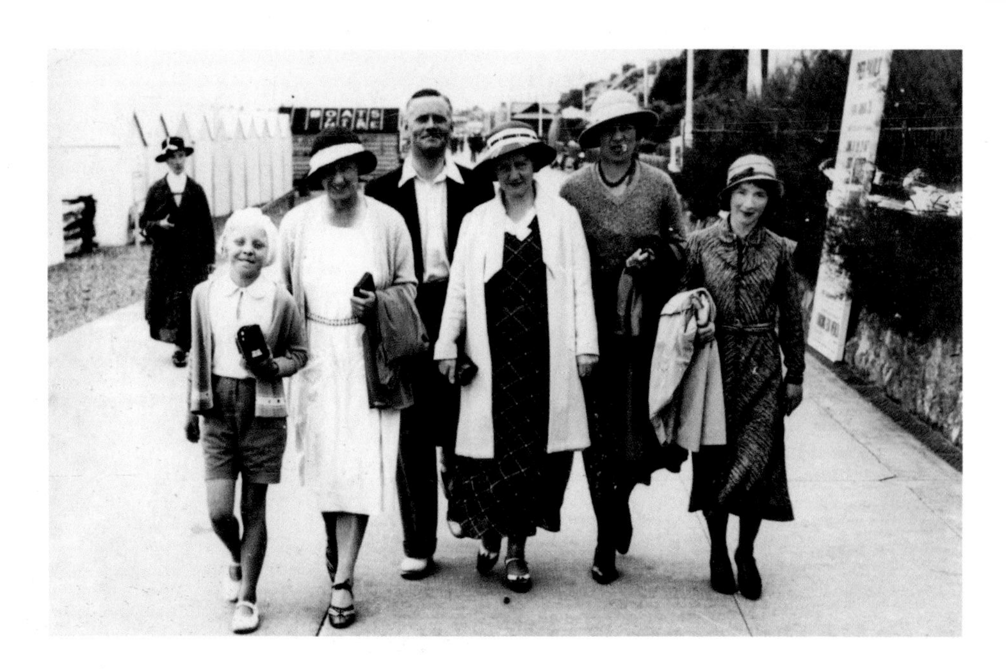

July 1934/July 2012
A family group captured by Mr Snaps of South Hill, while below Cassie and Mollie caught by me, separated by nearly eighty years, but all enjoying a walk by the sea in the sun. The gardens restoration, the multi million pound plans for the pier and the future of the Spa Pavilion resolved, could herald a new era for Felixstowe. It should be entirely possible to have the largest container port in the country and a successful holiday resort building on the heritage of the last one hundred or more years on this delightful bay on the Suffolk coast.

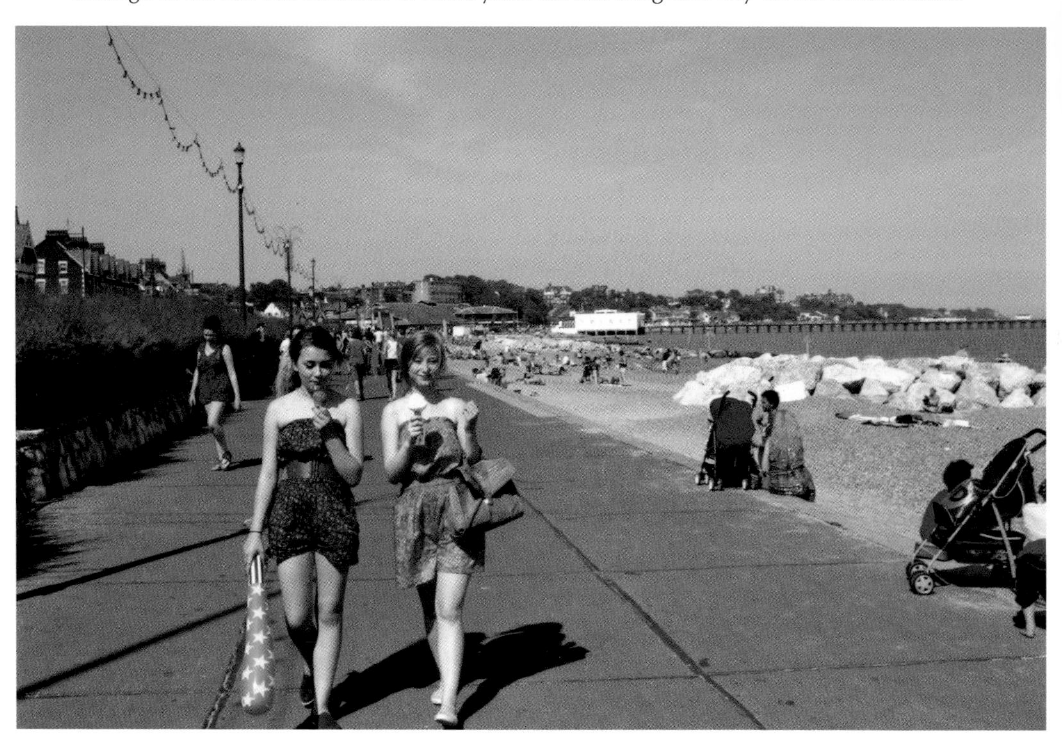